RINGING THE CHANGES

A Memoir

RINGING THE CHANGES

A Memoir

Richard Luce

MICHAEL RUSSELL

First published in Great Britain 2007
by Michael Russell (Publishing) Ltd
Wilby Hall, Wilby, Norwich NR16 2JP

Page makeup in Sabon by Waveney Typesetters
Wymondham, Norfolk
Printed and bound in Great Britain
by Biddles Ltd, King's Lynn, Norfolk

TO MY WIFE ROSE
WITHOUT WHOM I COULD NOT HAVE
MANAGED SUCH A FULL LIFE

Contents

	Author's Note	9
1	My Family	11
2	My Parents	13
3	Growing Up	22
4	National Service	31
5	Following the Flag	36
6	University and Marriage	42
7	The Last Days of Empire in Kenya	52
8	Getting into Parliament	62
9	Parliament	72
10	Rhodesia/Zimbabwe	79
11	Other Overseas Assignments – I	96
12	Other Overseas Assignments – II	104
13	The Arts, the British Library and the Civil Service	119
14	The Falklands	134
15	The University of Buckingham	148
16	Gibraltar	154
17	The Monarchy	166
	Epilogue	176
	Appendix: Address to Mark the End of Her Majesty's Overseas Civil Service etc	182
	Index	186

Author's Note

I have written this book principally for family and friends, though of course I will be delighted if it is of interest to specialists or others with whom I have worked over the years. I feel the need to describe what I have done in life and to add some reflections on these varied experiences. I have also been encouraged by a number of people over the years to put pen to paper.

I am greatly indebted to those who have given help and encouragement. Miranda Legard has patiently typed from tapes which I have regularly sent to her in Yorkshire and interpreted my instructions remarkably accurately. Sarah Dodsworth, who worked for me at the University of Buckingham as a very competent chief of staff, has given me very helpful and thorough editorial advice from her Cambridge home. Sharon Smith, my current personal assistant, has helped in typing the final drafts and has produced them with conmendable speed.

Above all my wife Rose has shown exceptional patience in reading the chapters, giving me her views, making detailed adjustments on the computer and generally giving me all the support that I needed. I am so grateful to her and our sons Alexander and Edward for encouraging me to write.

It is also a special pleasure to me that Michael Russell has taken on the task of publishing the book, having in earlier times published my mother's diaries, *From Aden to the Gulf*, as well as several books for my aunt Priscilla Napier.

I

My Family

My father's family came across from Normandy with William the Conqueror. They settled solidly and uncontroversially into English life and by the eighteenth century they were mainly farmers and hoteliers. Malmesbury became the family base in the early nineteenth century, so much so that the Abbey is packed with Luce plaques and memorials and the predictable joke was that there were far too many 'Luce' women in Malmesbury. Then we altered course to brewing, commerce, banking and Parliament. My great-grandfather became the first mayor of Malmesbury in 1887.

In the First World War my grandfather, Admiral John Luce, was captain of HMS *Glasgow* – the only ship to escape the defeat of the Battle of Coronel off Chile – and played a leading role in the first victory of the Battle of the Falkland Islands in 1914. His brother, Major General Sir Richard Luce, was a surgeon general, distinguished himself at Gallipoli and was Director of Medical Services for the Egyptian Expeditionary Force in Palestine. He ended up for a short spell as MP for Derby.

My grandfather had four sons, two of whom entered the Navy, one the family cloth business in Wiltshire and my father the Sudan Political Service. One naval son, David Luce, resigned as First Sea Lord in 1966 having advised the Prime Minister Harold Wilson that, since the Government's policy had been to maintain a British role east of Suez, it was wrong to phase out the aircraft carriers.

My mother's family are called Napier. Since in earlier centuries the Napiers were based in Scotland, many of them served the Scottish monarchs. John Napier, who invented logarithms, was a forebear. When I gave a lecture on higher education at the Napier University in Edinburgh, I had to confess that I had missed out on my forebear's genius for mathematics. Later there were many Napiers who distinguished themselves serving the Empire. Among them was Sir Charles Napier, the conqueror of Sindh and the author of the celebrated pun

'Peccavi' or 'I have sinned'. When I visited Karachi once I was agree-
ably surprised to be greeted warmly by Pakistanis as his descendant.
Lord Napier of Magdala features in my Gibraltar chapter since, as a
former Governor of Gibraltar, he built the west wing of the Convent in
which Rose and I lived. In later times, my mother's family produced
many naval leaders, not least my grandfather who died of typhoid in
Bermuda as Commander-in-Chief West Indies and North Atlantic. I am
proud of my Uncle Trevie who escorted King Haakon out of an embat-
tled Oslo in 1940 and died of septicaemia soon after. Eric Linklater
wrote a chapter on him in his book on budding leaders who died
young. I can remember seeing this tall reassuring figure at home, just
before he died.

Since I have served the monarchy it is worth mentioning that my
grandmother, then May Culme-Seymour, was caught up in the early
years of her marriage in an appalling court case, known as Rex v.
Mylius. Mylius, a republican journalist, alleged in 1910 that George V,
when Duke of York, had been secretly married to my grandmother in
the early '90s in Malta and had several children hidden away. The
court case was presided over by the Lord Chief Justice and the
Attorney General acted for the King. The photographs show my grandmother as a witness, giving her evidence from under an enormous hat.
Mylius was imprisoned. But it gave me and my cousins much amusement imagining ourselves as leading members of the Royal Family. It
seems that the media may not have changed too much.

Writing about my family highlights the depth of class consciousness
in Britain, with its various shades of interpretation. It is deep-rooted in
British history but today much less divisive: there is increased social
mobility and greater equality of opportunity. Certainly the younger
generation seems to be far less concerned with race and class.
Nevertheless I am conscious that my father's family were solid professional middle class and my mother's came from a more aristocratic
background. Somehow it was a reassurance to me in my earlier unconfident days that I knew my family history and was proud of their
achievements.

2
My Parents

The more I reflect on the lives of my parents, known to all their friends as Bill and Margaret, the more I am struck by the strength of their marriage and their characters. I am biased of course, but I think that they were a remarkable pair who complemented each other in every way, from talent to character.

I have already written something of my father's family. The Admiral and my grandmother Gar had four sons and lived at Cheverell in Wiltshire. My father and Ted were twins and the youngest. They had a solid middle-class, secure and disciplined upbringing. I know surprisingly little about my father's earlier years. He had a bad start in life, being confined to a wheelchair for much of the time until the age of twelve or so with what I believe was a form of rheumatic fever, which in turn affected his heart. It was all the more remarkable that in later days in the Sudan he was able to work in the toughest conditions and became strong and fit.

I know nothing of his earlier schooling, but he went to Clifton College for his public school education. I think, from my mother's description, he was often shy and diffident. Sometimes he could go through a whole meal without contributing to the conversation. By the time he entered Christ's College, Cambridge, he was showing real talent as a pianist; so much so that my mother told me that he was encouraged by some to become a professional. Faced with a choice between music or a traditional professional career in public life, he was urged – well, probably ordered – by his father to go off and play his part in running the Empire. The two elder brothers had gone into the Navy and Ted was to go into the somewhat ailing family cloth business.

After Cambridge my father chose the Sudan Political Service, regarded as the élite of the Imperial Service, second only to the Indian Civil Service. Rather unusually, the Sudan came under the Foreign Secretary's responsibilities and tended to recruit able all-rounders, with a good sprinkling of blues. For this reason the Sudan became known, a little heavy-handedly, as 'a country of blacks ruled by blues'. My father wasn't a blue, but could certainly be described as an all-rounder.

The Sudan, the largest country in Africa, had only 400 administrators in sixty years of British rule. District commissioners held enormous responsibilities for large areas at a young age. My father served in a number of areas in the 1930s, some of them very remote and with tough conditions. It was lonely for my mother and difficult if they were unwell. Indeed my father once did his work travelling by camel while in high fever from malaria. When he was a district commissioner at Hassa Heisa, near Khartoum in the cotton belt, there were diversions with other British colleagues that included a silent crime film with my father as a police inspector involved in chases through the desert.

The war of course meant prolonged separation for my parents, with my mother spending much of the time in the UK. They communicated by teleletter. My father, like so many others, fought to persuade the Civil Secretary to release him to fight in the war. There was much ill feeling and tension when the authorities refused. Instead he was made private secretary to the Governor General, General Sir Hubert Huddleston. He had an office in the famous palace where Gordon was killed and a small house in the grounds. He became devoted to Sir Hubert who had been both Kaid (Commander of the Sudan Defence Force) and GOC Northern Ireland. He was clearly a man of immense humanity and humility. Many visitors arrived, from the Duke of Gloucester to Field Marshal Smuts and Noël Coward. At a party for the Field Marshal my mother, in one of her expansive waves of her arms, threw a glass of sherry in his face, which he took with good grace; while on another occasion Noël Coward told my father that he had forgotten the tune of one of his own compositions: would my father play it for him.

My father worked his way through the Sudan Political Service, eventually becoming its senior British civil servant and the last to leave at independence on 1 January 1956. Immediately after the war he came to London and spent a year at the Imperial Defence College, returning to Khartoum as assistant civil secretary and then went to Equatoria Province as deputy and later acting governor based in Juba. My younger sister Diana (known as 'D') and I always loved our Christmas or summer holidays in the Sudan. The senior provincial governorship was the Blue Nile Province in Wad Medani, and my father was given that job and also made chairman of the Sudan Cotton Board. Government

House was attractive and we often travelled with him on trek through the desert and into greener areas, sometimes by Nile steamer. We would stop at villages and see the village chiefs or watch a camel race. There was sailing on the Nile, tennis and plenty of social life.

In 1953 Sir James Robertson, the civil secretary, left to become Governor General of Nigeria. That particular job was really the equivalent of Prime Minister of the Sudan and head of the Civil Service. In view of the progress towards independence it was decided to split the job, creating the posts of director of internal affairs and advisor to the Governor General on foreign and constitutional affairs. The advisor's role was that of the senior civil servant in the Sudan, and my father was asked to take it on. He returned to the palace, and for the next crucial three years helped to steer the Sudan through constitutional evolution and political minefields towards independence on the last day of December 1955.

The Sudan was an Anglo-Egyptian condominium (though in practice the British ruled), and the Egyptians needed delicate handling. On one occasion General Neguib, the President of Egypt who was half Sudanese, visited Khartoum. He stayed with the Governor General, Sir Robert Howe, and was joined there by Selwyn Lloyd, the Foreign Secretary. Soon after his arrival riots took place outside the palace and my father was asked to investigate. As he emerged by the Gordon steps his friend, the Commissioner of Police, was stabbed to death in front of him. My father leapt into his car and drove straight through the riot to the palace of the Mahdi, the leader of the Ansar sect, and ordered him to instruct his people to stop rioting or he would send in the troops. The Mahdi withdrew them and never realised there was only one company of British troops in Khartoum! Later my father called on Neguib in his room and found him praying and in tears that he had been the cause of so many casualties.

Those were politically stormy days. When Churchill became acting Foreign Secretary while Eden was ill, he did his best to delay independence but was thwarted by the Governor General and my father. There were serious difficulties in the south, where the Nilotic Christian and pagan tribes did not want to be part of the Arab north. A civil war was sparked by the south and my father spent much time in 1955 negotiating with the rebels and eventually receiving their surrender in Torit. He was in the news virtually every day.

In March 1955 a new Governor General, Sir Knox Helm, arrived. In the late summer he went home to deal with important family concerns and did not return. This left my father steering the Sudan through the final stages to independence, timing and handling it so as to thwart Egyptian plans to dominate the Sudan. The Chief Justice, 'Wob' Lindsay, tried unsuccessfully to become Acting Governor General – such rivalry just added to the burden in those last days.

Sir Douglas Dodds-Parker, Parliamentary Under Secretary for Foreign Affairs, flew out on behalf of the government and at a dinner on the eve of independence announced that my father was to be knighted for his services to the Sudan. After twenty-five years of service, he had left an indelible mark. The older generation still remember him well today, as they do in the Gulf. When I flew out to the Sudan as a new MP in the1970s, the rumour went round Khartoum and Omdurman, 'Sir William Luce is back'. It was something of a disappointment to them that it turned out to be his son.

While I was doing officer training at Eaton Hall during my National Service, my father told me he needed to decide between two job offers – Ambassador to Syria or Governor of Aden. I drove down to my parents' house in Wiltshire for the weekend and offered my strong opinion that Aden was the right one, knowing that he was a proconsul and not a diplomat. He would have been driven mad in the Foreign Office. He needed to be in charge. My father duly chose Aden. Syria was soon after absorbed into the United Arab Republic with Egypt.

He took on Aden for four years from 1956 at a time when the Arab world under Nasser in Egypt was becoming bitterly anti-colonialist. The Suez Canal had been nationalised just before my father arrived in Aden in August and I remember that he forecast a major international crisis. The Suez fiasco followed soon after and for a time Aden port lacked any commercial life. Nasser and Radio Cairo poured out vitriol about the British in Aden and elsewhere. Against this background, my father steered Aden towards a federation of the Eastern and Western Protectorates and made constitutional advances for the colony of Aden. Relations with the Yemen to the north were difficult and there was a measure of guerrilla activity in the Western Protectorate. He sacked the ruler of Lahej and installed a more moderate ruler.

The Colonial Secretary at this time, and a good friend of my father's, was Alan Lennox-Boyd. He lent us his yacht *Tawau* with a crew of five in the summer holidays. Lennox-Boyd was succeeded by Iain Macleod who congratulated my father warmly on his achievement in moving Aden forward while maintaining stability. For this he was awarded the GBE.

In 1959 he was summoned for discussions and found himself on a short list of three to be Governor of Kenya. He was invited to meet the Prime Minister, Harold Macmillan. In the end Sir Patrick Renison was given the job as the only one of the three who was a member of the Colonial Service. The third candidate was Field Marshal Templer. Soon after that my father was offered the job of High Commissioner to Pakistan. He turned that down and, despite his desire to leave the Middle East for the sake of my mother, accepted the senior Middle East job of Political Resident for the Persian Gulf under the Foreign Secretary. This he did for just over five years until retirement at sixty. Based in Bahrain, he became the only person to have responsibility over time for the whole of the Gulf Peninsula. With responsibilities for all the Gulf sheikdoms from Kuwait to the Oman he dealt with the first Kuwait crisis of 1961 when British troops pre-empted an attack by Iraq under General Kassem. Meanwhile there was a rebellion in the Oman and tensions over Buraimi oasis with Saudi Arabia. At the beginning of his time in the Gulf he forecast that Britain's role could last another ten years without loss of goodwill. He was right and was subsequently called out of retirement to negotiate our withdrawal in 1971.

Following his first retirement he received a surprising sounding from the Prime Minister of New Zealand as to whether he would like to be Governor General of that country. Principally for the sake of my mother he refused, but I think equally he had no desire to serve abroad again. His brother David was then offered the job and also refused.

After a few years on the board of various companies, including Inchcape, Chartered Bank, and Gray Mackenzie, the Conservatives returned to power and the Foreign Secretary, Alec Douglas-Home, recalled my father from retirement to be his Special Representative to the Gulf, in order to negotiate Britain's withdrawal. This meant a Kissinger-like role for eighteen months, with constant flights to see the Shah of Iran, King Faisal of Saudi Arabia and the Gulf Rulers. The most difficult task was to help create a new country, the United Arab Emirates, comprising all the former Trucial States. Few people can claim to have played a part in creating a new country. Enormous goodwill amongst the Gulf States has been retained towards the United Kingdom as a result of the way in which Britain withdrew.

Many of my father's friends thought that he should have been sent to the Lords. Instead he was offered a GCMG, which he turned down, saying he had 'too many gongs'. He accepted it all in good grace, and after explaining it to me over lunch said the matter was thereafter closed.

He only lived another five years, dying suddenly of a heart attack in the orchard in Fovant in 1977, aged sixty-nine. As Lennox-Boyd wrote in his obituary of my father in *The Times*, 'He folded up his tent like an Arab and stole away.'

I was forty when my father died. I felt his loss very keenly and was moved to tears in private in the weeks thereafter. Tributes to him spoke of his wisdom, common sense, the respect in which he was held and the immense care and interest that he took in all who served under him. At his memorial service in St Margaret's, Westminster, I recall walking out through a mass of tall, upright elderly men, many who had served the Empire with distinction.

Although I hardly began to know him till after the war when I was ten, he had been a wonderful father, though less close and intimate than my mother. His letters were always interesting about the political scene and encouraging to me throughout my awful school years. There was a quiet authority about him, but I felt close to him, felt that he was tolerant and concerned for me. I loved his laughter at some comedian or family joke when we were all together and relaxed. He played the piano beautifully, filling the house with music, above all Chopin. Perhaps what I appreciated as much as anything was the way in which he responded to my interest in international affairs, and in how he was handling his responsibilities. He took me completely into his confidence, showed me important documents, and talked to me about it all for as long as I wanted. I am enormously grateful to him for this as it taught me so much about international affairs, and I think perhaps contributed in some ways to my becoming a Minister of State for Foreign Affairs. He would never have pushed it on me, he was responding entirely to my own interest. I was very proud of him and loved to discuss his jobs and his challenges with him. His achievements did much to boost me at a time when I felt that I was a failure.

Now, my mother. 'I don't think anyone in the world could have asked for a more loving mother who, through her unique humour and perceptiveness, helped me always to keep life in perspective.' These feelings of mine were quoted by Sir William Hayter at his memorial address for my mother in 1989.

I have already described my mother's parents. I have a sad impression of her losing her father in Bermuda aged only twelve. As he was dying of typhoid my mother was taken out in a sailing dinghy and on her return at teatime found the flag at Admiralty House at half mast. Her elder sister Joan was seriously mentally retarded. This put an immense strain on my mother throughout Joan's life, though she took great care over her and often took her out from her residential home. It explained why in later years she campaigned for the Wiltshire Branch of the Mental Health Foundation. A building attached to a Salisbury mental hospital was named after her. Someone who worked with her in this area commented, 'She always made everything that we did such fun.'

My mother was educated at Downe House. She acted in many plays at school and in Wiltshire and especially at Wilton House. She went to Newnham College, Cambridge, and got a half-blue at lacrosse. However she failed to complete her degree course because she had a nervous breakdown, triggered probably by the strain of caring for her elder sister Joan, and particularly the effect of her epileptic fits. There was always a considerable amount of nervous tension in my mother, though frequently camouflaged by her humour. I used to think that she sometimes worried too much about minor issues.

She was a most gifted writer, principally of plays and diaries. While living at Rockingham Castle in her twenties she wrote *The Kingmaker*, a play set during the Wars of the Roses in the fifteenth century. Two families epitomise the conflict: the Nevilles, led by Warwick the Kingmaker, and the Woodvilles. The play focuses on the turmoil of the times and the rivalries between the warlords.

The play toured the country, appearing eventually at the St James's Theatre, London, on 14 May 1946. The cast was led by John Clements as Warwick and included Kay Hammond, Dame Irene Vanbrugh, Robert Eddison and Moira Lister. I saw it aged nine or so in several theatres round the country. Queen Mary was in the royal box when I saw it at the St James's. Whenever my mother attended a performance she would be summoned on the stage at the end by John Clements amidst loud applause, and she was always given many bouquets. It caused me immense worry and embarrassment to see the rather frail figure of my mother appearing on the stage. Our book of press cuttings shows the acclaim in which it was held. It certainly stimulated my interest in history, drawn out by Sir Jack Plumb, my tutor at Cambridge. She later wrote a few other plays, like *Harvest Time*, which I saw in the Kew Theatre and *Orange Island*, a comedy about life in an island colony, in the Salisbury Theatre. I remember also while at school at Wellington a play called *Chameleon*, which was viewed on television by a large audience on a snowy night, and which had appalling reviews. Her other plays were not in the same league as *The Kingmaker*.

After my parents married in 1934 my mother's life changed dramatically and she spent, on and off, over thirty years with my father in the Middle East. Although she lived for several months each year in Britain, she gave unstinted support to my father throughout his career, often at the expense of her health. He could not have achieved all that he did without her support, advice and presence. While this new focus in her life had an adverse effect on the writing of plays, it did encourage her to produce some remarkably entertaining and interesting diaries, mainly on the Sudan, Aden and the Gulf, which gave an insight into the last years of British rule and into what it was like to be the wife of a proconsul. An edited version of her diaries entitled *From Aden to the Gulf* was published with a foreword by Alec Home in 1987. Regrettably, Sir Anthony Parsons and I had to persuade her to take out some of the more sensitive descriptions of life for the women in the Rulers' harems. My mother was one of the first to penetrate these harems and was deeply shocked by the Arabs' cultural approach to women and by their lack of opportunities. However an unexpurgated version would undoubtedly have upset the Rulers, who were friends of the family and with whom I still had contact. Even then the diaries were not allowed in Qatar. Later on it might be appropriate to publish a much fuller version of those diaries.

My mother died in the autumn of 1989, twelve years after my father, in her early eighties. When I went over to see her in hospital one Sunday she thanked me for taking the trouble to come to see her. She died two or three hours after I left her. She had a well-attended memorial service in the church at Hambledon and my son Alexander read a delightful poem that he wrote in memory of her.

The letters I received after her death highlighted her character. They refer always to her special sense of humour, her charm, her lack of pomposity, her sense of informality, her intelligence and perspective. As one said: 'Margaret had that love in the deepest sense of interest and thought for everyone with whom she was in contact.' Although she wasn't a regular churchgoer she was spiritual in a simple way, and utterly confident of the world to come, and therefore unafraid of death. She once had a dream after her brother Trevie's death and woke up certain that she knew that he was all right, but could not describe it fully to me.

I owe her just about everything for my survival in my early life and especially at school. I've kept most of her letters. They were the one thing that sustained me through all those miserable days. Her understanding was deep, and she kept the flame of hope alive in me. She turned out also to be a superb teacher, taking me away from school for one term and instructing me in English and history in Khartoum.

Many rightly described her as an enchanting character and said that they felt all the better for having seen her. Her official parties in the Middle East became totally relaxed. She played bicycle polo on the terrace of Aden's Government House and fractured her skull. She was vivacious company, but often had to be ticked off by my father for revealing secret information absent-mindedly. She too played the piano and often sang familiar songs of those times, so carried away that her fingers frequently missed the note.

By the time my father died she was becoming an unhappy person, with all the consequences that can flow from that. Notwithstanding her sense of perspective of life, there was much nervous tension in her. She often became obsessive about particular subjects – such as the fear that our first child would be rhesus negative. I think she was probably pretty spoilt as a child, perhaps in compensation for Joan, which meant that she lacked a certain measure of self-discipline. I asked myself why she seemed so unhappy in the last ten years of her life and felt that one important reason, in addition to the loss of my father, was that she was a frustrated playwright whose talent had never been fulfilled. John Clements felt that she could have become one of the great women playwrights, but her life abroad with my father put paid to all that. She never again wrote anything of the same quality as *The Kingmaker*.

I look back on my parents with immense gratitude and inspiration.

3

Growing Up

There is a danger that memory – or lack of memory – will do odd things to the picture we have of childhood. All we can give is an impression. I have to say that the first eight years of my life strike me as almost the happiest and most secure.

I was born in London in 1936, where a few days later my mother, on leaving for Wiltshire, allegedly forgot about me and left me on the kitchen table by mistake before returning hastily to collect me. My early years were spent at Sedgehill, which was rented from the Rimington family in the 1930s and 1940s by my Napier grandmother. It was a peaceful, fairly isolated house in the countryside between Shaftesbury and East Knoyle. Nothing much happened down that lane, which led on to the church and to the very small local school and farms. My memories are of a peaceful family life in the quiet country-side. The garden was dominated by a vast elm tree with an enormous branch that came right down to the ground. I have a painting of it by my aunt Gim Luce. Our principal pastime seems to have been climbing the tree and playing in a wooden boat with wheels. Walks were down lanes to a stream where paper boats were made for me to float. I woke up in the morning to the loud cawing of rooks in and around the nests in the surrounding trees.

In those early days my father was in the Sudan for much of the time, so I have no impression of him at that stage. My mother was the central figure in my life, but a strong support was Glenys Snook, who looked after me until about 1941 when she became a wartime land girl. She must have been in her early twenties and was a very attractive character with a pretty and charming smile who did much to make me secure and happy. I never saw her again until the 1980s. One evening in Parliament the MP for a Gloucestershire seat, John Cope, told me he had been approached by my nanny in the market place whilst canvassing and asked to send a message to me. I got down to her home in Bristol as speedily as I could. There she was standing at the door. I hadn't seen her for over forty years. She sat me down on the sofa and said that there was only one thing she wanted to know: 'Do you still eat as much chocolate as you used to?' I told her that I still loved it. Nothing except time had changed our relationship and we carried on as before. Thereafter I kept in touch with her for I was devoted to her and owed her a great deal. She died at a good age in 2001.

The family atmosphere at Sedgehill was a lively and happy one. I and my sister D shared the house with my first cousins, the Napiers. Uncle Trevie, my mother's brother married to Aunt Priscilla, had three children, Miles, Lavinia and Anne. All five of us were brought up together. Miles was just like a brother to me and Vin was my contemporary. We all played together to our hearts' content, with the usual hair-raising consequences: on one occasion Miles drank some Jeyes Fluid, imagining it was beer, and was lucky to survive. We later threw some elephant bullets into a garden fire, which exploded in all directions. On another occasion my mentally handicapped Aunt Joan chased us round the garden with a shotgun. Fortunately I don't think it was loaded.

In 1944 my maternal grandmother died of cancer. She was a spiritual person, and I recall being summoned to her bedside on my birthday – two days, it so happened, before she died. She gave me a Bible and a prayer book. Our meeting left a deep impression on me and it was the last time I saw her. My mother explained that she had died. I inquired, 'What happens when you die?' She replied, 'You stop breathing and go to the next world.' For a long time after that I had breathless moments and was terrified that I could be on my way.

My awareness of the war came from occasional sightings, high in the sky, of aircraft chasing each other and smoke trails emerging. It was exciting rather than frightening. On one occasion, however, I was taken to the Cadogan Hotel in London, and while I was resting after lunch a flying bomb exploded nearby. That did succeed in frightening me. Many years later I discovered that early in the war my mother had sent a telegram to my father, stationed in a remote part of the Sudan, to say that if Hitler invaded she would shoot me. My sister was to be preserved but she thought that the Nazis would do unmentionable things to all British males. This caused me immense amusement afterwards but equally apprehension as to how my father, thousands of miles away, could have dissuaded her from such a finite ending for me!

My mother periodically arranged for us to visit places away from home. We went to Rockingham Castle, owned by my cousins the Culme-Seymours. There three or four families of relations lived in different parts of the castle. We all met for breakfast at King John's table in the Hall with our rations of sugar, marmalade and margarine. Rockingham helped to give me a great sense of history. Before she married, my mother spent ages in the Long Gallery writing *The Kingmaker*. We also visited Norton Conyers, the historic country house of Richard and Beatrice Graham, with a beautiful field including walnut trees in front and a lovely separate walled garden. This was reputed to be the original of the house of Mr Rochester in *Jane Eyre*. And then after the war when my mother was abroad I would stay at Stokehill near Buckland Monachorum in Devon with the Napiers. Aunt Priscilla took charge of me in those days and was a substitute mother to me when needed. I was devoted to her.

At Sedgehill's nearby church, my grandmother, mother, Priscilla and Trevie are all buried. My mother's grave looks out over the beautiful and peaceful countryside, bringing back memories for me of those happy early days of family life.

I felt safe and secure at Sedgehill until, aged eight in 1945, my parents made plans for me to go to a boarding prep school, The Old Malt House in Dorset, near Swanage. This was the convention in those days, and in addition my parents felt they had no alternative to my boarding since my father was in the Sudan, where my mother naturally wanted to join him.

The change was sudden, dramatic, and a turning point. It shattered me. I can clearly remember being left at the school feeling totally bereft and watching my mother drive away, obviously in agony. The only thing that really saved me over the many years at school was getting her magical letters. Each time a letter arrived I derived some comfort from reading her thoughts, which were always helpful and often inspiring. They helped give me the courage to continue.

I must have been a very timid boy. Certainly such self-confidence as I possessed disappeared at the Malt House. It was a nightmare. I was put into boxing in my first week and was dispatched right out of the ring. To this day I am haunted by a fear and dislike of being herded around, hating lessons and games and performing in front of others.

After some weeks of this, my mother took a big risk and extracted me from the Malt House for the whole of my second term. I was in Khartoum with her for three or four months, being taught history and English by her and maths by a tutor. Without doubt I was happy and started to enjoy learning, particularly writing. My mother was a wonderful teacher, far better than any others I had at prep school, and several terms later one of my essays was picked out by the headmaster as being exceptional. He read it aloud to the entire school.

I may have returned to the Malt House with a little more self-confidence. But it does not help when you are woken up late at night and sent down to the headmaster, Mr Haggard, for six strokes of the cane, the reason given being a poor standard of work. There was plenty of bullying, but I was lucky to have Miles Napier, my first cousin, at school with me. He was twice as tall as anyone else. On one occasion I was being chased around the grounds by a gang. Suddenly I realised they were no longer after me. Miles had waited behind a bush while I passed and then stepped out, whereupon the gang dispersed immediately. I owe much to Miles's friendship at both prep and public school. Once the whole school watched and cheered Miles in a fight with another boy in which he drew blood, reminiscent of *Tom Brown's Schooldays*.

My poor mother worried intensely about me. One day, during the holidays at Rockingham Castle, she took me into Kettering to shop. On the way she tried hard to get me to tell her why I was so unhappy at school. I was unable to tell her because I didn't know why, other than I was miserable. She became so exasperated that she made me get out of the car and stand by the road until I told her. At one point she started to drive off and then lost her nerve and backed the car towards me virtually into the ditch. I still couldn't tell her. Looking back I have every sympathy with my mother's exasperation. She had no alternative to sending me to boarding school if she was ever to see my father.

The headmaster, Mr Haggard, was a controversial character. He had a charming wife, and some of the other teachers were perfectly nice, and sometimes great fun. I always enjoyed the walk a mile or so to the sea in the summer at Dancing Ledge, but there we were made to jump into the rock pool, often out of our depth, or off the ledge into the sea. If we couldn't swim, a master would rescue us with a rod and loop. To my amazement I was made a school captain at the Malt House, although I can't think that I had much influence. Captains had the power to beat other boys, but I can't recall ever having done that. In 2000 when I sailed home from Gibraltar, the first sight of Britain on approaching Portsmouth was the Dancing Ledge and Swanage. It horrified me still.

In 1950 I moved on to Wellington College in Berkshire. My mother was keen for me to go to Eton, but I was quite clear that this was totally unacceptable, as I would have to dress up in those ghastly clothes. It was fortunate that my cousin Miles, as the son of a serviceman who had died in the war, had already been at Wellington for two or three years.

Wellington was for me no improvement on the Old Malt House. Very early on, bullying by a particular boy made me utterly miserable. On one occasion this character managed, just before bedtime, to suspend me with my dressing gown round my neck over the banisters on the top floor. Some fifty years after this incident, I had just arrived as Governor of Gibraltar when I received a call from this same character who was living in southern Spain just along the coast from Gibraltar. He wanted to meet. The call itself caused me a terrible shock, but Rose persuaded me that the best thing to do would be to invite him and his wife to tea. They came and were rather pathetic and sad. He persisted in congratulating me on succeeding in life and implying that he had made rather a mess of things. I think he was removed from Wellington during my days there. I concluded that he must have bullied a large number of boys and was oblivious of the fact that I had been one of his victims. Perhaps this indicates that there is a kind of rough justice in life.

The consequences of this bullying were serious at the time. I missed the beginning of the second term due to the delay in returning from the Sudan. I took the train alone from my parents' home in Fovant in Wiltshire to Crowthorne in Berkshire, changing at Waterloo. Whilst travelling from Waterloo I began to panic, wondering why I should return to a place where I was tortured and which was like a prison. By the time the train reached Crowthorne I was sweating profusely and people in the carriage looked concerned. The stationmaster was baffled but allowed me to cross the platform and catch the next train back to Waterloo. I eventually arrived back at Fovant in the middle of the night. In those days doors and windows were often left unlocked, and

I crept in through the drawing-room window so as not to disturb my grandmother, Gar. I awoke the next morning to hear her on the telephone, saying that she had told the police and there was no more she could do. I shouted out to her from upstairs and she answered quite calmly, 'Oh there you are, my dear. We had been wondering where you had got to.'

After some discussion she decided with me that we would have three nice days at home, go out for drives and relax, after which she would take me back to Wellington. I went back and never again did I hear from anyone in the school any reference to my running away. That was clearly my grandmother's influence. In the train I was defiant, blowed if I was going to be defeated by Wellington. Afterwards I felt utter shame and embarrassment at the worry I had caused my family. My parents wrote firm but encouraging letters from the Sudan which helped me put things in perspective, and my mother urged me in future to think like a general: 'Who looks at, and considers, every possibility, bad and good, carefully beforehand, and knows what he is in for. He is the one who wins.' She urged me not to worry and panic. My father commented 'It wasn't a very good thing to do', but urged me in future 'to talk things over with us in advance'. They must have been terribly anxious. In recent years it has become a matter of amusement to me, and my family, that I ran away from Wellington. It wasn't quite so funny at the time.

Correspondence with my parents reveals a timid, unconfident boy who disappeared like a tortoise into his shell, lacked much sense of humour, felt a sense of failure, and took life pretty seriously. In one letter to my parents I wrote about a biology film shown at school on the facts of life: 'It was the last straw. I don't think I need worry about it for another six or seven years, which is very relieving. You said in your letter it was just an ordinary thing that one need not worry about, but it seems to me to be the absolute end.'

Wellington was a matter of survival. I shone at nothing, whether academic or sporting, though I did take up fencing and became a glider pilot. I was absorbed by events overseas and I recorded in a book extracts from *The Times* on topical issues like the Korean war and developments in the Sudan. I hated exams and continued to have nightmares about them in later years. When I was seventeen my housemaster, Mr Horsley, told me that I wasn't capable of passing the necessary exams to get into university. Indeed he went much further than this by saying to me and a close friend, John Friedberger (who later became a general), 'You are the two most useless boys that Wellington has ever had.' I retorted that what he meant was that Wellington wasn't capable of getting me into university.

I left the College at the age of seventeen of my own accord, and studied at a tutorial college, Davies, Laing and Dick, where I got 'A' levels in History and Oral French. These enabled me to scrape into university.

Two or three years later my mother wrote me a most encouraging and inspiring letter. She listed all the things at both schools that various masters had said I would not achieve, all of which all had been proved wrong. She said, 'Everything you have achieved, you have achieved on your own, mostly by determination not to admit failure.' She concluded, 'You have got in yourself the foundation of a real assured and splendid future.'

I do not see how I could have got through school without the support of my mother and the calm and wise assurance of my father. I knew that I was loved by them both. I clung to that lifebelt. However I desperately needed to lose my introspection and shyness and to look outwards. During one school holiday my mother reproved me for shaking hands with guests and looking at the ground. She said to me, 'Instead of thinking of yourself and your reaction to the stranger, try looking at the person direct in the face and thinking about what he or she might be like, or interested in.' It was simple but remarkably effective advice.

Looking back, I can see that both schools taught me one thing, probably inadvertently: in the face of constant adversity I learnt how to deal with it in later life. I no longer feel any bitterness towards my schools and it wasn't their fault that I was miserable there; I would probably have been so at any school. School life engendered a permanent feeling of insecurity about big things as well as small things, but more importantly it equipped me to cope with the tough outside world. One great friend told me that it was a disaster for him that he was the outstanding scholar and sportsman of his school. He thought the world would be at his feet and it wasn't.

Once, when a rather pompous new peer was making his maiden speech, he said, 'I shall conclude by proposing a question to myself.' Quick as a flash the Lord Chancellor Lord Hailsham said, 'And you'll get a bloody silly answer!' In posing a question to myself about our education system I hope to avoid that fate. If we were starting from scratch I would not advocate our educational system. Boarding aged eight for most children, for example, could be disastrous. It certainly was for me. It was, however, considered appropriate in the time of our Empire, and an inevitable form of education for our aristocracy and upper middle class.

The educational pattern does not fit the contemporary requirement. Seven per cent of all students go to independent schools. Obviously their parents have the wealth to manage the formidable fees, which means that they tend to come from a particular social background and aren't encouraged to mix with children of all social backgrounds. Notwithstanding the high fees, parents have continued to find the money to send their children to public schools, reasoning that they want what they consider to be the best all-round education for their children. Many public schools do indeed offer a high level of academic teaching and a broad education, and thus a good preparation for the world outside. However the underlying resentment from those who rightly feel that it is a privilege which only money can buy and the continuing debate about the proportion of university places which go to independent as opposed to state schools continues to cause tension.

The problem isn't solved by abolishing independent schools or by withdrawing their charitable status. We have to preserve the best schools in both independent and state sectors and use them as a benchmark to improve standards for all and to broaden the prospects of children of all backgrounds to benefit from the best education. Various attempts have been made to broaden the base for those who are less well off. The Assisted Places Scheme in the 1980s and '90s meant that some academically able children from underprivileged backgrounds could go to independent schools. Now sadly that has gone. I would advocate its return. Similarly it was a profound mistake to have abolished grammar schools, for in doing so we have thereby succeeded in lowering the general standards of education. We will always need centres of academic excellence to set the pace. Perhaps the biggest educational tragedy of postwar years is that successive Governments have failed to ensure adequate standards in all state schools in this country. That must be our highest priority.

An additional problem is the obsessive concentration today on exams and academic achievement. What we need are children with a rounded education. Of course that must include an important academic challenge. But the development of the character is of overwhelmingly greater importance – a sense of commitment to fellow human beings, the development of natural talents in each individual, the qualities of self-discipline, learning to take initiatives to cope with adversity, to show courage and enterprise and to have a broad view and knowledge of the world outside. I'm glad that many employers are now looking for these broader characteristics. We have a long way to go to get the balance right.

4
National Service

I look back on National Service with mixed feelings. I am pleased to have experienced it, but found it at the time by turns difficult, agonising and exciting.

I was eighteen when I was called up in the summer of 1955. I was not considered physically fit enough for the infantry and was sent to Oswestry for basic training with the Royal Artillery. Life became a simple matter of survival. We rose at 5 am and worked hard until 11 pm. At that time my father's negotiations with the rebel leaders for their surrender in the South Sudan made the headlines each day. The RSM took one look at me on parade and said, 'Your father may be negotiating with the rebels, but you're a bloody rebel yourself!'

Fortunately I was able to persuade the authorities to transfer me to the infantry after a fortnight. I was despatched to a training camp at Exeter before joining my county regiment, The Wiltshires (The Duke of Edinburgh's Own). My time at Exeter nearly turned me into a communist. I loathed being shouted at and found the physical work very difficult. The assault course included a tunnel into which, once you were crawling inside, thunderflashes were thrown from both ends, causing a nightmare sensation of choking and claustrophobia. One day I was made to run across water on a narrow log with heavy equipment on my back. I fell in and rapidly sank, only to feel a hand grasp me by the neck. It was the Company Sergeant Major retrieving me.

I was in a rebellious mood at Exeter, caused by one officer whom I particularly disliked and who gave unnecessary orders to men in my hut where I was acting lance corporal in charge. Later he disciplined me for not implementing his order and withdrew my lance corporal's stripe. I was put on extra duties peeling potatoes. This was laborious but not too difficult as there was a machine which peeled them once I had washed them. I was clearly not a natural soldier: I detested marching around on parade, not to mention the endless cleaning of equipment, belt and boots. A few days doing military exercises was more enjoyable, even though the temperature in our tent at night was well below freezing.

My chance to appear before the War Office Selection Board and apply to be an officer seemed to be being postponed. I never quite got to the heart of this delay, but reluctantly had to ask my father's twin brother and former Army officer, Ted Luce, to intervene with the War Office to find out the cause.

The summons duly came through and I passed the three-day test and went to Eaton Hall for officer training. Here officer cadets were treated with a little more respect, though the course was tough and rigorous both intellectually and physically – considerably tougher than Exeter. I recall one training expedition where I managed only three hours' sleep during a seventy-hour exercise. One evening I got quite drunk and was seen singing merrily on a first-floor windowsill. The next moment I had disappeared. I had fallen out of the window and landed in a flowerbed below, fortunately uninjured.

My father, who had just been appointed Governor of Aden, came up to Cheshire to watch the passing out parade in July 1956. He stayed with the GOC Western Command, General Whistler. The RSM gave me permission to have tea with them, knowing it was with the General, but somewhat spitefully put me on extra duties very early the following morning. It was a huge relief to have survived the course. My fellow cadets were congenial and I made a lasting friendship with Christopher Tugendhat. He and I were later at Cambridge and then in Parliament together before he became a European commissioner in Brussels.

I joined the Wiltshire Regiment for a few days at their headquarters in Devizes where I settled in as a junior officer and gradually got used to the idea of command. In September I joined the regiment in Cyprus. This country could best be summed up as 'God's own country with the Devil's own problems', a description once used by a minister in Attlee's Government, I think about Kenya; but it was just as relevant then to Cyprus.

This eastern Mediterranean island has seen many historical changes over the centuries: Byzantine and Roman Empires, the Crusaders and more recently the Ottoman Empire. Following the Berlin Congress, towards the end of the nineteenth century, the British assumed responsibility. In the mid 1950s Greek Cypriot terrorists, led by Grivas, carried out a violent campaign against the British in favour of 'Enosis', or union with Greece. The campaign was conducted mainly from the Troodos mountains and the Kyrenia range. A state of emergency was declared and Field Marshal Sir John Harding, former CIGS, was sent out as Governor and Commander-in-Chief. Along with other colonies Cyprus was moving slowly but ineluctably towards independence. This campaign however threatened the stability of the island because the Turkish Government was clearly opposed to 'Enosis' and, without decisive British action, might have been tempted to invade northern Cyprus to protect the Turkish Cypriots.

The Wiltshire Regiment battalion was stationed in Kyrenia, the largest town on the northern coast, and along the hills and coast on either side of the town. Headquarters was at Aghirda camp, which controlled the St Hilarion pass leading from Nicosia down to Kyrenia, looking across the forty miles to Turkey. Although the area was inhabited mainly by Turkish Cypriots there were some mixed villages scattered in the hills and coastal areas, and some which were Greek Cypriot or Turkish Cypriot only.

It was a challenge for any nineteen-year-old to arrive in these circumstances and take command of a platoon of forty men in a state of emergency. I was based in the historic Kyrenia Castle both at the beginning and the end of my posting, but I spent several months with my company in the hills. Later my platoon encamped on the top of the mountain range. Internal security required special and wide-ranging skills dealing with demonstrations, searching houses and coffee houses, laying ambushes at night to try and catch the terrorists, trying to extract intelligence information from captured terrorists, building a rapport with the population through visits to cafés, schools and churches – and setting up roadblocks and searches.

There were three identified Eoka gangs operating in the Kyrenia range. They threw bombs, set time bombs and engineered demonstrations, and then melted back into the villages or the hills. In the Castle we held up to fifty terrorist suspects in cages. Our fingers seemed too often on the trigger in this tense atmosphere. There were a few casualties which included two or three men from my platoon. Looking back I am sure that at times we were unnecessarily tough and perhaps patronising towards the Cypriots. Certainly prisoners were tortured to gain information. But in an emergency and facing violence it is difficult not to get angry with people who shelter terrorists. All the same I and my platoon attempted to get to know and understand the local population.

Archbishop Makarios was behind much of the violence. In one week in November eighteen people were killed and another eighteen injured by Eoka. The Greek Orthodox Church, of which Makarios was head in Cyprus, ran the secondary schools or gymnasiums. Children, after a good primary education, moved on to these at fourteen where they were indoctrinated by the Church with hatred for the British, and no doubt the Turks. The children were given leaflets to distribute and were often participants in demonstrations. The Greek Cypriots in particular were sullen and difficult to talk to, though I made a considerable effort to do so. It seemed so incongruous that in the sleepy villages of these beautiful hills – Lapithos, Karmi, Bellapais, Templos, Ayios Ambrosis – were terrorists, supported and sustained by the Greek Cypriot population.

Life in such circumstances was tough and challenging, sometimes exciting, sometimes merely exasperating and exhausting. I was on duty with my platoon for four and a half months every day without a break. We lived in tents in the mountains, marched up to twenty miles a day and were often on night duty and ambushes. I became very fond of the men and learnt a lot about their home lives. I was lucky to have Sergeant Puffett to help me and we formed a strong bond with each other. Quite apart from the emergency we were able to enjoy training and sports together. When I was posted back to Kyrenia to a new platoon, I was touched to discover that my platoon had petitioned the regiment for me to stay with them.

I visited the regimental headquarters very seldom, except at the beginning and end of my stay. On my last day the adjutant informed me that I was entitled to read the report of General Coad, the honorary colonel of the regiment, which he wrote after an interview with me when I applied to join the regiment. In it he said that he was only recommending me to the regiment due to my Uncle Ted Luce's distinguished record with them; that I had strong views and should be kept with my platoon in the mountains and out of headquarters!

I can't say that I had much in common with the senior officers of my regiment. The commanding officer, Colonel Hunter, did however take some trouble to keep in touch with me during my time there, and Major 'Dim' Robbins was most kind and spent time talking to me as much about current affairs as regimental business.

We were lucky to have Harding as our Governor. He was kind enough to invite me to lunch with other guests and promised to help me, if I needed it. Later I acted as his ADC for the day when he visited Kyrenia Castle for the regimental celebration. He was brilliant with people and remembered them and their names.

In the autumn of 1956, on the outbreak of the Suez War, the regiment, part of the 51st Brigade, was put on forty-eight hours' notice to fly to the Canal Zone in Egypt. Tensions ran high, and one Labour MP urged the cutting off of supplies to British troops in the Middle East in order to end the conflict. This scarcely endeared the Labour Party to me. However the abrupt termination of the war meant that we continued our work in Cyprus.

In March 1957 Archbishop Makarios was released from exile in the Seychelles and flew to Athens. A most untrustworthy character, he was regarded by the Greek Cypriots as their religious and political leader. I felt at the time that the only way to achieve peace and progress was to get Makarios on board and to try to isolate the terrorists. I hoped that we could negotiate for a military base after independence.

National Service helped the individual to mature very quickly. I remember at Cambridge how immature the new undergraduates seemed who had not done National Service. My diaries show a demonstrable change from embarrassing immaturity to a growing sense of responsibility. But I can understand the reason why Service leaders have never wanted to revive National Service. The conscripted are counting the days to departure and therefore undermine the professionals. I felt that the two-year experience was good for me but bad for the Army. It is a pity, however, that there appears to be no alternative for young people today, except for the gap year.

Cyprus is a beautiful country, especially in the spring, with the flowers and the views, as Lawrence Durrell described so well in *Bitter Lemons*. Although Britain did well to negotiate independence under the leadership of the new Governor, Sir Hugh Foot, and to retain the bases of Akrotiri and Dhekelia, Cyprus has not lived at peace since. The subsequent occupation by Turkish troops of the north including Kyrenia led to partition and the unhappy migration of families. They deserve better. Perhaps one day Cyprus will become God's own country after all.

5

Following the Flag

My early days in the Sudan have had a lifelong effect on me. I loved the Sudanese, Arab and Nilotic alike. Imagine the excitement of boarding a flying boat in Poole Harbour in 1947, aged eleven, on my first flight to the Sudan for the Christmas holidays. The flying boat was often bumpy as it flew through clouds, but we could lie down on a bunk on the top deck. The first night was spent in Marseilles with the sensation of a soft landing in the sea; the next morning we flew onwards across the Mediterranean with lunch in a restaurant in Augusta with a lovely view of Mount Etna. The second night's stop was Alexandria and the next day we flew to Cairo, landing on the Nile. Airsickness and earaches due to aircraft pressure were inevitable but these were nothing to the exhilaration of the adventure. We finally transferred to a train to cross the Sudan desert from Wadi Halfa. In later years we flew from Blackbushe Airport near Camberley by Viking aircraft, with one night only in Malta. We were all children of members of the Sudan Political Service; a night in the Phoenicia Hotel in Malta was uncontrollably riotous and enjoyable.

Khartoum, designed in the shape of the Union Jack, was a lovely city where the White and Blue Nile converged, with the Palace, where Gordon was killed, dominating the river. Christmas was a very social time, with tennis and plenty of swimming at the Club. The houses had flat roofs on which, in the heat, we could sleep enshrouded in mosquito nets. Local prisoners irrigated the garden once a week. I learnt to sail in dinghies moored by the *Malik*, the ship in which Kitchener sailed up the Nile too late to rescue Gordon. We would set off with picnics and land on some deserted sandy Nile shore, or sail down to Tuti Island, avoiding crocodiles, and hoping not to get bilharzia from walking on the river's edge. Christmas, in particular, was a very social time, with tennis and plenty of swimming at the Club.

In Wad Medani, where my father was based as Governor of Blue Nile Province, Government House had a generous garden and wide verandahs where we sat for lunch, tea and supper. Picnics in the desert or on the site of the Battle of Omdurman were fun. Several days on a Nile steamer were tremendous, watching my father deal with local problems at different stops. In the Sudd area, islands of grass would float past us. The braying of donkeys, the superior look of camels and the active birdlife were all part of the scene.

In Equatoria Province we experienced the different views and smells of real Africa and enjoyed the mass of wildlife, including elephants, lions, rhinos, hippos and gazelle, around our house in Juba and on trek in the Nimule Reserve. We would call on the local missionaries for breakfast and camp in rest houses in Nimule or in the Ngong Hills where the undergrowth was thick and green with plenty of rain. In the cool evenings a log fire would burn in our rest house.

There was rough shooting in abundance and it was almost impossible to miss a fat guinea fowl. I joined my father on an organised shoot early one morning with the Governor General's party: at the crack of dawn we shot sand grouse as they came in to drink. This made me rather despise the mass slaughter of formal shoots in Britain.

Servants were a daily feature of life. Sayed Osman was my parents' senior servant and we had absorbing conversations in a mixture of Arabic and English. We were talking intensely once about religion, Jesus and Mohamed. Suddenly Sayed said, 'I know! Jesus and Mohamed were brothers, one for the whites and one for the blacks.' The thought that we all share one God but are represented on earth by the experiences of different prophets and messiahs has stayed with me. Sayed stayed on with the British embassy after independence, making the tea for the ambassador and staff. When I returned for the first time to the Sudan as an MP in 1971, there outside my Nile hotel room was Sayed who arrived in the night and waited for me to emerge. We hugged each other. Later, as Minister of State, I visited the Sudan and took part in a ceremony at which the ambassador, Sir Alexander Stirling, awarded Sayed the BEM for his services. I was asked to say a few words in front of the embassy staff and Sayed's family. As words were translated, Sayed constantly interrupted my speech to add his comments or to disagree with the dates. It caused great amusement. His son was later employed as an office manager at the embassy. One morning he rang me in Britain, simply to say all was well. It was only later that I realised he could not bring himself to tell me that his father had died.

There was no shortage of parties among the British community and we occasionally dined or had tea with distinguished Sudanese. My sister D and I could hardly contain ourselves as our Sudanese hosts burped constantly in appreciation of their food. We had tea sometimes with the Mahdi, the grandson of the famous Mahdi, at his palace, where he gave us delicious cake for tea and paraded his racehorses below the verandah. I remember the Governor General arriving at our home for dinner in a Rolls-Royce and Lady Howe stepping into the hedge, making a rather undignified arrival.

My father took me to the opening of Parliament after the first full-scale elections. Afterwards the PM, Mr Azhari, asked me to join my father for tea with him. I took the opportunity to ask him how he won the election. I have used his answer ever since: 'Oh, it was very easy,' he said, 'I asked my supporters to call on all houses and identify if they were going to vote for the opposition. If so, they were to offer transport in the early morning of polling day. At 0700 hours they put them into lorries, took them twenty-five miles into the desert, and told them to make their own way home, thus missing the vote!'

For me the Sudan is the charm of the Arabs in their *galibiyahs* and in contrast the naked, or semi-naked, Nilotic tribesmen of the Africa south of the Sahara. They never got on well together, as the Arabs, encouraged by the Egyptians, wanted to control the South and the source of the Nile. It has been a deeply unhappy story ever since and disturbing to see these good people destroying themselves by civil wars and conflict in the South, Darfur and elsewhere. I loved the Sudan. They deserve a better future.

ADEN AND THE GULF

My father was Governor of Aden from 1956 to 1960, arriving as the Suez Canal crisis was erupting.

There was a flow of visitors through Aden both by air and sea. I remember the former Governor General of Australia, Lord Slim, coming for breakfast off his ship en route for Australia. Before my father could say 'Good morning, sir', Lord Slim had got it in first to the serving Governor. There were frequent dinner parties for guests in Government House or for leaders in the community. I remember lighting a very large Havana cigar and turning to a general to ask him a polite question, whereupon I burnt his moustache – to his horror, and mine.

Sometimes I would fly out on an RAF plane if there was a spare seat; otherwise by BOAC. Returning to England from Christmas one year, I was accompanied by Lord Tedder. As we flew over Italy, he said that he wanted to go and sit somewhere else, and would I mind. A few minutes later I saw him on his own in tears looking at the land below, remembering all the wartime casualties when he was Deputy Supreme Allied Commander to Eisenhower.

While on National Service in Cyprus, the Commander-in-Chief Middle East, Air Marshal Patch, arranged for me to fly down in his aircraft to see my father over a long weekend. Duncan Sandys, the Defence Minister, came to stay. On leaving for the airport he became bossy and started to tell my father how to do his job, whereupon he was quickly rebuked: 'Secretary of State, you do your job and I'll do mine.'

On one occasion while I was at university I flew out with friends, Mark Coe (who was later murdered by the IRA) and John Friedberger. Together we were nicknamed 'The Three Musketeers'. When the ADC, Tony Ramus, offered to take us up in turn in a Mosquito fighter, Mark, rather unwisely, said that he wanted Tony to do everything he could with the aircraft. We watched them take off and disappear into the clouds only to emerge upside down just above the sea. Mark had to be carried out, pea green. When my turn came I asked Tony to take it easy, only to be rewarded with a hair-raising dive down towards an Arab fort.

My father arranged for the three of us to fly over to Hargeisa, the capital of British Somaliland, where the Chief Secretary kindly arranged for us to go trekking in the Haud Reserve area. Accompanied by camels carrying our tents and equipment, we walked ten or fifteen miles each day, shooting sand grouse at dawn. On one occasion some Somali women appeared, took one look at us and ran. They had never seen a white man before.

Aden Colony was not very exciting. Government House occupied a commanding position on a promontory and looked like an ugly cinema. My father's office and those of the staff were in the house. There were private quarters upstairs for my parents and large rooms including a ballroom. There were tennis courts in the grounds and swimming in the sea from a private beach below. The harbour was packed with ships. In Aden I often accompanied my father on engagements. On one occasion he told me to go ahead to a reception whilst he had a haircut. As I stepped out of the car a band struck up the National Anthem which gradually petered out as they realised that I was not the Governor. Occasionally I visited the Eastern and Western Aden Protectorates, driving up once in a military convoy to the Yemen border. While crossing a pass surrounded by mountains on either side we were fired on by rebel forces and I was ordered to take cover beneath our land-rover.

My first visit to the Gulf was in 1959 accompanying my parents in an RAF aircraft. As we flew over the desert to Bahrain, I was reading Thesiger's magical book on the Empty Quarter, *Arabian Sands*. Sir George Middleton was the Political Resident. After staying with him we visited Sharjah, Abu Dhabi and Dubai, small towns now unrecognisably transformed into the modern cities of today. And then to the beautifully mountainous Oman where the Consul General's historic house, now dismantled, used to be in the harbour of Muscat below the prison. The Gulf in those days had far fewer British citizens but Britain had disproportionate influence. Today there are thousands more citizens, but we no longer have direct responsibility for the area. We paid a few visits to Bahrain when my father was Political Resident. In those days the Residency was by the sea. Today the house is derelict and the land reclaimed with tallish buildings all round. I can picture the ghosts of my parents reminding me of an imperial past. The Gulf has changed dramatically. But it was fascinating to witness the twilight of the Raj. The relationship between my father and the Rulers of the Gulf States was a mutually respectful one, though it was absolutely clear that the British were dominant still. The friendly atmosphere continues today.

On one occasion, after I was married, Rose and I flew to the Gulf from Kenya in General Goodwin's aircraft. He was GOC East Africa. We stayed a night with my father's successor in Aden, Sir Charles Johnston. I recall feeling how quiet and unlively it was at Government House now that my parents had moved on. We then had a wonderful Christmas at the Residency in Bahrain.

I am glad that I had a taste of the British Empire in the Middle East, just before it faded. I learnt an immense amount about the Middle East and international affairs generally. I can count myself as supremely fortunate in having had a bird's-eye view of that region from a very privileged position. My affection for and link with the area lives on today in my being patron of the Sir William Luce Memorial Fund based in Durham University (the first chairman having been Sir Donald Hawley, a former colleague of my father). The Fund finances research and fellowships to study subjects of importance concerning the Gulf, South Yemen and the Sudan. These were the countries to which my father gave devoted service.

6

University and Marriage

University life started immediately after my two years of National Service. In those two years most of us had matured very fast and could enjoy the university as young men rather than as grown up schoolboys. Unlike my schooldays, it was a time of happy memories.

Only now do I appreciate how lucky I was to have three years at Cambridge, and a fourth year at Wadham College, Oxford, to complete the Overseas Civil Service Course. My father had been at Christ's College as had other Luces. Yes, there was still a bias in favour of a family link, though it was a narrow squeak for me as I had poor 'A' level qualifications.

The key to both my success and enjoyment was my tutor, Jack Plumb. I was influenced to study history by my mother. Jack, who was a brilliant eighteenth-century historian and an authority on Walpole, brought history alive in his tutorials and lectures. There were never more than three students in his weekly tutorial, at which we would be asked to read out essays in turn and then be challenged, with our arguments frequently torn to pieces.

Cambridge offered a wide range of opportunities and I was soon making new friends, talking over coffee late into the night, playing squash and tennis, taking part in political societies and debating in the Union. I joined the Liberals at one point, largely because I liked Jo Grimond and was attracted by his views, but I gradually became more active with the Conservatives. I aspired to making my mark in the Union, but the truth was that I was too diffident and nervous about public speaking. I did, however, take part in a debate on the question of the ending of debutante presentations at Buckingham Palace. The motion was that 'this House welcomes the twilight of the debs', to which I moved an amendment that 'this House prefers the deb by twilight'.

There were occasional celebrity excitements. I recall being invited to a small gathering of students to meet Dean Acheson. He had been a distinguished American Secretary of State, responsible for the dictum

'Britain has lost an Empire, but has not yet found a role'. But he was a good friend of our country and indeed rather old-style English in his looks and approach. Another memory is of E. M. Forster. He lived in King's College. I met him at Rockingham Castle with the Culme-Seymours and then took him out to tea in my digs at Cambridge with Christopher Tugendhat. He had immense charm. Meanwhile St Mary's Church was very popular under the leadership of Mervyn Stockwood; I remember being very excited to hear Nye Bevan preaching from the pulpit one Sunday evening. Unusually for me, I once walked out of a play. It was Samuel Beckett's *Waiting for Godot*. I couldn't wait that long.

An important opportunity was offered to student historians when Professor Nicholas Mansergh introduced the first course at a British university on the Anglo-Irish Treaty of 1922. I don't quite know what led me to join one of a small group who took it up in my last year, other than a desire to study a contemporary subject. In any event I asked whether three or four of us could go over to Dublin and interview the then President de Valera. To my amazement my request was granted after we had been introduced to Conor Cruise O'Brien, then a Dublin civil servant. We were told we could have half an hour with de Valera, but ended up spending three or four hours with him at his residence in Phoenix Park. He spoke freely, stimulated by a glass or two of sherry. He was almost totally blind by then. It was enthralling to hear his stories of the Easter Uprising (he was only saved from execution because his mother was American) and of Lloyd George and other British statesmen. After the interview I went to Tallow to stay with my Protestant godfather, who was horrified to hear that I had been talking to de Valera.

Life at Cambridge was enlivened by Rose's occasional visits. She stayed in digs around the corner from my own digs in Newmarket Road and I once took her to a May Ball. While I knew other women as student friends, none became girlfriends. For me Rose's visits were very special. I probably hid from her the existence of a brothel opposite my digs, which lent a certain unsavoury cachet to the area.

In the autumn of 1960 I persuaded Rose Nicholson to marry me and the wedding took place at the Temple Church in London on 5 April 1961. I first met Rose seven years earlier, when we were both seventeen and my mother had sent me to live with Madame Sallier du Pin in Blois for three months to learn French. She stressed that I would have to speak French every day as there would only be French people there. On the train down I carefully rehearsed my opening remarks. When I arrived at this lovely house above the Loire on the edge of Blois I was introduced to an attractive girl and boldly announced 'Le soleil brille.' She looked at me as though I was mad. It was Rose who was staying there with three other English girls. So much for learning French! I wrote in my diary that night that one day I would marry her. It took me seven years and a volatile engagement to achieve it. We got engaged in the Lebanon, while we were on a tour of the Middle East with John Friedberger and Iona Macdonald, disengaged in Egypt, and finally engaged a few weeks later on Dartmoor. On that occasion I took her to the top of a tor in rain and wind and told her that she could not descend until she had said 'Yes'. When tensions still continued my father intervened at breakfast one day and said 'I have only one question. Do you want to marry Rose or not?' I replied that I did and he simply said 'Well, get on with it then.' That was the best thing that ever happened to me.

Rose's father was Godfrey Nicholson who served some thirty-five years in Parliament. The Nicholson family came from a solid middle-class background originating from Cumbria. For over 200 years they ran a family gin distilling business, which was eventually sold in the 1980s. In the late nineteenth century the family branched out into Parliament and the Army. Godfrey's only brother Claude commanded the brigade that defended Calais in 1940. By holding out so valiantly and for so long before surrendering he ensured that many thousands more British troops were able to get home from Dunkirk. Sadly he died while still a prisoner of war. Godfrey's uncle Willie Nicholson, who served in Parliament, was once asked by Baldwin what honour he would like to be put up for. He replied 'All I want is to be left alone.'

Rose's mother's family are called Lindsay, stemming originally from Normandy and becoming landed aristocracy in Scotland. In more recent times the family have made a major contribution to the arts, heritage and politics. I got to know the present Earl of Crawford, Rose's first cousin, when he was in the Commons as Lord Balneil. Later, when he was Lord Chamberlain to Queen Elizabeth the Queen Mother, he and I took leading roles in the State Funeral and, with the Dean of Windsor, presided over the final burial alongside George VI in a side crypt of St George's Chapel. Rose's grandfather 'Bal' Crawford was Chief Whip and a minister around the time of the First World War. He is said to have turned down the job of Viceroy of India on the grounds that his wife did not want to go. Earlier he had been instrumental in setting up the National Arts Collection Fund and later the Council for the Protection of Rural England. To add to the political involvement of the family, Rose's aunt Mary married Reggie Manningham-Buller who served in the Macmillan and Home governments as Attorney General and later Lord Chancellor. He was a tough figure in public life and not known as 'Bullingham Manner' for nothing; but in private life he often showed great kindness.

My parents-in- law, Godfrey and Katharine Nicholson, whom I first met in Blois in 1954 when they were on their way to taste and buy wine for the family business. They lived at Bussock Hill House in Berkshire. I first stayed there in the late 1950s, and marrying Rose felt like breaking into a Jane Austen re-enactment. I thought that persuading the first daughter to marry me, and becoming the first son-in-law, was a triumph. With the four daughters – Rose, Laura, Emma and Hatty – the setting was inevitably feminine and domestic. The continual conversation was oriented towards areas of family and domestic interest and often the whole family would join in. For example, the telephone was in the drawing room and no matter who was speaking, everyone seemed to participate. Katharine was the anchor of the household, setting the pace and standard and providing Godfrey with all the peace of family life. This gave him the security and comfort that he needed after the exhaustion of Parliamentary demands. He often spoke of how happy he was at having a united family. He regularly retired to his beloved wood where he would light a fire and chop away to his heart's content. Katharine, too, would disappear to garden for hours on end. Family conversation may have been a little strange to me and sometimes difficult to handle, but there was laughter and happiness in the household.

In his private writings Godfrey recalled the early 1900s in London; he had a small whistle which he employed to summon taxis or hansom cabs, while buses could be stopped anywhere on the road. This was a London still dominated by horses rather than cars. He moved with his parents in 1910 to Woodcott in Hampshire, where his nephew, Dickie Nicholson, has lived in recent times. The head gardener at Woodcott,

Hutchins, had worked at Osborne House on the Isle of Wight as a young man. He told Godfrey that on seeing Queen Victoria one day he said, 'I 'ope as 'ow you'll excuse me but I've been spreading mook.' He reported that the Queen replied, ''Utchins, 'asn't somebody got to spread the mook?'

Godfrey's prep school was St Peter's Court in Broadstairs, also attended by the former Dukes of Kent and Gloucester. He recalled a visit by King George V, who told Godfrey that he thought his writing was very good, a considerable boost to morale. After prep school Godfrey went on to Winchester, which he loved despite a spartan life of cold baths and poor food. But disaster struck him at the end of his time at Winchester when he caught encephalitis lethargica or sleeping sickness. In those days about half of those who caught this disease died immediately, the remainder tending to die of Parkinson's in their forties. In the event Godfrey developed Parkinson's in his eighties and died aged eighty-nine. For the rest of his life an immobile face, clumsy hands, and a lack of concentration affected him, but in every other way he lived a very full and active life.

After obtaining a third class degree in History from Christ Church, Oxford – having been advised not to work too hard as a result of his illness – Godfrey entered the family distillery business, J. & W. Nicholson, which provided an independent job and source of income for the rest of his career. He was later chairman of the company. I remember calling on him there and finding it a very old-fashioned family business.

It was Parliament, however, that was Godfrey's life and career. He loved it and thought that there was no more rewarding job than being an MP. This he did for thirty-five years. He entered Parliament in the 1931 landslide election for Morpeth, which was marked by the extraordinary scene of both Labour and Conservative candidates utterly distressed on the town hall balcony, the Labour candidate because he had lost his majority of 16,500, and Godfrey because he had promised his father that he wouldn't win it and could stay in the family business. He was devoted to the constituents of Morpeth, many of whom were miners and their families, and was very proud of his achievement in getting the Workmen's Compensation Coal Miners Act through Parliament, to compensate miners for health problems. Godfrey appreciated his constituents' sense of humour and enjoyed telling anecdotes about them. During the 1931 election campaign he was speaking rather lengthily at a meeting where he was continually heckled by someone at the back who kept on saying how bored he was. Eventually Godfrey said, 'If you're so bored, why don't you leave?' The man immediately retorted, 'Can't, I'm the caretaker.'

Inevitably politics resumed its traditional party structure and he lost his seat at the next election, but was elected for Farnham in a by-election in 1937 and remained its MP until 1966. His heart, however, was always with the people of Morpeth and it gave him immense pleasure when his daughter Emma fought that constituency in 1979. I used to enjoy my chats about politics with Godfrey, often over a gin and orange before supper. He was a true Parliamentarian and believed deeply in the need for national unity. Baldwin was in many ways the peacetime prime minister he most admired, in particular for his humility, honesty and love of his country. Godfrey believed that Churchill had unfairly maligned Baldwin for not preparing the country for war. Many years later, during a general election in the 1970s, I met one of Baldwin's daughters. She was a reclusive figure who had been deeply wounded by the public criticism of her father. But her face lit up when I said Godfrey was my father-in-law.

Godfrey had a quick wit and was celebrated in the Chamber for his repartee. On one occasion there was a row in the chamber when Macmillan was answering questions. A charge by one MP was that the catering staff of the house had 'cooked the books'. Godfrey leapt up and said, 'If they have cooked the books, then we must book the cooks.' The House proceeded to other business. When I arranged with Rose to sit in the public gallery at Question Time, one backbencher asked the Minister of Agriculture, 'Does the minister realise that warthogs are sensitive animals?' Little did I then know that the MP was to be my future father-in-law!

Godfrey was held in wide affection among MPs of all parties. Throughout my time in Parliament there were many Labour and Liberal MPs who told me how much they had appreciated his warmth and friendliness. A Labour MP once said to him, 'You will find that the House is a bloody X-ray machine.' How absolutely true this is. Others are quietly observing all your strengths and weaknesses and there is no way that you can hide from them.

Godfrey had interesting views about some of the other political leaders. He was struck by Neville Chamberlain's vanity. After a Toscanini concert, which they both attended, Godfrey asked him in the lobby whether he had enjoyed it. He replied, 'Of course, I've heard it all before.' Godfrey felt he was jealous of his half brother, Austen Chamberlain, who was a Midland businessman and had been described as 'a good Lord Mayor of Birmingham in a lean year'. Godfrey had supported the Munich Agreement in 1938 on the grounds that Britain needed time both to prepare for war and to test the prospect for peace as far as possible. He had the courage to be one of the thirty-three Conservative rebels who voted against Chamberlain on 8 May 1940, leading to Chamberlain's downfall. Godfrey's father had just died, but he came up to Parliament to vote.

His relationship with Churchill was a difficult one and indeed may have been one of the reasons why Godfrey never became a minister. They fell out over India: while Winston was arguing in the 1930s for continuing British control over India, Godfrey contended that the country should be moving towards self-governance and independence. But they became friends much later, after Winston's retirement, and on one occasion Winston asked Godfrey to lunch. With tears in his eyes he said, 'When I think of you, I think of your heroic brother [Claude, who defended Calais]'. Godfrey described Winston as 'boyish' and recalled that Winston once said to Eddie Marsh, his private secretary, 'I like things to happen and if they don't happen I like to make them happen.' When Winston was pretty gaga Godfrey would look after him in the Chamber or in the smoking room. Once Attlee came up for a chat, and as he walked away, Winston said, 'Nice man. What was his name?'

Godfrey thought Attlee powerful, impressive and laconic. When Arthur Greenwood asked why he had been sacked as a minister, Attlee said, 'Not up to the job. Sorry. Good morning!'

In the war Godfrey often went on Home Guard duties. But in Parliament he was liked and admired as a colourful backbencher and served on the Public Accounts Committee and was chairman of the Estimates Committee. He wrote of his own 'basic mediocrity' in Parliament. I think he did himself an injustice. He was inclined in life to be ruled by his heart rather than his head and this may have been another reason for not being a minister. But he left his mark on Parliament and made a distinct contribution to Parliamentary life.

During his career he accompanied many delegations abroad. He started visiting India in the 1930s. In 1946 he accompanied an all-party delegation and stayed with Wavell, the Viceroy. The purpose was to help relax the atmosphere while HMG prepared for independence. He went in a boat on the Ganges with Nehru and also met Jinnah. He told the story that when meeting Gandhi a Labour MP, Bob Richards, said, 'Now tell me Mr Jinnah!' Gandhi burst out laughing.

Godfrey was active in Africa and supported the steady progress of African colonies towards independence. He formed a great friendship with Doctor Banda and they were once both seen dancing hand in hand in their dark suits in the stadium during independence celebrations. When I later called on Banda in Malawi as Minister for Africa, he told me of a conversation with Rab Butler in which he vowed that he would double the standard of living in twenty-five years. Rab had refuted Banda's claim, but he achieved it. Banda warmed to Godfrey and listened to his advice. Godfrey also led a delegation to Japan in 1954 to help them re-establish links with the Western world. And he went to the then Rhodesia when tensions were high over their Declaration of Unilateral Independence. He was to the left of the party on Africa and voted for the imposition of sanctions on Rhodesia at a time when the party was split three ways.

Godfrey continued to lead a very full life after he left Parliament. He became a district councillor for Newbury, but grew bored by all the committee work. He was chairman of the St Birinus Group of six psychiatric hospitals with 1,700 beds in all, and found this almost the most satisfying thing that he ever did. He just treated the patients as human beings and showed how much he cared for them. He thought it important to shake hands with them all. To one he said, 'Are you off to have your tea?' To which the reply was, 'What the hell has this got to do with you?' Both Godfrey and Katharine devoted themselves to these hospitals: it was no wonder they were so missed on their departure.

Godfrey was immensely active in a wide range of activities, yet I think he felt most at peace in his beloved wood at home. He writes movingly in his memoirs of the hazels mixed with thorn, maple, ash, elder and whitebeam; the panoply of bluebells, primroses and wood anemones; and the cuckoos. I can picture him in his old jacket and torn trousers reappearing for tea with a sack full of wood, and his chopper or axe. He was also well known in Berkshire as a beekeeper and for his interesting observations on the behaviour of bees.

He took to parachuting at the age of sixty. One day in Kenya the air-mail edition of *The Times* arrived and there, to Rose's horror, was Godfrey pictured on the front page jumping into Poole Harbour. He made several hot air balloon trips and jumped from hydrogen balloons at Kidlington, near Oxford. He invented a new activity called parascending and became president of the Parascending Club.

In his earlier days he loved climbing in the Alps and walked for miles in the country until his early eighties. He was very widely read in the classics and history, like his mother, with a fine memory. Christianity for him was an act of faith. He had a deep faith, but was not ostentatious or judgemental. He would regularly read the lesson in church.

It would not be true to say that I always found Godfrey easy. Indeed, he was a very emotional person. He wanted me to go into the family business, which I was unwilling to do. This resulted in upsetting scenes. I think that because he didn't have a son he wanted to have a son-in-law who would join the business, particularly as Rose didn't want to join Nicholsons. He was inclined to be self-centred and demanding. I found him difficult to cope with in my younger days, but later on I became very fond of him and enjoyed his company. I regard myself as very lucky to have had such a colourful, warm and amusing father-in-law.

Katharine provided a wonderful contrast and balance to Godfrey. She was the anchor to the family and provided Godfrey with a secure and happy home. She had two brothers and five sisters and had spent a happy childhood, although quite detached from her parents. She never went to school and was taught entirely by a governess. She was very knowledgeable and well educated and indeed was quite an advertisement for not going to school. She had missed mixing with her contemporaries but was close to three of her sisters – Barbara Hurst, Mary Dilhorne and Elizabeth, who died young. The family tradition was to move seasonally to Balcarres for the summer, to London for the spring and autumn and to Haigh Hall at Christmas – rather like the Queen's routine. Katharine was twenty-three when she married Godfrey in 1936. He was twelve years older. During the war they lived in Bussock Mayne in Berkshire and Katharine worked three days a week at India House sorting clothes for the troops. After the war she became a governor of Dr Barnado's and then chairman of its Finance and General Purposes Committee. She evidently made a major contribution to this charitable cause with her common sense approach.

She was a shy and reserved person who enjoyed nothing better than to be at home with her beloved family and her gardening. She did her duty by accompanying Godfrey to constituency events and she was popular and respected in the Farnham constituency, but she was not a social person and avoided parties if she could; and later her daughters began to take her place. To me Katharine seemed more like my father, while Godfrey and my mother had quite a lot in common. Katharine was perceptive and very widely read in literature and poetry. She was artistic and she painted, like so many of the Lindsays. She also had a very nice sense of humour. I always enjoyed my chats with her and found her very understanding and helpful; indeed I became very attached to her. It was a tragedy when in 1972, at the age of sixty, she developed a tumour on the brain and died later that year. Her death was a terrible blow for the family and above all deprived Godfrey of the support and love he so much needed. She died with immense dignity and set an example to us all.

7

The Last Days of Empire in Kenya

We are so much more adventurous when we are young. School holidays spent with my father in Sudan and visits to Aden were enough to decide me embarking on a brief dalliance with the Overseas Civil Service. I had attempted and failed the Foreign Office entrance exam; something led me inexorably to the old Colonial Service. I knew any opportunity would be short-lived because the Empire was coming rapidly to an end. I could not miss the venture for anything.

I took part in the last full year of the Devonshire training course at Queen Elizabeth House, Oxford, in 1960. This was my fourth university year and I was attached to Wadham College. The course included some thirteen subjects, with exams were taken at the end of the year. Subjects included Swahili, local government, East African history, law and agriculture. I wanted to go to Kenya because I loved Africa, and this was the most beautiful and challenging of countries. There was a tricky time when, as I have already recounted, my father was short-listed to be Governor of Kenya. In such circumstances I would have opted for Tanganyika (now Tanzania). But when Sir Patrick Renison duly got the job I could go to the country of my first choice.

In the summer of 1961 I set off on my own. Rose had undergone a minor operation and stayed behind in England for a few weeks to recuperate. We had only married in early April and it was a difficult start.

Robin Paul, who later joined BP, and Robin Williamson, who later taught at Hurstpierpoint College, accompanied me on the journey. We were the last three British administrators to join the Kenya Service. In Nairobi I stayed with the Commissioner, Robin Wainwright. He and his wife were very welcoming, for I was upset not having Rose with me.

I bought a simple yellow car and drove to Isiolo, a long way north of Nairobi, where I was to be the last British District Officer. Isiolo is the capital of the Northern Frontier District (NFD) and lies in the desert scrubland to the north of Mount Kenya. It is the only proper entry point to the Northern Province. It was a small trading post and headquarters of both Province and the District.

I occupied the District Officer's house straightaway in the *boma* (compound). After supper with Michael Power, the District Commissioner, and his wife, I walked back in the dark only to see what looked like a mobile crane leave my garden as I tried to enter. In fact it was a giraffe. This was real Africa at last!

Mike Power was a strong and impressive man. He gave me policy papers to study and sent me on a fortnight's trek round the District where only Swahili was spoken. When I returned I was put in charge of security, agriculture, local government, and made a grade three magistrate. The District was the size of southern Ireland, with a population of 70,000. I was second in command. There are few jobs in the world where at the age of twenty-four one could be given so many responsibilities.

By 1961 a growing number of British Colonies in Africa were achieving independence. The Sudan and Ghana had already done so. Kenya was moving rapidly in the same direction. Macmillan had already made his famous speech in Cape Town about the wind of change. As John Johnson, a former administrator has said, 'British rule was a pinprick in Kenya's history.' It lasted for less than seventy years, from 1895 when a Protectorate was declared over British East Africa until 1963. Unlike Rhodesia, a positive turning point came in 1923 with the Devonshire Declaration, which declared the paramountcy 'of the interests of the African Natives' in Kenya. The interests of the European farming settlers were subsidiary to the development of the African. In Rhodesia it was the direct opposite and Britain was to pay a heavy price.

In the 1950s the country was dominated by the Mau Mau Emergency under the Governorship of Lord Howick. The Mau Mau rebellion was mainly a movement of protest by the Kikuyu, Embu and Meru peoples. It originated with the alienation of African land for European settlement in the early twentieth century, thus creating a landless and socially deprived community. Once peace had been restored the Swynnerton Proposals created a hugely ambitious plan for African land resettlement and the creation of smallholdings for the purchase of European farms. The price of the inevitable rebellion was heavy. 11,000 terrorists and 1,920 African loyalists were killed and 95 Europeans and 29 Asians also died. The emergency ended just before I arrived, but their leader, Jomo Kenyatta, who had been sentenced to seven years in prison, was still under house arrest in Maralal. I remembered in 1956 my father being telephoned at home in Fovant and asked whether he would lead an inquiry into the origins of Mau Mau. He refused but recommended a Mr Corfield from the Sudan Political Service, who subsequently became the author of the Report.

Today the Mau Mau rebellion and our handling of the Emergency remain highly controversial. At the time I regarded the Mau Mau as a group of bloodthirsty oath takers who murdered more of their own people than Europeans. Kenya was already moving towards independence, even though the first African ministers had been appointed only in the mid-1950s. Was Mau Mau a freedom movement or a battle to win back land? In Kenya much was owed to the enlightened views of some of the European farmers, led by Sir Michael Blundell, Minister for Agriculture, who became a friend in later years when I was Minister for African Affairs. An old Wellingtonian, he loved Africa and the Africans. As a farmer and minister he had the foresight to lead European farmers into an independent Kenya which put Africans first. We owe him a great deal.

I committed the crime of failing to keep a diary to describe the role of the District Officer in the evening of the Empire. However a book entitled *Colony to Nation*, edited by Sir John Johnson, has a wide range of descriptions of life as a District Officer that has reminded me of that way of life.

It is my view that the District Officer was the heart of the Empire. I was honoured to give the address in Westminster Abbey on 25 May 1999 in a service of thanksgiving to mark the end of Her Majesty's Overseas Civil Service, in the presence of the Queen and the Duke of Edinburgh. I could see from the pulpit 2,000 faces of elderly people who had served the Empire in different capacities. They looked an admirable collection. To enable me to give this address, I read the diaries of a cross section of former administrators in the nineteenth and twentieth centuries. The address summarises some of my views about the Empire and is incorporated in the Appendix.

I had of course travelled with my father in Equatoria and the Blue Nile Provinces of the Sudan and had seen for myself how he governed a large area. This helped to make the role a little easier for me. Each morning I would set off early to the office, often inspecting the *dubas* (the police guard of honour) en route. It was a harsh life for the local tribes since the green only came with the rain and their goats and cows, on whom their existence depended, only survived by moving around. Sir Michael Blundell regularly warned publicly of the danger of soil erosion and over-grazing, which meant the desert was creeping southwards. I tried hard to teach the Africans that grazing control and rotation was the only way to conserve grassland. They took no notice and continued to over-graze areas. When I returned in the 1990s to the Northern Frontier the desert was even more extended.

Much of life was spent on safari and Rose, who had by now flown out to join me, usually came with me accompanied by our dachshund, Nutkin. We toured the District with my staff, a Somali interpreter and the *dubas*. We talked to the local people and tried to unravel their problems and disputes, and worked with the local leaders and their headmen to set up a form of local government. We usually pitched camp and heard through the night the noise of all the wild life. In those days big game surrounded us everywhere: elephant, giraffe, gazelle and rhino. They loved to wallow and drink the water of the River Uaso Nyiro near Buffalo Springs.

Quite often the game warden, Terence Adamson, would accompany us. Brother-in-law of the famous Joy Adamson, like her he had a magical way with animals. He would talk to them, particularly the elephants, as we drove through the bush. He told us that he once found an elephant wedged and stuck fast in a water hole. Many Africans were trying to release him by throwing stones into the well to enable him to climb out. When the elephant neared the top of the well Terence told the Africans to run off quickly, for the animal would be likely to charge them in frustration. He then completed the job on his own. The elephant stepped out, genuflected to Terence in gratitude and wandered off.

One day I was walking through the bush near Isiolo with the acting Provincial Commissioner, John Dowson. Suddenly we heard an alarming noise of what sounded like a steam engine pounding towards us. It was a charging rhino. My experienced companion ordered me to stand absolutely still until he gave me an order to dive into a thorn bush immediately to my left. On came the rhino, closer and closer. It was within ten yards of us before he shouted to me to dive. The heavy animal thundered past us, its blinkered vision and enormous weight making it difficult to swerve easily. At such close range he had no chance to adjust his course. Shaken and covered in thorns, John Dowson and I returned urgently to our house for a strong drink with Rose.

It was the animal life of Isiolo that I mentioned years later in a conversation with the Queen Mother over dinner at Windsor Castle in 1992. She suddenly lit up and revealed that part of her honeymoon with Prince Albert was spent at Buffalo Springs in 1924/5. This shared love of Kenya led to a friendship for the remaining years of her life. She invited Rose and me to lunch at the Royal Lodge to show us her photographs of that visit. Prince William also visited the district during his gap year and told me how much he enjoyed it.

While we usually travelled in small trucks, I sometimes walked; and on one occasion Rose and I made a camel safari to visit the nomadic people. The swaying was wearing. As the day began to heat up we thought we saw a village shimmering in the hot sun and looked forward to seeing the villagers. An hour later the village was still shimmering the same distance away, and so it continued. Eventually we discovered that it was quite literally a village on the move. The villagers had heard that the District Officer was coming to collect taxes, and had put the humble mats and sticks of their home on their backs and were doing a runner.

A typical day might involve dealing with grazing control, soil conservation, cash crops, water holes and irrigation, damage caused by wild life, cattle auctions, tribal disputes, local government issues, licences to trade, control of movement into the Northern Frontier, the marking of tribal boundaries, school and road building and the maintenance of law and order. In addition my duties as a grade three magistrate gave me powers to deport, to sentence up to twenty-four strokes of the cane or to imprison for three months. I never sentenced more than six strokes of the cane, usually for stealing. I had to witness the administration of the strokes by the police. Stealing stopped pretty quickly. However when I reached the Embu District there was a sudden upsurge of petty crime. When I sentenced the thieves to a month in prison they were led away grinning broadly, looking forward to a Christmas with good food in the 'Queen's Hotel', the local name for the prison. The Turkana would often come illegally to the Isiolo

District to shop. They would be arrested and sentenced to deportation to their own district, thus getting a free ride back!

African humour, conscious and unconscious, was one of the many joys of the job. One particular District Officer had the experience of helping an African to complete an application form for a job. In one section in answer to questions, 'What is your father's name?' he had written, 'nevertheless'. For 'What is your father's place of birth?' he had written again 'nevertheless'. Finally after 'What is your father's date of birth?' he had written yet again 'nevertheless'. At the bottom of the section was a note in small print which read 'If your father is dead, these answers should be answered nevertheless.'

Sometimes the humour was more than a little disconcerting. On one of my earlier days in Isiolo there were severe floods, during which three Africans including our houseboy came running to our house rocking with laughter. They said they were having a competition to see which of their friends could manage to swim a flooded river without drowning. Horrified, I asked what had happened. Again rocking with laughter they said three had already drowned. I rang the Provincial Commissioner who simply said this was typical African behaviour!

Isiolo was very tough for Rose. It was isolated and lonely and gave her a taste of what it had been like for my mother and all the thousands of wives of administrators stuck in some remote district, often miles from any companionship, proper shops, and all the normal enjoyments of the Western world. It was not easy to take a break even at weekends, but we did sometimes drive up to the nearby mountains to stay with Andrew Brooks, the District Administrator of Maui, and his wife Helen. The coolness and greenery were in wonderful contrast to Isiolo. On one occasion I was stung by an African hornet and very soon I collapsed. Rose drove as fast as she could the fifty miles to Nanyuki. The doctor flew down in a small plane, injected me several times with adrenalin and then flew me round Mount Kenya and over Nanyuki airstrip to Nairobi while Rose, still on the ground, wondered whether I was alive.

On another occasion, when Rose was pregnant and couldn't come, my sister-in-law Laura and I flew with Gilfrid Powys, a neighbouring farmer, to Lake Rudolf (now Lake Turkana). En route we got stuck in a valley with heavy rain, so flew to Marsabit and stayed with the District Commissioner for the night. Marsabit is like a green island emerging from the desert with forests and elephants. The next day we flew on to fish for Nile perch from a launch on the lake. A Cambridge expedition had completely disappeared there in the 1930s, eaten overnight by crocodiles. On the flight back Gilfrid unwisely told Laura she could land the aircraft. The plane rapidly went into a nosedive. Before I blacked out I hit Gilfrid on the shoulder and ordered him to take the controls.

Wilfred Thesiger was an old family friend. He came to me not long after I had arrived in Isiolo and asked me to arrange six camels, six guides and supplies for an expedition. I asked him how far he was walking. He replied, 'It's only a stroll of 700 miles – in fact to Lake Rudolf.' He then became angry with me because one camel went sick. I responded robustly, after which we became lifetime friends. He admired my father, and Rose and I in our turn admired his uniqueness, courage and enterprise. Wilfred was one of the last great travellers and explorers to walk through areas still virtually unknown to the Westerner. His books *Arabian Sands* and *The Marsh Arabs*, superbly written, bring to life his travels in the Empty Quarter and amongst the Marsh Arabs of southern Iraq. One tribe described him as 'the old bull elephant, who walked by himself'. Today's generation would not produce such a man. We were privileged to know him.

Isiolo provided me with my first political challenge. As Kenya's independence approached, Somalis of the Northern Frontier campaigned to secede from Kenya. About 270,000 semi-nomadic Somalis lived mainly on the eastern side of the Northern Frontier. They had nothing in common with the Bantu to the south whom they despised, but everything with the Somalis who lived in the neighbouring region of the Horn of Africa. They shared a flag with five stars, which was the emblem of Greater Somalia symbolising the five regions of former British, French, and Italian Somaliland, the Ogaden and the Northern Frontier. Somalia became an independent unified Republic in 1960. It was perfectly natural for the Somalis, who had never been properly integrated into Kenya, to want to live with their own kind in Somalia, rather than under an alien administration based on Nairobi. Indeed as District Officer of Isiolo I controlled all movement in and out of the Province. It gave me considerable pleasure to delay passes for the arrogant Robert Ruark, the author of *Uhuru*, and other notable people. When Reggie Maudling, then Colonial Secretary, visited Kenya, I was asked to bring a Somali delegation to see him in Government House. I did not attend the meeting, but they emerged triumphantly to claim that they had put their case for secession and had been listened to. We drove back to Isiolo in a long convoy. That evening there was a Somali party in an area outside Isiolo, which I attended. They were delighted, but the Provincial Commissioner was not pleased as he felt I had jeopardised my impartiality. Like many other Northern Frontier administrators I was very sympathetic to the Somali cause. I felt that the only opportunity to facilitate secession was at independence and only Her Majesty's Government could do the deed since Kenyatta could not be expected to agree to cut off one limb and survive politically. Kenyatta was not liked by the Somalis. Once the Governor asked me to let him know when Kenyatta could safely make a speech in Isiolo. After consulting security advisors, I said rather unwisely that he would only be safe there if he was kept in a cage.

Soon after I had returned from Kenya, I started a campaign to support Somali secession. My letters were published in *The Times* and other papers and Godfrey Nicholson arranged for me to see Nigel Fisher, the junior Minister for the Colonies. While conceding that it was a dangerous precedent to start adjusting national boundaries in Africa, I felt that there was a worse danger in that failure to make these adjustments would lay the foundations for ethnic violence and boundary disputes. The Europeans had created totally artificial boundaries in the scramble for Africa with no regard for tribal interests. A classic case was the Sudan, where the Nilotic tribes of the south had nothing in common with the Arabs of the north.

But ministers ruled against secession, and independence for Kenya followed in 1963. Sadly the prognosis of violence, of which I and other administrators had warned, came true. Shifta Somali raids led to a breakdown of law and order in the Northern Frontier, and two District Officers were murdered.

The other potential political problem was the position of Asians in Kenya. These were the entrepreneurs, traders and professional classes who, with their families, had come to Kenya from India in the early part of the twentieth century. There were many Asian shopkeepers, even in Isiolo. One of them said to me when I left Isiolo, 'See you on the British motorway', meaning that he wanted to emigrate to Britain and would like to run a shop on the motorway! During the 1960s and

1970s many Asians left Uganda and Kenya to settle in Britain. We had been instructed by the Colonial Secretary to make it clear to Asians that they had a right to settle in Britain if they were driven out of East Africa. In 1971, as a new MP, I recall having a sharp exchange with Enoch Powell in the Conservative Foreign Affairs Committee, who had denied that the Government had ever given such a commitment. I had to say that this was untrue, for which he found it hard to forgive me. Today these Asians make a major contribution to our economy. Equally their departure from East Africa was very damaging economically to those countries, even though they probably stood in the way of African advancement in both trade and the Civil Service.

I recall my days in Isiolo with some nostalgia, despite one occasion when there was a demonstration outside my office with placards saying, 'Luce, go back to Siberia!' I am still puzzled as to why I should go to Siberia – where I had never been before. Nor can I recall why the demonstrators were so angry with me. In the end however the wonderful African humour saved the day.

After leaving Isiolo we spent a few months in Embu, where I was the District Officer. The District was on the southern slopes of Mount Kenya and extended as far as the River Tana. Our house, which was in the same garden as the District Commissioner's, was constructed in about 1909. Everything about it was dark and depressing, including the furniture, but the garden was lush and green with a variety of fruit trees, including avocado, mango and banana. The town was full of jacaranda and nandi flame trees. As in Isiolo most of the issues I dealt with were agricultural, trading and local government or security, in addition to the courts. There was an Anglican church just by our house and one Sunday I set off to early morning Holy Communion. Rose was surprised to see me return within a matter of minutes. I had been the only member of the congregation whereupon the charming African clergyman said, 'Where two or three are gathered together... and as there is only one...we shall now dismiss.'

My District Commissioner was Geoff Mackley, an agreeable but weak man. He would not take measures to maintain law and order and the resulting upsurge of gang warfare had rather too much of the Mau Mau flavour for my liking. In the end I went to Nyeri to see the Provincial Commissioner, Dick Wilson. I informed him that it was intolerable to have a District Commissioner who could not endorse the maintenance of law and order and that it was our job to uphold order to enable the District to develop. I unwisely added that if Mackley wasn't removed within a month, I would go instead. The Provincial Commissioner indicated that he would act – but he didn't. I was therefore compelled to leave, knowing that Kenya was on the verge of independence and that I wouldn't be there for much longer anyway. The District Commissioner was eventually removed on the day I left Kenya. I learnt very quickly never to make such silly threats again.

Rose, who was pregnant, went ahead by air in the autumn of 1962. I began my journey home by the cheapest route, travelling on a bus through Uganda to the River Nile on the Sudan border and then by air via Juba and Khartoum. It took four days to reach London.

I would not have missed those eighteen months for anything. It gave me a glimpse of another age, almost as though we were on another planet. It was a good foundation for later times when I was Minister for Africa and a real pleasure to work amongst Africans in a remote region. It was very tough and lonely for Rose but she helped to make it possible and tolerable for me.

It is perhaps appropriate to complete this chapter by describing a particular experience. One day in Isiolo I was told that two tribes were killing each other over the use of a water hole some seventy miles away. I drove speedily to the site, escorted by police, where I summoned the two tribes to sit under a baobab tree so that I could lecture them in Swahili, no doubt rather patronisingly, that rather than killing each other they should share the water hole and stop fighting. Whereupon, a hand went up from the back and a man said in Swahili, 'Bwana, you tell us to stop fighting. Can you explain how it is that in Europe you have fought two world wars this century?' I replied, 'You win', and they all left peacefully in peals of laughter – to share the water hole. Perhaps it really was time for the British to leave Africa.

8

Getting into Parliament

In my early teens my ambition was to be Foreign Secretary. Anthony Eden, who had retired nearby in Wiltshire, was something of a model for me and back in Fovant we made a cine film with the Napiers and Luces acting the roles that we wanted to play in life. I am seen marching around in a dark suit, umbrella and bowler hat, graciously acknowledging the public! I'm not sure to what extent it had occurred to me that, in order to be Foreign Secretary, you had to be an MP first. At university I tried to get into the Foreign Office and while at Cambridge took their tailor-made exams, which I failed. At the time it was a bitter disappointment, but I put aside my sorrow and decided to apply for the Overseas Civil Service.

At this time I had only a limited experience of politics. I had learned a little about it from Godfrey and Rose, and from occasional visits to Parliament. I attended my first political meetings during the 1959 election, first in Compton Chamberlayne where I heard the MP John Morrison (later Lord Margadale). He was asked from the audience whether the Conservatives would abolish Schedule A, a housing tax. He replied, 'Schedule A; Schedule A', searched through his pockets and swiftly turned over the pages of a policy guide book before announcing, 'We will abolish it.'

From there I went to Devizes where Henry Percivall Pott was the Conservative member. I canvassed for the first time and learned, at considerable pain, not to put a foot in the door to prevent it from being closed by the owner. Nor was it a good idea to put my hand in the letterbox, in case a dog bit my fingers. At a meeting one evening, a man at the back of the hall who was irritated by the MP called out, 'Pott, go back under the bed where you belong.' I later joined Alan Lennox-Boyd and his team in his Mid Beds constituency. I toured round with him in his open car and observed the friendly and expansive manner in which he would greet people at their windows and in the streets. Alan was in trouble following the Hola Camp scandal involving the deaths of ten Kikuyu inmates. People shouted at him, 'Hola, Hola.' He disarmed them by replying simply, 'How lovely to see you.' I learned how a candidate ran his campaign and gained much valuable information from him as we lunched in pubs, canvassed and attended meetings.

My experiences in Cyprus and Kenya strengthened my interest in international affairs and politics. I must have bored Rose stiff in my Kenya days by endless discussion of political matters and expressions of anger about the state of the world. She was very patient, but hinted from time to time and rather reluctantly that the best place to express these views might be Parliament. It was noble of her to say so since she was not keen on a political career for me, perhaps especially because she knew how much it affected family life.

Instinctively the Conservative Party was natural to me because it was a broad 'church' and I tended to be left of centre within it. The philosophy of the party involves creating an environment which channels constructively all the strengths and weaknesses of human nature. Socialism did not appeal to me, as their philosophy would lead to the State trying to run and control the lives of individuals. The Liberals were no longer a serious party but more a home for political refugees from the two main parties.

By the time that I returned to the UK from Kenya in 1963 I was clear that my preference would be to stand for Parliament. But I needed a job and a base before trying, and it was Godfrey Nicholson's idea that I should join the family business, to which end I became a management trainee at Glyn Mills (now part of the Royal Bank of Scotland). Very soon I realised that this was not for me, and I left to join Gallahers as a marketing manager, where I was heavily involved in the marketing of cigarettes and cigars. However I became bored with this and – again with Godfrey's help – I was introduced to John Cuckney (now Lord Cuckney), managing director of the Standard Industrial Group. He asked me to join Spirella, a subsidiary selling women's clothes, including corsets, based in Letchworth. I was appointed marketing manager of a company which faced the threat of intense competition. Spirella's marketing director was Denys Hodson, who in later years managed the arts in local government and voluntarily served the Arts Council.

My mother had a difficult time explaining to people that I was selling cigarettes or corsets! No doubt it was a great relief to her when I left Spirella, though they had been generous enough to allow me to stand for Parliament.

Becoming a Parliamentary candidate is undoubtedly the toughest part of getting into Parliament. We lived in the Hitchin constituency where Martin Madden had been the most recent Conservative MP, losing his seat in 1964 to Labour's Shirley Williams. John Stokes, a headhunter, had become the Conservative prospective Parliamentary candidate. During the spring of the 1966 general election I canvassed for John Stokes in Hitchin. I heard him speak in our village hall and thought he was rather good – very robust and traditional. I was particularly pleased when he praised my uncle, David Luce, who had just resigned as First Sea Lord over the phasing out of aircraft carriers, and attacked Harold Wilson for jeopardising our defences. Nevertheless Shirley Williams was returned with a majority of over 10,000. Boundary changes had led to the constituency's inclusion of Stevenage, which had a large Labour vote. Shirley, later Baroness Williams of Crosby and a Liberal Democrat, was Minister of State at the Home Office and a very popular MP. She worked extremely hard in the constituency and was widely liked and respected.

Suddenly an opportunity opened up for me when John Stokes decided not to continue in Hitchin. He left and later became an MP in the Midlands. In later years, when we were in Parliament together, he became a slightly eccentric but popular figure of fun, always standing up for the best of English traditions and his interventions producing affectionate laughter from all sides.

In the Conservative Party it was regarded as a part of the learning experience that a hopeless seat should be fought before going for a safer one. Hitchin was therefore the obvious choice. However there was a problem: in order to be recommended and supported by Central Office for interviews for a candidacy by a constituency association, you had to be on the Office's candidates list. To be on the list, you must first have served the Party in some capacity or other, either as a Young Conservative or a member of a constituency association, or as a councillor in local government. I had done none of these because I had been in Africa and had then moved from a job in London to Hertfordshire. I thought the Central Office's view very narrow because it seemed to me that both the Party and Parliament needed the broadest experience that they could get. Godfrey Nicholson and James Ramsden intervened on my behalf with Central Office to no avail, although I did have an interview with Geoffrey Johnson Smith, deputy chairman of the Party in charge of candidates. He was perfectly friendly but would not put me on the all-important list. Eventually, under determined pressure and because the constituency association led by Bill Kirk, the agent, had asked me to apply to join the long list of applicants as the local candidate, they reluctantly agreed to support my application for the Hitchin constituency only, leaving my name off the general candidates list.

To my surprise, after a pretty rigorous interviewing process, I was put on the short list of four people. The others included Neil Crichton-Miller and John Wauchope. Crichton-Miller was favourite and I felt sure that he would win, because I had heard much laughter from the association members. He apparently informed them that he would not live in the constituency but would stay in his mother-in-law's caravan during the election. But such flippancy did not pay off. I really worked on preparing my speech and worked out my thoughts on every anticipated question. When I was declared the winner it was the most exciting – and surprising – breakthrough. Here I was, aged thirty, set to challenge Shirley Williams at the next election. The local press made much of it, and the association was very supportive. None of those other competing candidates ever got into Parliament and it was one in the eye for the Conservative Central Office's narrow-minded attitude to recruiting.

Rose had seen too much of the effects of Parliamentary life on the family through her relations, particularly her father, who spent so much time away from home, returning exhausted at weekends. Nevertheless throughout my political life she was unfailingly helpful and an extremely accomplished source of support in the constituency. At the time of my selection, however, she looked horrified. When asked by the press what her comments were, the agent quickly replied on her behalf, 'Surprised, and delighted.' In fact, such was her panic that I would be selected that she fell down the steps as we entered the hall for the interview.

I spent four years nursing the constituency on behalf of the Conservatives, and I think that the effort paid dividends. We grew to know and feel close to the constituency and all our supporters. The constituency association's chairman was Peter McMurtrie. He was highly efficient and businesslike and gave strong leadership, but he portrayed the wrong image: as a businessman he had a chauffeur-driven Rolls-Royce and during the election constantly insisted on driving me to speaking engagements. There were many officers of the association who were full of fun and the Young Conservatives were strong and lively, making the Party a good social outlet as well as a chance to experience politics. The first six months were strenuous. About four evenings a week were committed to speaking to Conservative branches and at weekends I visited farms, factories and fêtes in order to meet people, learn about their lives and win their support. I joined forces with Shirley Williams in the campaign against Nuthampstead being a new airport site and spoke with her on this subject at public meetings. We succeeded and the plan was dropped. I was a very nervous speaker and spent much time painstakingly preparing my subjects. The strain resulted in a depression, to such an extent that I would have to be dragged to meetings by Rose, where I would sweat on each occasion. I couldn't sleep properly and didn't know how I could carry on. Rose suggested two topics for each speech, gave me briefing notes and forced me both off to work and to meetings. At the end of the first six months I had a wonderful holiday with the family, after which I recovered and never really looked back. I had undergone the most difficult stage in my political life and it was entirely due to Rose that I got through it. I can only think that it must have stemmed from a complete lack of confidence in myself which can only be overcome by keeping at it. I learnt much later on that Rose's parents had come over one day to support her when she herself was feeling in despair.

Each week I put out press statements, challenging Shirley Williams or setting out Conservative arguments or policy. Harold Wilson's Government was running into difficulties and gave us a great deal of ammunition. Many outside speakers visited Hitchin including Keith Joseph, who attracted a large audience. At one point a small man at the back asked a question about overseas aid. Joseph gave an erudite answer based on the contrasting positions on the subject of Barbara Jackson and one Professor Bauer. After a pause the questioner from the back said, 'But I am Professor Bauer.' Joseph conceded amidst much laughter. A brilliant thinker, he also had charm. He was kind enough to tell me 'I hear you are doing very well here.' I was stunned into silence, whereupon he continued 'I know it's our wives who do the trick for us really.' He was the philosopher of the Conservative Party and was later responsible for many of the policy successes of Thatcher's Government.

Ted Heath, as Leader, came one day to Letchworth and I took him to a parachute production factory. As we drove through the streets of Letchworth, he ordered, 'Lower the windows so that I can wave to the crowds.' We did so, but the streets were empty. Later on, during the general election of June 1970, Margaret Thatcher, Shadow Education

Secretary, visited the constituency and we drove her round in an open car. She was horrified as she thought it would wreck her hair. Peter Carrington came and spoke for me; this was my first meeting with him. With the Young Conservatives we marched through the streets and the parks giving the many people leaflets and asking them for their support. I challenged Shirley Williams to public meetings, though normally the sitting member declines on the grounds that it gives the opposition candidate publicity. To her credit she accepted and we held two such meetings sponsored by the local press, with a good 800 people present each time. They were stimulating and exciting occasions, with strong audience participation. My son Alexander, then aged five, came to a meeting for the first time. He sat on a chair in the front row, his feet not touching the ground, clapping Shirley Williams each time the audience applauded, but not me when I spoke. He hadn't quite got the right idea. He was puzzled because, as he told me afterwards, he thought that a meeting had something to do with meat.

I continued to challenge Shirley through the letters page in *The Times*. There were masses of posters saying 'Vote Fast and Luce' and there was marvellous support in getting us round the constituency and opening doors for us to canvass. The outcome of the election was uncertain and many were surprised when the Labour Government was defeated and Ted Heath became Prime Minister. In Hitchin I reduced Shirley's majority from over 10,000 to about 4,000. It was regarded as a good result and no doubt helped when, some nine months later, I was selected as the Arundel and Shoreham candidate. I remember Shirley Williams being in tears as she learnt that many of her friends had lost their seats. I on the other hand was cheerful with the result.

The experience in Hitchin was the best possible preparation for politics. The constituency association tried to persuade me to stay on with them, but I was anxious to move on and get into Parliament. I accepted re-adoption, but on the understanding that I could stand down if given an opportunity to go to a safe Conservative seat.

I was still marketing manager of Spirella when I was adopted for Hitchin, but was getting restless with the company and the job. It was therefore a great relief when an opportunity arose in 1968 to break away and take a job which fitted more easily with a future Parliamentary career. I forget exactly how the contact was made, but I was put in touch with Dr Michael Young, who wanted to appoint a director for one of his new projects, the National Suggestions Centre (later known as the National Innovations Centre). Since it was a new and risky project he felt that I would be the best person to do it since I hoped to get into Parliament before too long and could afford to take a chance on a job that might be of a limited duration and on which I would not be dependent. For me there was the additional advantage of having a challenge that was far more interesting than Spirella, and which would cover every aspect of life in the public and private sector – a good preparation for Parliament.

Michael Young was already by then well known as the founder of the Consumers Association and as the consumer's champion in both the public and private sectors. He had already done much distinguished work for the Labour Party and I was struck by his open-mindedness and breadth of approach in appointing me. He was a most stimulating and interesting, but difficult, man to work for. The office was at 18, Victoria Park Square in the basement of Michael's building accommodating his Institute of Community Studies, of which he was a partner. He had already used his energy and persuasive powers to get a number of organisations to sponsor the Centre at £1,000 a year for three years each. The Beecham Group, Black and Decker, Marks and Spencer, I.C.I., the National Coal Board, the Department of Health and Social Security and the Post Office Corporation had all agreed to be sponsors. In addition Michael's own organisation put in about £20,000 to get us off the ground.

My task was to set up the non-profit-making organisation, recruit a team, raise more resources and get the Centre established. It was the most stimulating but hair-raising four year stint. The purpose of the Centre was to canvass ideas for doing things better, more efficiently or humanely in all walks of life. The means for publishing and generating these ideas was a magazine called *What?*, to complement *Which?* and *Where?*. The best ideas were then researched to see whether it was practicable to implement them. Adrian Moyes, who had worked for a charity, came in to head the research and Rudolph Klein, a most talented journalist, arrived to edit *What?*. £50 was offered for the most constructive or best-planned proposals, and there were lesser rewards for other particularly original or striking ideas. We negotiated a weekly programme on Thames Television which ran for three months every

Monday between 6 and 6.45 pm and was hosted by Eamonn Andrews. It was called 'What? Spot' and attracted three and a half million viewers in the south east. I was interviewed occasionally for this programme.

I was both startled and encouraged by the immense amount of publicity generated by the national and regional media. I spent quite a lot of time communicating with the media, as did Rudolph Klein. We received over 1,000 suggestions within six months and nearly 3,000 within ten months. As Michael had correctly forecast, there was a reservoir of ideas to be tapped. Soon our ten full- and part-timers at the Centre were working flat out investigating the best of the ideas. I reckoned that half were worth looking at and 1% were really outstanding.

Before long we realised the importance of local campaigning to generate more community involvement. The Hertfordshire regional evening newspaper, the *Evening Echo*, launched an intensive campaign which generated 200 ideas for improvements in south west Hertfordshire. Alma Williams, an attractive and energetic campaigner living in Watford, set up a regional suggestions centre. Later other regional centres were established in Newcastle and other cities. Ideas covered a broad range of areas; the most popular were road transport, housing and taxation, followed closely by the Post Office, welfare services, British Rail, crime prevention, health services, shopping and education, reflecting the concerns and problems of the time.

So what ideas did we follow up? They covered a broad area. Marks and Spencer agreed to mark the size of sheets on the label to help housewives. Her Majesty's Stationery Office and other publishers agreed to print all their titles consistently from the top down alphabetically. The Post Office introduced a telephone guide for food shopping. The Federation of Registered House Builders agreed to sponsor on a national scale a guide for each house purchased by an individual, called *You and Your Home*. Community schemes were introduced, for example in Westminster, for the milkman on his rounds to provide details to the Welfare Department of anyone who would like help or a visit. In Hull telephones were installed experimentally free of charge in the homes of a hundred old people to enable them to keep in touch if they had any problems. In the field of social services it was clear that many people had no idea of their rights. After a survey in Newham, the centre concluded there was a need for more citizens advice bureaux and free legal advice centres.

One project which attracted much publicity was the Working

Association of Mothers (WAM) set up by a Mrs Priestley of Teddington, with our support. It was in effect a cooperative of mothers who provided the services of a playgroup and crèche, an employment agency for part-time work at home and help with illness or the purchase of consumer goods. One year later there were twenty regional WAMs throughout the country. A need was being met.

The desire in urban areas for the equivalent of a rural parish council was identified in order to promote the communal interests of the neighbourhood. In 1970 a National Association for Neighbourhood Councils was launched at the House of Commons, following research undertaken in Camden and Hornsey. Above all it was intended to encourage citizens to participate in their own local communities.

The demand to improve services offered by local authority museums led to the setting up of National Heritage. This was the idea of John Letts, who has campaigned for museums to be improved ever since and who achieved the opening of the Museum of the Empire in Bristol in 1991. Surveys were carried out to give a rating of services in local authority museums. All the campaigning acted as a spur to the improvement of standards.

Our experience at the Centre often revealed the need for new organisations to help improve things in particular areas. When Stansted, a small village, was proposed as the preferred site for the third London Airport, it became obvious that those adversely affected by the proposal had to grapple with professional experts, whose arguments they were not equipped to counter. So we set up the Planning Advice Service to 'put the planned on an equal footing with the planners'. The service provided a network of consultant specialists who were available to help residents counter the arguments of the planners and to develop various alternative suggestions, which would reconcile the varying interests.

I recruited John Mathews, who was manager of the Ford's Suggestion Scheme, to provide Ideas for Action, a consultancy service run on a commercial basis for clients advising them on how to improve the flow of information and ideas at work. This led to increased communications between staff and managers. The profits of the organisation were ploughed back into strengthening the Centre. Ideas for Action also led to the formation of a National Suggestions Schemes Association to exchange views on successful suggestions schemes. Over 200 organisations joined the Association.

Another major project was the Community Innovations Register, based in Leicester. With grants from the King Edward's Hospital Fund and the Joseph Rowntree Memorial Trust, the Register was established in order to improve communications on innovations in the field of welfare which had already been implemented by voluntary bodies and local authorities. This identified a real need in the social welfare area but would have been equally relevant in many other areas: how often has a new idea been thought of that has already been implemented somewhere else? The problem is a general lack of information about local success stories.

By the time I left to become an MP in 1971, Michael Young was keen to change the Centre's emphasis to one which concentrated on social welfare, where there was a need to improve the willingness to explore new ideas and to disseminate information about existing ideas which had been successfully implemented. Dame Elizabeth Ackroyd was recruited as my successor. She was well known as the Director of the Consumer Association and a former civil servant. The publication of *What?* ceased and all resources were channelled into social welfare and the Community Innovations Register. The organisation quietly disappeared not long afterwards. Dame Elizabeth was a formidable and competent individual, but she was really not the right person to provide the creative energy to expand the National Innovations Centre and to help it develop its areas of greatest potential. Moreover Michael Young's heart was no longer in it. He was moving off in other directions.

When Asa Briggs wrote a biography of Michael, there was no mention whatsoever of the National Innovations Centre. This is a pity because it was a notable experiment and it would have been interesting to assess why it failed, unlike *Which?* and his many other ventures.

We have a reputation in Britain for producing ideas, but not for implementing them. It should be a fundamental role of any managerial leadership to stimulate creative thinking in both the public and private sectors. In order to adapt and strive to do things better, we need to live in a culture of continuous improvement. The alternative is to stagnate, and stagnation means decline. But people need to feel that their ideas will be taken seriously. I would have liked to have had a little longer in the 1970s to see if it would have been possible to get the Centre off the ground in the right direction. I count myself lucky to have worked there and I'm glad that there were some long-lasting changes as the result of the Centre's work.

9
Parliament

After the June 1970 election I assumed that I would have to wait four years or so before having another chance to enter Parliament. I continued to work with Michael Young as Director of the National Innovations Centre. Within months, however, I received a call from the Conservative Central Office and was asked whether I would like to be considered for Arundel and Shoreham on a long list. The MP, Henry Kerby, had dropped dead aged fifty-six. At that time this was the safest Tory seat in England, with an electorate of about 120,000. This was only the second by-election since the general election in 1970. Cecil Parkinson had been the first to win a by-election following the sudden and tragic death of Iain Macleod, the Chancellor of the Exchequer. The initial list was several hundred names long but was quickly whittled down, and I appeared for interview on long- and short-lists in Shoreham in front of the selection panel, comprising admirably bright and mainly retired people. The two who stood out were Noel Barker, chairman of the panel, and Denis Morris, a former head of BBC Light Services. The questions were helpful and not hostile. The final short list consisted of me, Douglas Hurd and John Stanley. The national media focused on our wives for several days before the final selection. They attended a fork lunch at the Beach Hotel in Littlehampton and had to answer a few questions. Outside the hotel was Maureen Colquhoun, later a Labour MP, who carried a placard saying to our wives, 'Are you a man or woman?' This was her idea of a feminist protest against the treatment of wives. I replied as I entered the hotel that I had some experience and was convinced that Rose was a woman.

To my amazement I was selected. Douglas Hurd was at that time Ted Heath's political advisor and the constituency did not want a Number 10 man imposed on them. John Stanley was in his late twenties and was just too young. Both later became successful Parliamentarians.

Rose was in tears of horror at my selection, which the agent told the press were tears of joy! The *Sunday Times* headline read, 'Mrs Luce's Husband Wins'. This upset Rose even more. Events then moved very fast as the by-election was on 1 April 1971, of all dates. It was a big upheaval for Rose and the boys, who were well settled in Hertfordshire. Rose's aunt, Barbara Hurst, kindly put us up at Rusper and we fought a vigorous campaign in this large constituency. *The Times* described me as 'barnstorming' my way to victory. I was flown over the constituency in a small aircraft from Shoreham to get an over-all view of the area. Unfortunately we had to fly above the clouds and I could see virtually nothing.

Amongst the many retired people living in Arundel were those who had been in the Armed Forces, the Diplomatic Service or Intelligence. Many of them pointed out to me that Kerby, my predecessor, had a rather unusual link with the Soviet Union. His mother was Russian and he had interpreted for Bulganin and Khrushchev on their visit to Britain. But to my mind he was not a very significant backbencher. He made only two Commons speeches in his last several years, and spent much of his time in Fleet Street. He portrayed himself as a rather sim-ple, rabid right-winger who wanted to bring back capital punishment.

The result of the by-election was declared in Littlehampton – a majority of some 22,000. Suddenly I was propelled into Parliament at the age of thirty-four. The adrenalin was flowing. Soon afterwards I took the Parliamentary oath, my two sponsors being Francis Pym, the Chief Whip, and Martin Madden who had represented Hitchin. Martin was to die suddenly and tragically aged fifty-two a year or two later. My father was sitting in the Civil Service box on one side of the floor of the House, and my father-in-law was in the ex-MPs' box by the Bar of the House. As I paced forward to face the Speaker and to take the oath, there was a considerable roar in the Chamber. The Conservative Sir Gerald Nabarro was shouting at the Leader of the Opposition, Harold Wilson, 'Three point eight per cent, Harold, three point eight!' This was the biggest swing to a sitting Conservative Government for a considerable time. A few days later I queued outside the members' telephone to ring Rose, only to be greeted by Sir Gerald walking out and saying, 'This is only for members, you know.' I had made less of an impact than I had hoped!

I was taken to the smoking room to meet Willy Whitelaw, who urged me always to drink lime juice and soda late at night. He did not always follow his own advice! I was greeted by Alec Home, then Foreign Secretary, who said, 'May I introduce myself? You won't know me, but I know you as I saw you being introduced to the House. My name is Alec Home.' I replied that I knew exactly who the Foreign Secretary was.

Entering Parliament is rather like going to school. Nobody takes much notice of you as you walk through endless corridors; you are given a locker and a room to share with others. In my case these were in an old building where the smart Portcullis House now is. In those days members spent more time in the smoking room, the tea room, or Annie's Bar downstairs. There was much less correspondence to deal with then, but later articulate constituents took to writing more and in an average week I might receive over 200 letters.

Early on I was asked to join Nick's Diner. This was a club founded by Nicholas Scott, whose membership were mainly on the left of centre of the Conservative Party; but it also included Ken Clarke, John Gummer, Charles Morrison, Barney Hayhoe and Tom King. To my disappointment I was never asked to join the One Nation Group. I did however join the Progress Trust, then chaired by Tufton Beamish. This group was more to the centre of the Party and met secretly outside Parliament. We had a flow of intelligence that gave us a picture of what was going on behind the scenes. If we felt strongly about something, the chairman would talk to the Chief Whip very privately. Being a member of groups of this kind gave me something of a base and a sounding board within which to operate in Parliament.

It was nerve-wracking to make my maiden speech. The Chamber was fairly empty, though Boyd-Carpenter was there to encourage me. My mother was listening with Rose in the Gallery. I was speaking, as is traditional, about the constituency and the fact that it was largely composed of retired people or, as I foolishly described it, 'the Costa Geriatrica'. I realised my mistake immediately but to my relief subsequently received letters from old ladies who thought the reference to them was very funny. My mother apparently went to sleep during my speech. Rose jogged her and she said, 'Oh! What a pity. I thought I was in a railway carriage.' I was relieved when it was all over. Perhaps the nicest aspect of the occasion was the support given by Alec Home. We had lunch with him and his wife Elizabeth that day, an event organised by his nice PPS Martin Maclaren, to give him a chance to meet some new MPs. Alec was very easy to chat to, more especially because my father worked for him at that stage as his Special Representative for Gulf Affairs. While I was making my maiden speech, out of the corner of my eye I saw Alec standing beside the Speaker's Chair, listening. For a busy Foreign Secretary to take the time to do so was an indication of his humility. I love the story of him travelling back to Northumberland, when an old lady sitting opposite him said, 'You know, Lord Home, you would have made a very good Prime Minister.' His reply was typical: 'Well, as a matter of fact, I was Prime Minister, but only for a year you know.'

I entered the House just after the Industrial Relations Bill had been completed. Since it was designed to start bringing the trades unions back under the rule of law and to stop union anarchy, there had been a mass of all-night sittings. I was fortunate to miss this because I found late-night sittings the most debilitating aspect of parliamentary work. In those days, on average we sat twice a week after midnight, unlike the early twenty-first century. I remember Nicholas Soames saying over lunch, 'Nowadays if there are votes at midnight, Labour members start blubbing!' As a minister I usually worked on boxes into the night when not in the chamber or voting, which meant I wasted less time hanging around talking or having cocoa in the tearoom. But more often than not I found myself having to complete the red box work in the early morning, sitting up in bed. Although the adrenalin often flowed, there was no doubt that I felt more tired and flabby as a backbencher in the '70s than at almost any other time, except perhaps as a minister.

I made a few speeches early on, mainly on foreign policy or consumer affairs. I became involved in writing a pamphlet about consumer affairs with Nicholas Ridley, Sally Oppenheim and Teddy Taylor, my interest stemming from my time at the National Innovations Centre. I knew how important it was to have well-informed consumers of goods and services to help enhance competition and to redress the balance between the interests of producer and consumer. It was my work on this campaign which led to my first step up the ladder: Geoffrey Howe was a successful Solicitor General who had helped to push the legislation on the Common Market through Parliament. Suddenly he was made Minister for Trade and Consumer Affairs in the Cabinet, the Consumer portfolio being a direct result of our pamphlet and campaigning. I was thrilled to be asked to be his Parliamentary Private

Secretary. I became heavily involved in his working life, often studying his red box papers with him, accompanying him to engagements and occasionally speaking on his behalf. He was the second Cabinet Minister under the Secretary of State, Peter Walker, at the Department of Trade and Industry, where other ministers included Pat Limerick, Peter Emery and Chris Chataway. My work with Geoffrey centred on seeing the Fair Trading Bill through Parliament. It laid the framework for a more consumer-orientated society, with the new Director General of Fair Trading having powers to ensure that trading practices had the consumers' interest as a priority. For the first time ever, the Bill was televised on Channel 4 to demonstrate to the public the processes that we had to go through, and turned out, in my view, to be singularly boring.

Geoffrey was a wonderful boss. However he was inclined to mumble when he spoke in public and I tried to persuade him to speak more clearly and not to use legal jargon. While working on his boxes in the middle of one night I told him that it was intolerable to write all his comments in classical Greek. Although his civil servants might be classicists, I wasn't. He stopped doing it. He was a thoroughly civilised, intelligent and thoughtful politician. When staying with us once in Sussex I asked him whether he wanted to be Prime Minister. He replied that he would like the challenge but, failing that, he would wish to be Lord Chancellor. In the end he did many things, but neither of those. His modest, humble, thoughtful and measured approach to public life is rarely seen in today's politicians.

The Common Market dominated Edward Heath's Parliament. The innovation of a referendum was a challenge, and in response I set up an all-party committee in my constituency, which organised large public meetings. Lord Hailsham came to address one in Shoreham, which I chaired, during which I had to stop him bullying some harmless lady. After the Arundel meeting we dined with the old Duke of Norfolk (Bernard) and his wife Lavinia. He said to me 'I don't understand the Common Market issue. Which way would you advise my tenants to vote?' Lavinia told him to stop being so stupid. In fact he had loads of commonsense and a twinkle in his eye. When the time came, I voted in the Commons for the Common Market, mainly on the grounds that I never again wanted to see a world war started in Europe. There would be the added advantage of creating more prosperity in a free single market and binding ourselves together more closely. In later years it didn't evolve in the way that I would most have wanted to see, with inadequate democratic checks, and too fast a development towards ever closer union.

My constituency, meanwhile, was exercised by three common issues: supporting the whites in Rhodesia, bringing back hanging and opposing the construction of a Channel tunnel. On Rhodesia Alec Home's name always saved the day, as the constituents worshipped him, and I would invoke his views if necessary. I found constituency work a good down-to-earth contrast to Parliament. Advice services for constituents were rewarding because it was possible to help a surprising number of people. Elections involved intense canvassing and usually two or three meetings in the evening. Personal contact with people is essential, and it is important to ask people to vote for you. Television is reducing the spark of contact in elections.

Michael Heseltine was already a colourful character in Parliament but, once he had swung the mace dangerously in front of the left-wingers in the Chamber, I found it hard to think that he could show much in the way of measured judgement. Heath, known by many of us as 'Morning Cloud' after his yacht, was not easily approachable; I had a meeting with him in 1974 when he was Leader of the Opposition, to tell him that the Crown Agents were about to go into liquidation and found him exceedingly stiff and detached.

The country squires were the stalwarts of the Tory Party. Harry Legg-Bourke was a very firm chairman of the 1922 Committee, and allowed virtually no discussion. Edward du Cann was unlike the traditional Tory. Probably the most memorable Parliamentary occasion was the vote that turned out the Callaghan Labour Government in the spring of 1979. When the Government surprisingly lost a vote of confidence by one vote, I found myself on my feet waving the order paper like every other Tory MP. We realised that it was a historic moment, as did Callaghan. The time had come for the country to change direction. This brought about eighteen years of Conservative Government.

Soon after we lost the first 1974 election, I became an Opposition Whip. Humphrey Atkins (later Lord Colnbrook) was Chief Whip and Jack Weatherill the Deputy. Other whips included Cecil Parkinson, Bob Boscawen and Carol Mather. There were two types of whip – the stalwarts who remained there for many years, and those who were 'greenhousing', gaining experience before going on to other tasks. I was one of the latter group, looking after the south-eastern region of MPs, and decided not to spend too long there before seeking the freedom of the backbenches. However it was an important experience. I learnt a great deal about the nature of the Party, the MPs and how Parliament works. Jack Weatherill was a particularly colourful disciplinarian with a splendid sense of humour, who would begin his briefings with the words, 'Stand by your beds'. Many years later I was delighted when he, with Robert Fellowes, was one of my sponsors on my introduction to the Lords in 2000.

After a period on the backbenches I joined the Shadow team as spokesman for all non-European affairs. Francis Pym was in charge, with Douglas Hurd looking after European matters. Later John Davies succeeded Francis. A former head of the Confederation of British Industry, he was a brilliant businessman, highly intelligent and an accomplished linguist. Some months before the 1979 election campaign he developed a brain tumour and died within a year. It all started during the Party Conference in October 1978. I was sitting just behind him as he was speaking in a tense debate on Rhodesia. His wife, Georgie, was next to me and grew alarmed when his speech started to become inarticulate. John was whisked into hospital for an emergency operation and I had to take his place as the main speaker in the next day's foreign policy debate. Typically John rang me the next day from his hospital bed to tell me how well I had performed. In the event this turned out to be the only main Party Conference speech I ever made.

Taking part in debates and answering questions was unnerving and much time was spent preparing with advisors. Dennis Skinner, known as 'the Beast of Bolsover', was a constant presence in the Commons, trying to trip up the speakers with his running commentary. In fact I got on well with him after we had appeared together on TV. On this occasion he had not won the argument, but I told him a few days later that he had done well and thereafter we always had a word when we passed each other. Enoch Powell was a frightening prospect for any minister. On one occasion I spotted him preparing to intervene with those large staring eyes. The question was on the Gulf, and he asked me if the Government had learnt the lessons of some unknown admiral in the Dardanelles. I replied that I was sure that we had. Meeting him afterwards, I asked him what he had meant. With his eyes gleaming he said, 'I thought you wouldn't know. He secured both flanks!'

My constituency faced boundary changes twice during my time in Parliament, eventually comprising mainly the coastal belt surrounding Worthing, with Findon linking the two sides. I became very fond of many of those in the Conservative Association with whom I worked, including successive chairmen Noel Barker, Denis Morris, Harold Rogers, Ian Elliott and Greta Brown, and knew that on retirement I would miss the many characters in the constituency. I was immensely pleased when the Garter King of Arms allowed me to use the title Lord Luce of Adur, named after the district in my constituency through which the River Adur flowed. The Association gave Rose and me a lovely farewell in the form of a painting of Shoreham and the harbour by Phyllis Pearsall, which will always hang in our house as a reminder of those days.

Do I miss being in Parliament? The answer is no – but I am profoundly grateful to have had the opportunity to serve there for twenty-one years. It gave me an insight into the widest range of issues, and enabled me to meet a cross-section of society in a way that would not otherwise be possible. There was a buzz about being at the centre of history-making and one found friends among MPs from all parties. So there was excitement; but there was also drudgery: committee proceedings or bills could be deadly, particularly if you were on the Government side as a backbencher, rarely able to say anything. Constituency correspondence increased during my time but I owed a great deal to my two personal assistants, Janis Downey and Sally Merrick, for their excellent support. When I left in 1992, I missed the company and the drama but not really the way of life. I disliked late-night sittings intensely and never felt that we were improving things in the middle of the night because we were all too tired; to me it was important to feel that it was possible to achieve things, to make progress. I was very lucky to have been a minister for ten years, just under half my time in Parliament, and to have been on the inside of the Party as a PPS, Whip and Opposition Spokesman for a further four years or so. I am by nature someone who prefers responsibility and action. I'm not really a club man, and I realise that I would have found it rather difficult to remain in Parliament as a frustrated backbencher, as I had originally planned to do after my retirement as a minister. It is, however, very rewarding to serve in the House of Lords and to contribute in a small way my experience from a varied life.

10

Rhodesia/Zimbabwe

A frica has featured much in my life ever since my first flight, at the age of eleven, to the Sudan by flying boat in the Christmas school holidays of 1947. It seemed entirely natural therefore when, in November 1977, Margaret Thatcher asked me to be Opposition Spokesman on all non-European affairs and subsequently, after the May 1979 election, to be Minister for Africa in my capacity as Parliamentary Under Secretary of State for Foreign and Commonwealth Affairs.

The big political issue which faced me was Rhodesia. Peter Carrington, as new Foreign Secretary, was my boss and took overall charge with a view to working for a settlement. Ian Gilmour was Lord Privy Seal in the Cabinet, and answered for the Secretary of State in the Commons, giving extra political support to Peter on Rhodesia.

When I had first entered Parliament in April 1971 Rhodesia was already a hot political issue which divided the country and certainly the Tory Party. In the 1960s Ian Smith had announced the Unilateral Declaration of Independence, stating that he would not tolerate African majority rule in his lifetime. He defied efforts by successive Prime Ministers Harold Wilson, Ted Heath and Jim Callaghan to restore legality and achieve African majority rule. The big difference in Rhodesia, compared with the rest of Africa and most notably Kenya, was that the interests of the Africans were not paramount. The white settlers, inspired no doubt by the ghost of Cecil Rhodes, had decided that they would run the country, and the Governor, Sir Humphrey Gibbs, was powerless to impose the authority of the Crown without military backing from Britain.

By the time I entered Parliament the situation was deteriorating. African guerrilla violence was increasing, particularly in the north, and Robert Mugabe was preparing to lead the movement to fight for independence from Mozambique. Africans both in Rhodesia and the international community were looking to Britain, as their colonial power, to take responsibility on their shoulders and to impose their will on the whites. Prime Ministers were not prepared to risk sending armed forces to impose a settlement; partly perhaps for fear that servicemen would not be prepared to kill white settlers or Rhodesian servicemen. Meanwhile African movements in the surrounding countries were growing more militant – and no doubt the Soviet Union were exploiting this to their advantage. Sanctions had been imposed in the 1960s which had initially helped Smith to rally people behind him. Later, when Mozambique joined the boycott, the economic pressures became intense and even the apartheid South African Government began to worry about the effects of a continuing conflict. This was already besmirching Britain's otherwise proud record of leading many African countries to independence before the inhabitants turned to violence.

The Tory Party was very divided. In the '60s, for example, Godfrey Nicholson had voted firmly for sanctions and had visited Rhodesia, but on this issue he was regarded as left of centre. Each year the Government had to put forward regulations to renew sanctions. The Party was divided between those who approved sanctions, the opponents and the abstainers. In the '70s there was a hard right wing led by Julian Amery, Patrick Wall and Stephen Hastings, who wanted the continuation of the British Empire and who supported the white settlers. They used the weapon of communist subversion mercilessly. Julian cut a nineteenth-century figure, often seen in the lobbies of Parliament plotting and whispering like a medieval monk. His brother-in-law, Maurice Macmillan, told me that the problem with Julian was that he had Armenian blood in him! He was a very mixed-up person whose burning ambition was to be Foreign Secretary. He was also a sad man, for his brother was executed in the Second World War as a traitor working for the Germans. (Albert Pierrepoint, the famous hangman, said that of all the people he had executed John Amery had been the bravest by far.) For this reason Julian was against capital punishment. One evening, just before a vote on this subject, I was standing with him at the bar of the Chamber, when an unwittingly tactless Tory came up to us and said that he assumed Julian would be voting for capital punishment. With tears in his eyes, Julian said no.

As leader of the right wing faction of the Tory Party, Julian did everything possible in the '70s to persuade the Tory Party to support Ian Smith and the white settlers, and continued to create difficulties when Margaret Thatcher formed a government. His target was Peter Carrington, in whose place he would have liked to have been.

In April 1975 Malcolm Rifkind and I visited Rhodesia and South Africa. We were regular travelling companions in the '70s and became great friends. An Edinburgh man, Malcolm had been a lecturer at Salisbury University and did his PhD on the Rhodesian Land Apportionment Act. During our visit we had a meeting with the most unattractive Minister for Foreign Affairs and Defence, Mr van der Byl, son of one of Smuts's South African Cabinet ministers. Apparently unaware of our experiences of Africa, he lectured us on the primitiveness of the natives who he declared had only just come down from the trees. He was a tall, dandified figure, with a shock of black hair and a nonchalantly arrogant manner. A real hard liner, he was totally against contemplating African majority rule. He presumably thought that this was our first day in the Continent and was rather shaken when, after twenty minutes of lecturing from him, I introduced Malcolm and myself, explaining our experiences of Africa.

During that visit we met a good cross-section of people, but it was clear that Smith did not want to see us, even though we saw him drive off to his farm. There was a solid African middle class whose standard of living was quite high. The political leaders were very hard line and told us that they wanted majority rule immediately, with only a short transition to independence. We were quite impressed by the calibre of some civil servants and felt that the political infrastructure was there for any new leader.

We relaxed one day by being taken to a football match. It was years earlier that John Stonehouse, Postmaster General, had disappeared. The African manager, who greeted us at the match, said 'You must be Mr Stonehouse!' There was little racial tension and everyone mixed together during the match – in stark contrast to South Africa.

On our return Malcolm and I had a meeting with Margaret Thatcher who read my report carefully and was understanding and sensible. She too stressed that the transition to independence must be short.

I returned to Rhodesia in 1978 after I had become Party spokesman. I recall a fairly stiff meeting with Ian Smith. He had a curiously masked face, rather like Alec Guinness, which effectively hid any expression. The cause of this was a war wound, which was also probably rather convenient.

When we got to the 1978 vote in the Commons on the renewal of sanctions, I had a rather tough time from our backbenchers in the wind up speech. Eventually twenty-three rebelled and opposed sanctions. Winston Churchill, the Defence spokesman, voted against. Instead of resigning he waited to be sacked by Margaret, and never again returned to the Front Bench.

During the late '70s I found myself in the position of advising and helping to work out Tory policy on Rhodesia. I stressed that we should do nothing to jeopardise the prospects of negotiating a settlement if we were to become the next Government. African leaders were already suspicious of us, but they would be looking to us to end the war and settle the dispute by negotiating legitimate independence. Indeed the whole problem would be an albatross around our necks if we failed to settle it. If we abdicated responsibility we would still be blamed for the war. It was essential to be in a position to bring about majority rule and independence, if we wanted to be free to play a more constructive role in the world.

Throughout the 1970s I regularly attended seminars at the Anglo-American Ariel Foundation. We met either in the USA or in the UK. Parliamentarians, academics, businessmen and journalists from both sides of the Atlantic met for a few days in pleasant surroundings to discuss Africa and in particular Southern Africa. We tended to be moderate politicians who had some knowledge of Africa. The real purpose for the British participants was to educate the US Congressmen about Rhodesia and South Africa, and to help prepare common ground on these issues.

Margaret Thatcher formed a Government in May 1979. I waited nervously to hear whether or not I was to join it as a minister. Eventually Peter Carrington rang me and asked me to join his team as the Minister for Africa. I was thrilled although I didn't know Peter at all well. I had first met him during the 1970 election when he spoke for me at a campaign meeting in Stevenage. I saw him occasionally in the Lords during the '70s. He always spoke warmly of my father, and of David Luce whom he had appointed as First Sea Lord.

Peter was an outstanding Foreign Secretary, delegating as much as he could to his ministers, but always with his finger on the pulse. He had a quick and sharp brain, immense common sense and wisdom acquired through many years of experience. His weekly meetings with ministers were always fun; I recall him once expressing exasperation with the 'dancing master'. We were all puzzled until Peter revealed that this was François Poncet, the French Foreign Minister, who indeed strongly resembled a ballroom dancing professional. Mugabe, less puzzlingly, was known by Peter as 'Ebagum'.

For that first year in office my life was dominated by the Rhodesian problem. 25,000 people, black and white, had died in conflict. All sides were getting weary. There was a desire to end the dispute. Bishop Muzorewa had become the first black Prime Minister with Smith serving in his Cabinet. This was the moment for us to grab it by the scruff of the neck.

Throughout this period my role varied. It was eventful. I was privileged to be at the centre when we were able to take the historic decision to end the war, hold elections and grant independence. It removed a major obstacle in the way of a more constructive foreign policy. From the beginning we faced strong opposition from the right wing and Peter had a very difficult time persuading Margaret Thatcher that it was in Britain's interest to settle.

Within ten days of my becoming a minister, Peter despatched me on the first of a series of tours to Zambia, South Africa and Namibia. My main purpose was to look at the Namibian situation but, naturally, in both Lusaka and Cape Town I discussed Rhodesia thoroughly. Just before departure, I joined other junior ministers in visiting Buckingham Palace to meet the Queen. She was puzzled at seeing me since she said that it was reported that I was already in Africa!

In Lusaka I received a very cold reception from the press and the Foreign Minister, Mr Chakulya. He was a very dreary man and seemed to sulk a great deal at the beginning of our talks, and especially in front of the press. While they photographed us I talked about the weather. The next day the headline in the Zambian *Times* read 'Minister talks about the weather rather than about Rhodesia'. The clear implication was that I was trying to evade the issue and that this was merely a foretaste of what was to come. In fact, the ninety-minute meeting with Chakulya helped to set the scene and reassure African leaders that Britain would not recognise Muzorewa, who had just become their first black Prime Minister, without seeking international support. Chakulya made one point which particularly struck me: that he was very proud of Britain's decolonising record and the magnificent and fair way in which we had handled the negotiations for independence in Zambia at Lancaster House. All he was asking was for Britain to do the same for Rhodesia.

In Cape Town I had a three-hour meeting and lunch with Pik Botha, the Foreign Minister. I was the first Conservative minister to establish contact with him and discuss Rhodesia's problems. He tended to lecture me in a tiresome way, but in fact his views were far more moderate than those of his colleagues. On a later occasion I decided to see him alone, leaving the British ambassador, Sir John Leahy, listening through the keyhole to what proved an unsuccessful conversation.

When I returned home Lord Harlech had already started on a front line tour as Britain's main envoy for Rhodesian affairs. A delightful man, he had been a minister and later ambassador in Washington. I was asked to complement his effort by visiting the more moderate African leaders in June 1979. I travelled first to Zaire, flying overnight in a very uncomfortable DC8 from Brussels, and spent one night with the British ambassador, Alan Donald, who was later our man in China. He had a pleasant house with a swimming pool overlooking the wide River Congo. In the evening I saw Mr Nguza, Zaire's Foreign Minister. Nguza was suspicious at first, but eventually relaxed and we had an easy conversation, during which I managed to dissuade him from making a big noise and sending an envoy to Rhodesia, which would undoubtedly have been counterproductive.

On a later visit to Zaire, I set off with the new ambassador and Keith Manning, my private secretary, for the presidential palace to see Mobutu. It was surrounded by military barracks and overlooked the rapids of the river; a dramatic sight. After a careful briefing from the head of protocol on the President's desire to keep a considerable distance from his guests at meetings, I was introduced to him in the principal sitting room. He sat on a sofa and I duly seated myself some distance away, in a chair. I found myself almost having to shout so that he could hear me, and after a while Mobutu suggested helpfully that we might talk at the breakfast table. I readily agreed since I would have a better chance of hearing him. We then proceeded to a small table on the verandah laid with various courses of fruit, omelettes and toast where the ambassador and Mr Nguza joined us.

A year earlier Nguza had been sentenced to execution for treason by Mobutu. At the last moment the President changed his mind and reappointed him Foreign Minister. Consequently Nguza was rather silent at breakfast, only speaking when told to do so. We sat there for over an hour. Mobutu began to lecture me angrily about the perfidious British in a rather odd French accent. As he grew more and more angry and excited I riskily asked him if I was on his black list for liquidation. He rocked with laughter and said that I was. Thereafter the atmosphere was far more relaxed.

Mobutu had been President for some time and was quite a quick and intelligent man, but also pretty tough. He was anxious to help by taking a lead over Rhodesia and it was important to convince him that we meant business on Rhodesia and to reduce feelings of mistrust. From this point of view I think the visit was relatively successful.

Some time later Nguza paid an official visit to Britain. I took him, at his request, to the musical *Hello Dolly*. He knew every line. Unfortunately he was inclined to sing the line just in advance of the cast, causing considerable consternation in the audience. Later over dinner at the Savoy he ordered '*kuku*' the Swahili for 'chicken' for the main course. The head waiter was desperately determined to counter the assumption that we eat cuckoos in this country. Eventually I intervened and we all enjoyed the chicken.

I flew from Zaire by Air Cameroons to the Ivory Coast. There the ambassador met me with the message that President Houphouet-Boigny was ill, but that he had recalled his Foreign Minister, Monsieur Ake, who had provided me with a police escort complete with very noisy sirens. We drove all round Abidjan with the awful wailing noise of the escort ringing in our ears. I met Monsieur Ake in his offices and he then hosted lunch for me, by which time we were getting on exceedingly well. The ambassador declared himself pleased with the outcome of our meeting. I then flew on to Dakar, the capital of Senegal, and a fascinating meeting place of African and Muslim worlds. I was greeted by colourful soldiers in red uniform against the background of a pure white palace. I spent an hour with President Senghor who was charming, very sophisticated and cultivated and spoke in the best Loire Valley French. He was certainly the elder statesman of Francophone Africa and very proud of his poetry and connection with Europe. He was a French Deputy and Cabinet Minister at one stage. I found him sympathetic to our approach on Rhodesia, but even he was not prepared to recognise Bishop Muzorewa without a change in the Constitution, and wanted closer ties with Britain

The British ambassador met me in Liberia and we had talks with Mr Dennis, the Foreign Minister, who was initially very suspicious of our intentions and wondered why I wanted to see the President. As the discussions proceeded he became more relaxed, and joined our meeting with President Tolbert who sat behind an enormous desk while four of us sat in a row in front of him, like children. Tolbert was friendly and clearly wanted to be helpful, particularly as he was to be the next chairman of the Organisation of African Unity.

I got to know Tolbert better when he paid an official visit to London in December that year with his wife and son, just a week before the final agreement on Rhodesia was reached. He was most helpful and prayed regularly for peace. His son sat next to Rose at a Mansion House banquet and murmured to her, 'You need not talk. I will meditate and probably levitate.' We took them to *Swan Lake*, which Mrs Tolbert said was just like *My Fair Lady*. Only a few days afterwards, back in Liberia, Tolbert was assassinated in his bed. The country has never recovered from this tragedy.

Soon after this I flew to Khartoum to see President Nimeiry, then also President of the Organisation of African Unity. Accompanied by our ambassador, Bill Carden, we had a very friendly talk at the palace with the President, though there was consternation when in response to the President's wish to receive a report on my forthcoming meeting with Muzorewa, Mr Carden asked the President if he could have his telephone number in order to keep him up to date. This caused much confusion, as the President had no idea what his number was.

The next significant development was the Commonwealth Heads of Government Conference held in Lusaka in 1979. The Prime Minister did not want to go because she thought that the Africans mistrusted her so much that they might be very aggressive and even throw acid at her! Peter Carrington persuaded her to accompany him, which proved a farsighted decision. Kaunda, at the big dinner and reception held to mark the end of the Conference, danced with Margaret. Such a public show of unity proved a turning point and the other leaders began to realise that Britain was serious in wanting to lead Rhodesia to majority rule and independence.

We then set in train negotiations for independence at Lancaster House. These began on 10 September and concluded successfully just before Christmas. Peter Carrington took me out to lunch beforehand and warned that I might get somewhat frustrated at times over precisely what role I was to play, but that, as Minister for Africa, I would participate in the proceedings and stand by to undertake particular tasks as and when they emerged.

Each Conference delegation had twelve members. There were three ministers in the British team: Carrington, Gilmour and myself. The other members were civil servants, principally Sir Anthony Duff, Sir Michael Palliser and Robin Renwick. The advisors said that negotiations would last between two to three weeks. I told them they were wrong. In fact they took fourteen weeks.

The procedure was as follows: every day Peter Carrington held a meeting of the British team at about 9 am. We would consider the invaluable overnight intelligence reports which provided information about the activities and views of the delegations. We would review the situation and in particular the tactics for the day before proceeding to Lancaster House for a plenary or bilateral session.

On the first afternoon we adjourned for tea and I suddenly found myself standing between Ian Smith and General Josiah Tongogara, Mugabe's Commander-in-Chief in Mozambique. I was temporarily stunned and wondered what to do. Then I decided to introduce them. There was a tense pause and then, to my amazement and pleasure, they suddenly hugged each other. They came from the same village of Selukwe. Tongagara wanted to know how the school was and to hear all the news of the village. A cup of tea had broken the ice.

On the whole I found the Conference difficult to handle as Peter Carrington had forewarned, because I don't much like not having a clear role. However there were certain tasks that I could undertake: for example, I hosted a considerable amount of private entertainment for people like David Smith, Nyandoro, Chinamano, Msika, and Chambati. I pressed other British ministers and MPs to help out, and Gilmour proved particularly good at this. I am sure that it helped to break down barriers.

What of the characters at the Conference? Peter Carrington was fairly dominating throughout and kept a firm grip on discussions, both private and public; his handling of the Conference was outstanding. His humour was an immense asset, and his occasional lightning flashes of temper no bad thing. On the whole he was respected by the participants, though not liked by Smith and Mugabe. It was to his great credit that the Conference was a success. Duff played a leading role and was brilliant. Renwick was the leading co-ordinator and mastermind. Both were skilled Whitehall operators. Palliser threw in very wise and sensible thoughts and commanded my admiration more than any other civil servant. He was always level-headed and constructive. Gilmour made contributions in a rather lethargic way, but was nonetheless effective in his support of Peter. At one point in the proceedings, he and I realised that the advisors had persuaded Peter to try to settle with Nkomo, excluding Mugabe. Gilmour and I took the view that the consequences of this would be catastrophic and cause the war to continue. We told Peter that we would resign if he came to an agreement with Nkomo. We heard no more of it.

Muzorewa was mainly silent and never spoke spontaneously. When he did speak, which was hardly ever, he read from a prepared text very badly as though he didn't understand it. At one stage, so far as we could establish, he sat in his hotel room for three weeks without once emerging. He was no politician, but a very honourable and decent man who believed firmly that what he was trying to do was right. When I entertained him to supper one evening, we chatted together for a long time and he told me that he felt he was taking part in an exciting experiment with the aim of achieving a peaceful adjustment to a multi-racial society. He also spoke of Smith and van der Byl's surprise at discovering that the African participants were as intelligent, or more so, than the whites in the Cabinet. He wanted time to prove that they could all work together. But it was too late for him. On the evening of 21 December I rang him before his departure. He was very nice and sent his blessing to the family for a happy Christmas. He had all the right aspirations, but didn't have the drive and political skills to achieve them.

Smith remained impassive throughout and tended to be sulky and morose. He clearly hated the British team and especially Peter Carrington, but was realistic enough to see that there was no future for the whites in holding out against increasing violence.

Mugabe was uncharacteristic for an Africa leader in lacking a sense of humour. And it flopped when he tried. One day he arrived in the morning for a meeting of his team with the British delegation. He had decided to break the ice. He said to Peter 'And what has our Lord to say to us today?' Peter was in a bad mood and didn't laugh. Mugabe never tried to crack a joke again. Fortunately his first wife Sally had an infectious sense of humour. Rose got to know her later in Zimbabwe. She and Christopher Soames had a good influence on him. In later years, well after Soames and Sally had died, power corrupted him and disaster followed. In the '90s I visited Zimbabwe and called on him. He had spent taxpayers' money on entertaining 14,000 guests at his marriage to his second wife. When I asked him what was his biggest problem he said, 'Poverty and land ownership.' He hadn't grasped the contrast between his own behaviour and the issue of poverty for his people.

One of the roles that I could play was to help work on Heads of States and Foreign Ministers. Kaunda remained an important link between us and Rhodesian leaders like Nkomo and Mugabe. On one occasion I accompanied him to London Airport immediately following a meeting with the PM and Peter Carrington. All the way down he was talking and laughing about the meeting. He said that Margaret was in a stormy mood. Peter Carrington had said to everybody, 'Fasten your safety belts!' Throughout the drive he held a white handkerchief to wipe away his tears of laughter. When he got to the top of the steps of the aircraft to wave goodbye, he shouted to me, 'Fasten your safety belts!' Really the African sense of humour so often saved the day.

Halfway through the Conference, in mid-October 1979, Peter announced that he wanted me to embark immediately on a tour of the front line states to brief Heads of State on the progress of the Conference and to seek their active support and co-operation. I was to visit seven countries in six days, meeting President Kaunda in Zambia, Foreign Minister Archie Mogwe in Botswana, Foreign Minister Chissano (later President) in Mozambique, President Nyerere in Tanzania, Foreign Minister Jorge in Angola, President Shagari in Nigeria and Foreign Minister Dennis in Liberia. An eight-seater jet aircraft HS125 was put at the disposal of our team. It had a desk and a bunk for resting. The speed of the tour was made possible by having this aircraft, and was further assisted by very welcoming ambassadors and high commissioners. I think that it helped to establish trust among some African leaders and demonstrated that we were serious in looking to an end to conflict and that we needed their constructive help. In discussions over how we proposed to conduct the transition I found both Kaunda and Nyerere to be delightful company and anxious to be helpful. Kaunda was more interested in his close link with Nkomo than with Mugabe. Chissano became a friend and later back in London I took him to see *Evita*. With his little beard he resembled the guerrilla leader Che Guevara and thought that the musical was portraying him, turning to me to say 'That's me.' Much later on Chissano succeeded Machel as President of Mozambique.

In Angola, Jorge was a tough nut and on that occasion I was not given an opportunity to meet the President, dos Santos. In Botswana Seretse Khama, the President, was recovering after the election. In the 1970s I had taken Margaret Thatcher, as Leader of the Opposition, to meet him at the Hyde Park Hotel. While we were talking to him in his sitting room, the door was opened by a female cleaner who said impatiently 'Haven't you finished yet?' before promptly shutting the door. President Shagari of Nigeria was charming and humble, but having restored civilian rule, he was unwise to work in the military compound rather than a civilian headquarters. He was not strong, and it was not long before he was deposed by the military. Foreign Minister Dennis in Liberia was an important link, particularly as President Tolbert was then President of the Organisation of African Unity. On my return to London, I felt that the tour had helped consolidate our work at the Conference. In a crisis there is no better alternative to trying to know and understand all the parties involved.

At a critical stage during the Conference I recruited a team of former colonial administrators to monitor and supervise the elections. I asked an old friend, John Cumber, to be deputy leader and provide expertise on Africa and administration, to complement the local government man, Boynton, who headed the team. When I briefed them it was quite something to see these distinguished men pleased to be asked to help, many of whom had been very senior to me in Kenya. I later accompanied Willie Whitelaw to a mass rally of policemen with striped umbrellas, all volunteering to help secure a successful election. They gave Willie a standing ovation, no doubt as an expression of their gratitude for being allowed to go on an exciting expedition.

DEPUTY GOVERNORSHIP

One Friday evening in November 1979, at the end of a long week, Peter Carrington and I drove with George Walden, the private secretary, to see President Kaunda at his hotel. After a rather brief meeting at which nothing transpired we left. The understanding was that Peter wanted an evening off, was very tired indeed and that if necessary I should stay on for a short chat with Kaunda if he had anything useful to say. In the event he had nothing whatsoever to reveal.

So we left the hotel at about 7 pm. I was about to get into my car when Peter drew me to one side of the pavement and made the most astonishing offer: he said, 'If there is a comprehensive settlement, then I want you to be Deputy Governor of Rhodesia.' I was so amazed by this that I was totally unable to reply. He broke the silence, repeating, 'Well, will you?' I replied, 'Yes, of course; I will do whatever you ask me to do.' 'Fine,' he said, and disappeared into his car to go home. I was, to say the least, pretty stunned. It seemed scarcely credible that as a member of Parliament and a junior minister, I was being asked to disappear for three months as a Deputy Governor.

That evening I arrived home late. My mother was staying, and clearly I couldn't tell her the news at this stage. I told Rose, who was as stunned as I. Over the weekend I remained in something of a daze. I felt enormously flattered to have been asked, and it seemed a unique challenge. I soon began to realise that this was a job that I could do quite well – drawing on my combined experiences of Africa as a District Officer, as a politician and as a minister. Rose started to plan, faced with the distinct prospect of having to leave in two weeks.

When I returned to the office the following week I heard no further mention of it from Peter, so on Wednesday I asked to see him alone. By then I was beginning to wonder if he had really meant it. But there was no doubt about it. He said that he was sorry to have rushed the offer on a Friday night but he had wanted me to have the weekend to adjust to the idea. I confirmed that I was looking forward to the challenge, and was told that the PM and Lord Soames, who was to be the Governor of Rhodesia, were pleased about it. I left Peter's office with renewed confidence and immediately went over to see Christopher Soames to start making plans.

I met him in his room in the Lords, where he was Lord President and Leader of the House. He was very friendly and expressed his pleasure that we were to work together. We had a general chat and he encouraged me to begin some of the day-to-day planning in preparation for our departure. By then it seemed possible that we would fly out in the PM's VC10 the following week.

I immediately set plans in hand both from the office and domestically. My close relations were informed of the news, as were our sons' headmasters because Rose and I wanted to take the boys out for the weekend before we left. I had a brief chat with Ian Gilmour who remarked nonchalantly, 'This will be good for your career.' The next day I returned to see Soames, this time in the office of the Lord President in the Old Admiralty. When I told him that we must have a dignified ceremony on arrival in Salisbury, with a band, he said, 'But what tune will they play?' I replied, 'There is only one tune I can think of: "God Save the Queen".' I paused and asked, 'What would you have chosen?' Quick as a flash he replied, '"Abide with Me".' We both dissolved into laughter. I pointed out that they probably didn't want to abide with him. We discussed many other issues, some important, others trivial. He focused on food and drink and asked who would do the shopping and how he might find a good pastry cook.

Mr Butler, Soames's private secretary, said that the main task for me was to be the 'Prime Minister' and Soames was to be the 'President' and that I would get on with the day-to-day caretaker administration of the country. 'And by the way,' said Mr Butler, 'would your wife like a bed in the VC10 on your flight out?' My reply was positive.

On the Friday of the same week Peter Carrington summoned me to a late afternoon meeting with Soames, General Walls, Rhodesian Chief of the Armed Forces, Police Commissioner Allan and civil servants. It was a somewhat uneasy meeting, concerning as it did the degree of control that HMG and the Governor would have over the Rhodesian Forces. In fact Peter gave Walls full freedom to patrol anywhere during the interim. This was risky but he doubtless felt it preferable to trust the general rather than try and exert control from a distance.

The following Monday morning I walked into the office and found myself pursued hot foot by Paul Fifoot, a legal advisor, who had in his hand a copy of the 1975 Disqualification Act. He told me that he had only just been informed of my appointment and wondered whether I realised that it was not possible under the law to be both a civil servant under the Crown and also an MP. I was shaken, but replied that I assumed the Prime Minister's advisors and the Foreign Secretary had been into this and cleared it. Paul however seemed doubtful, so I asked him to investigate with the legal advisors immediately and if necessary to consult the Attorney General. In the meantime I attended the Secretary of State's usual morning meeting on Rhodesia, where Peter Carrington seemed to realise that it was all off.

Shortly after this Michael Havers, the Attorney General, advised me that the risk was too great; if I took it I would be challenged and have to resign my seat. I had a conversation with Peter where we both expressed disappointment and unhappiness with this new situation. The very able Sir Anthony Duff took my place. This in some ways made more sense as it was not particularly appropriate to have politicians as both Governor and Deputy Governor. Rose and I were undoubtedly disappointed but were cheered up that evening by a performance of *La Bohème* to which my cousin Vin Robinson took us.

That experience perhaps strengthened my ability to take political disappointments more robustly in the future. There is no doubt that the settlement was a great achievement for Peter Carrington.

On Friday 21 December 1979 the final historic Lancaster House ceremony took place. The PM and Carrington were seeing Bishop Muzorewa, Mugabe and Nkomo beforehand and I was asked to receive the guests on behalf of the Government. For an hour I shook hands upstairs with ambassadors and high commissioners and other distinguished guests. Muzorewa was very friendly and looked quite cheerful. Mugabe arrived on his own, wrapped as usual in his scarf and seeming rather sober. Nkomo was very sunny and arrived last. I said, 'Thank God you've arrived. I thought you might have refused to come.' He rocked with laughter and when he left for the loo for a few minutes was very amused when I accused him of trying to escape.

Then the PM arrived with Peter. A little earlier she had changed the seating arrangements so that I could sit up front with her and Francis Pym, the Defence Secretary. This was generous recognition of the modest role I had played at the Conference.

The ceremony of signing and making speeches was speedy. The PM and I decided beforehand that we would stand and lead the clapping, once the ceremony was completed. We did so, there was a round of handshaking and so ended a most historic occasion. I wrote afterwards, 'All we have done is to create the conditions which will enable the parties to achieve peace. It will now be up to them to demonstrate that they do want it and will work for it.'

Looking back, nearly thirty years later, it seems that the first decade after independence was relatively successful. Mugabe broadly kept to the spirit and letter of the Constitution, and allowed the whites to continue as farmers to contribute to the prosperity of his country, though he did commit some atrocities on the Matabele. It was perhaps rather surprising that he didn't follow the Kenya example of land redistribution to give Africans a chance to farm more fully. We gave him that opportunity. Things began to slip by the early '90s. Two people were a positive influence on him in those early years after Independence – his first wife Sally and Christopher Soames. When I lunched with Mary and Christopher Soames and Mugabe at their flat, I realised that he had an enormous respect for Christopher.

But the truth is that so often power corrupts, as it has Mugabe. That has had the devastating effect of destroying and undermining Zimbabwe, causing misery to millions. At that time we had no other choice than to negotiate a peaceful settlement and independence. It brought the war to an end and gave both black and white people of Zimbabwe the chance to create a new nation within the Commonwealth. Britain, and Peter Carrington in particular, was given the credit for this and the Government was freed from a major albatross around its neck to concentrate on the problems of apartheid South Africa, the threat from the Soviet Union and the future of the European Union.

Other Overseas Assignments – I

THE MIDDLE EAST

M y lifetime's involvement in the Middle East is set against the background of my father's prominent role as the last real proconsul in the Gulf, and the fact that he was the only man to have responsibility at one time or another for the whole Gulf area from Aden (now South Yemen) to Kuwait. I came to know the area fairly well through family visits there from an early age.

I naturally took an interest in the Middle East once I was in Parliament, although I was never as absorbed with the Arab world as Parliamentarians such as Dennis Walters and Ian Gilmour. I had to point out to many that my father liked and respected Arabs but was perfectly balanced about them, warts and all. Julian Amery used to talk around in the House speculating why my father, a prominent figure in the Empire, had brought it to an end in the Gulf. Had he lost his marbles? In truth he was a farsighted man who saw that it was better to retain the goodwill of the Gulf Arabs by leaving before being asked to leave.

It was against this background that I decided to keep up the family link with the Middle East and to build on all that my father had taught me. In 1972 I accompanied two other Tory MPs, Brandon Rhys Williams and Albert Cooper, on a Parliamentary visit to Israel which gave me the first picture of this new home for the Jews. A night spent in a kibbutz conveyed a flavour of the pioneering Israel and meeting politicians like Abba Eban made me realise their extraordinary energy and intellectual power and to sense that the harnessing of the talents of Jews and Palestinians could make for a powerful force. The Government's decision in the early twentieth century to create a home for the Jews in Palestine has created the most prolonged, intractable and dangerous international crisis – with the exception of the Cold War – in my lifetime.

Over ten years later, in May 1983, when I returned to Government following my resignation over the Falklands crisis (which I recount in a later chapter), the new Foreign Secretary, Geoffrey Howe, asked me to take responsibility for the Middle East as Minister of State. For several months I played a leading role, as Geoffrey was preoccupied with other issues, not least the European Union.

There were many problems to grapple with, not least of which was whether to recommend keeping our 200 troops in the Lebanon, a country in the turmoil of a civil war. I sat in my summer house over the first weekend reading all the background papers and concluded that if we were to have any influence over the Americans in this area we would have to play a part ourselves, however modest. Geoffrey and the Prime Minister, Margaret Thatcher, agreed and in September that year I decided to visit the Lebanon. I spent a night in Dhekelia, the British base in Cyprus, and flew in the next morning by helicopter. The crew insisted on keeping the doors open because the pilot felt that it would be safer, if necessary, for me to drop into the sea! I pointed out that it was difficult to read my briefing papers with all that wind but the pilot prevailed. I was driven in an armoured car through the city of Beirut to a small fortress in the centre, where our soldiers were positioned. Bullets were flying in all directions as the colonel in charge introduced me to his team. I observed that he appeared to be under considerable stress. On my return to Britain the next day the papers suggested that I had a role in sacking the colonel, who unbeknownst to me had been removed immediately after my departure.

Over the following months the Americans were drawn deeper into the snake's pit, becoming a major target for Palestinian terrorists and achieving nothing. Eventually I was with the PM when she talked to President Reagan on the telephone to try to persuade the Americans to pull out of Lebanon with us. It was quite clear that we were on a hiding to nothing. As we know, Lebanon later depended on the Syrians to keep the peace.

Rose and I visited Israel for Balfour Day in 1983 where I made an off-the-cuff speech at a banquet which nearly caused the ambassador, Patrick Moberly, a heart attack. He thought that everything should be carefully drafted and read beforehand in such a delicate situation. I had meetings with all the leading politicians from Peres, Labour leader of the Opposition, to Shamir, the former terrorist leader, who was both Prime Minister and Foreign Minister. I met Palestinian leaders in the Jerusalem area under the auspices of our consul general, with the exception of Arafat, someone I have always found it difficult to respect or appreciate. Back in London King Hussein of Jordan told me that he was most anxious for Margaret Thatcher to offer greater recognition to Arafat and the PLO. I said I would take him to see her over tea at Number 10 and told him to repeat his views to her so that it came directly from him. He promised that he would do so, but on the day was too courteous to carry it out, probably believing that he should be polite to women. Stronger dialogue with Israel and with the PLO was all that I could hope for at that stage.

In March 1984 I accompanied the Queen on a state visit to Jordan. Rose came too. Before departure, the PM summoned me, Geoffrey Howe and Michael Heseltine, then Defence Secretary, to Chequers to discuss warnings that the Queen's life was threatened in Jordan. I was in favour of going. The others were not. We were unable to reach a conclusion. Margaret summoned Denis. Over a glass of whisky he concluded, 'Elizabeth I would have gone. So shall Elizabeth II.' So off we set, though on the first morning in Amman the ambassador, Alan Urwick, came rushing round to say that the Cabinet had further evidence of a plan to blow up the Queen on the road from Amman to the University that afternoon. As minister in attendance I was responsible for her security. I kept close to General Shaker, the Commander-in-Chief, who convinced me that they were in adequate control. Later King Hussein said to me that, if it would help, he would sleep on a mat outside the Queen's bedroom. I assured him that it was not necessary! All went well.

Elsewhere in the Middle East the war between Iraq and Iran, sparked by a dispute over ownership of land in Iraq at the head of the Gulf, lasted eventually for eight years and posed a threat to stability in the region. In Geoffrey Howe's absence I attended a Cabinet committee under Margaret Thatcher's chairmanship and argued that Britain and America would need to send ships to help stabilise the area. I knew that Michael Heseltine opposed this suggestion so I attended to argue the case, and got approval. The Cabinet instructed me to fly in March 1984 to Washington for discussions with Schultz, Secretary of State, Weinberger, Defence Secretary, and Vice-President Bush. We agreed on a strategy to send ships to police the Gulf. We have been in the region ever since.

At the time Iran posed a more significant threat to peace than Iraq because the country was in the hands of irrational ayatollahs. I had visited Teheran in 1978 in an all-party delegation and we had met the

Shah who appeared to be out of touch with his people; I never forgot his patent lack of knowledge of what was going on in his country. It was a blow to Western interests when he fell in 1979.

At the request of the Prime Minister I visited Iraq to try and assess their position and the chances of ending the war. The British ambassador, John Moberly, arranged for me to have lengthy talks with Tariq Aziz, then Foreign Minister. It was eventually discovered which palace Saddam Hussein was living in and I duly met him. He was imposing and his staff were clearly frightened of him. He wanted friendly relations with us but my visit gave me no cause for optimism.

Arab leaders attach great importance to developing personal relations with politicians from other countries. On one occasion the PM asked me to take a special message from her to King Fahd of Saudi Arabia. The King was at that time in the desert seeking peace and solitude, but he asked for me to be flown from Riyadh to his caravan headquarters in his own aircraft. I was told that it would be a twenty-minute flight. After forty minutes the pilot announced that he had overflown the site and was being guided back on the instructions of the King. On arrival I joined him in his caravan where he expressed relief that he had not been responsible for 'losing one of Mrs Thatcher's ministers'!

It was important for me to make full use of family ties with the Amirs when it came to Britain's relationship with the Gulf States. I regularly visited all the Gulf States to see the Amirs and their teams. I recall finding the Sultan of Oman on his annual pilgrimage to the desert. I sat in his tent with him on the ground and we talked frankly to one another about relations with the UK, the Iran-Iraq war and the Arab-Israel dispute. After two hours he leapt up. I tried to follow his example but my back was paralysed. I had to haul myself up by the central tent pole.

I was very touched when Sheikh Zaid, the President of the United Arab Emirates, said that he would like to meet the third generation of the family. So after Christmas 1991 Rose, Alexander, Edward and I set off on a tour of the Gulf to visit all except Kuwait's Rulers. This tour enabled Alexander and Edward to see for themselves their grandfather's legacy. We all felt very proud, for he had laid the foundation of the post-imperial age in the Gulf and to this day its goodwill towards Britain remains strong.

HONG KONG

I first visited Hong Kong with Rose in the 1970s when I was Shadow spokesman for non-European affairs. The Governor, Murray MacLehose, had been there for many years and was a tall, rather dominating proconsular figure, which I found rather surprising as he came from the Diplomatic Service. We had a rather stiff and formal lunch with him and his wife. He presided over a guided democracy – a bit too much guided and not enough democracy in my view. Had MacLehose advanced the franchise more rapidly during his time, Chris Patten would have had less of a battle with the Chinese later.

I was disappointed after the general election of 1979 not to be given Hong Kong to handle. That responsibility came, however, in June 1983 on my return to Parliament as Minister of State. By this time Hong Kong was entering a critical stage for, unless early agreement was reached with China to ensure a stable, long-term future after the handover in 1997, there would be a rapid collapse in confidence, a decline in business activity, and the probable emigration of the skilled middle classes of Hong Kong.

Margaret Thatcher was agonising increasingly over the prospect of handing over Hong Kong to China. After all, a large proportion of Hong Kong's population had fled Communism and never wanted to experience it again. However Margaret was also respectful of international legal obligations, under which Britain would hand Hong Kong back to China in 1997 with the exception of the island itself and Kowloon. She toyed with the idea of retaining the latter, but since we all knew perfectly well that the Chinese would soon have isolated the area and cut off the water supplies, it was clearly unfeasible. So the next thing to do was to find a way to persuade China to agree at the earliest possible stage to preserve the basic way of life of Hong Kong – its measure of democracy, freedom under the law, free press, and respect for individual rights, and most importantly its free market capitalist economy.

Under the overall guidance of the Prime Minister, Geoffrey Howe decided that he should take charge of negotiations with China, and that I as Minister of State should be the link with the people of Hong Kong. This meant that I needed to visit Hong Kong regularly and to see their political leaders in London when necessary. The prominent members of the Executive Council and Legislative Assembly included Sir S. Y. Chung and Lydia Dunn. S. Y., as he was known, was not very articulate, whereas Lydia, married to a former Attorney General, was dynamic and sharp in our discussions. The Governor at this time was Teddy Youde, a former ambassador to China. He was a quiet, calm, modest man with a charming wife, Pamela. He had the most difficult and painful job of keeping Hong Kong steady without revealing to the leaders or public anything of the negotiations with China. I think the strain literally killed him for he died on the job while visiting Peking, by which time I had become Minister for the Arts. The news of his death led me to shed tears for a good man. He received a state funeral in Hong Kong.

Each time I arrived in Hong Kong I could guarantee the stock market would decline, and then improve on my departure. Those visits were not easy and much tension was in the air. The press were always waiting for me at the airport and expected me to say something. Teddy Youde would give me excellent and thorough briefings at Government House before I started intensive discussions. The most difficult part was attending a meeting of the Executive Council, where I would be subjected to polite but detailed questioning about the talks with China. It was agonising not to be able to share anything substantial with them. On one occasion when I arrived for a meeting, I recall a sea of Chinese faces surrounding me and looking out of every window. The stony silence revealed their true anxieties about their future. On another occasion when driving with Teddy to the Executive Council, he said I was in for a surprise, and there, as I got out of the car, I found myself surrounded not by people, but by animals and birds, including pigs, ducks and geese, which were unleashed on me from behind pillars by farmers from the New Territory who were deeply worried by farm prices. On my return home Rose said she had wondered what on earth I had been doing when she read reports on this unusual attack.

In the meantime I was working very closely with Geoffrey Howe and diplomatic advisors on our negotiating cards with China. We were aiming for a set of guarantees on basic law and freedoms, to which China would be committed, notwithstanding the fact that the Chinese communists opposed such freedoms. Tensions were high and we had very little confidence that we could get the Chinese to agree. The turning point came suddenly, while Geoffrey Howe was negotiating in Peking. One Saturday morning I received a message saying that the PM would like me to go to the Foreign Office, to be on duty over the weekend to deal with any fall-out from Geoffrey's discussions, particularly if they failed. While there, a dramatic message came through from our ambassador announcing that the Chinese Government had unexpectedly suddenly accepted the importance of agreeing a basic law and had authorised speedy discussions to agree in detail the way of life for Hong Kong after 1997, realising that this was necessary if stability was to be preserved. The key to this change of heart was Deng Xiaoping, China's ageing leader, whom Geoffrey met that day. Deng told the British ambassador afterwards that he could trust Geoffrey Howe and from then on things went smoothly. The extent of Geoffrey's achievement should not be underestimated; his patent integrity and trustworthiness had been the key to unlock the door, for the Chinese are innately suspicious. Geoffrey's work led to the 1984 Declaration, and a reassurance about the future of Hong Kong. I was proud to have played a part in this, however modest, and to have had the opportunity to work with the people of Hong Kong.

By September 1985 I had been made Minister for the Arts and for the Civil Service. As Arts Minister I visited China with Rose and spent time in Beijing, Xian and Shanghai. We paid a short visit to Hong Kong, principally to view their arts but also to renew contact with old friends. It was the last time we stayed with Teddy Youde.

Sir David Wilson, another sinologist, succeeded Teddy as Governor on his death. He and his wife Natasha were friends of ours. In the early 1990s, after I had resigned from the Government, I discussed with the Foreign Secretary, Douglas Hurd, the possibility of my becoming Governor of Hong Kong. Despite the fact that the job would have been very difficult and a hiding to nothing, it appealed to my colonial past and experience of international relations. Douglas toyed with the idea for some time and discussed it with the Prime Minister, John Major, but the latter decided to postpone making any decision until after the 1992 election, and then offered the position to Chris Patten. Douglas meantime asked if I would be prepared to take on a High Commissionership in the Commonwealth, perhaps Canada or India, but by then I had decided to take on the job as Vice-Chancellor of the University of Buckingham and to leave Parliament.

We visited Hong Kong again three times and more than once stayed with David and Natasha Wilson. On one visit in the early 1990s we went to Fanling, their New Territory residence, for the weekend, and after lunch set off for a longish and enjoyable walk across the hills of the New Territory. Rose and Natasha stayed behind but planned to meet us at the bottom. While descending a fairly steep and rocky slope, David asked whether I would mind his running down ahead of me accompanied by his security guard policeman. I said that was fine provided I could be allowed to walk. A moment later I heard a cry and there down below me was David lying face down on the rocks, unconscious, with the policeman distraught. I thought David was dead or dying and told the policeman to radio for a helicopter. Meanwhile I ran downhill to tell Natasha. On climbing up the slope again, there was David walking carefully down hill, looking somewhat dazed. There was considerable public speculation over the next few days as to what he had done. In fact he had fractured a cheekbone and had been very lucky.

We stayed with Chris and Lavender Patten twice in the late 1990s. Chris had fast become a hated figure by China because he fought for an extension of democracy, which became a seriously divisive issue in Britain. Many politicians, including Geoffrey Howe and Michael Heseltine, and the majority of businessmen, were more concerned by longer-term relations with China than with Hong Kong. Chris Patten's priority was to secure the maximum amount of democratic freedom before Britain's departure. Sir Percy Cradock, a most distinguished sinologist, ambassador in Peking and advisor to the Prime Minister, led a very forthright attack on Chris in public. I felt he had no right to undermine the Governor in public and corresponded and lunched with him to try to dissuade him, without success. Cradock was a brilliant man but very critical of politicians. Chris probably made a mistake in dismissing all sinologist advisors and not attempting to negotiate secretly with China over democratic reform.

The situation in Hong Kong now is as good as it could be. The economy has its ups and downs and there is still debate about the level of democratic reform. But at least we know that the Chinese do not want Hong Kong to collapse, for this would cause serious economic damage; further, China wishes to hold out to Taiwan the prospect of adopting the same theme of one country but two different systems of governance. Both Britain and China have shown sufficient common sense to give Hong Kong at least a chance to succeed. Perhaps Hong Kong's basic freedoms will eventually influence China to adjust gradually to a freer life for all.

12

Other Overseas Assignments – II

Although Rhodesia dominated my time as Africa Minister, I did manage to visit several other countries and grapple with a few problems. Namibia remained to be settled much later. As South West Africa it was formerly German territory. Later the South African Government administered the country while SWAPO under Nujoma were fighting for their independence. I did one visit to Windhoek in the 1970s to meet some of the political leaders and the South African Administrator. I would have enjoyed seeing some of the desert and wildlife as well as Walvis Bay but there was no time. At Peter Carrington's request I paid an official visit to Namibia and South Africa, very soon after becoming a minister. On the flight back I wrote a full report, recommending what action we should take to facilitate an end to the conflict and independence. Peter was very complimentary and sent the report to the PM. In the end it was decided to concentrate on settling Rhodesia first.

In January 1981 a conference on the future of Namibia took place in Geneva. Due to our success in settling Rhodesia, there were many who felt we should take the lead on trying to settle Namibia. It was somewhat embarrassing when speculation grew in the press that I was flying into the Geneva Conference to help bring it to a conclusion. This is a good example of where it is helpful to understate expectations. Brian Urquhart, Britain's most senior and experienced UN hand, was chairman. I found a very negative situation with no will to achieve anything. They were on the verge of breakdown. I worked with Brian to avoid a total impasse so we got agreement to suspend the Conference and wait for a more propitious opportunity. However it was a chance for me to get alongside a number of notable people, including the UN Commissioner for Nambia, Mr Ahtisaari, a rather large Finnish diplomat who later became President of his country; the smooth and confident South African diplomat Brand Fourie; political leaders in Namibia Sam Nujoma and

Dirk Mudge; and Donald McHenry, the black American ambassador to the UN. The country achieved its independence later on, and I had no further role to play. It is now a member of the Commonwealth.

I was on holiday at home in early August 1980 when I decided to call on the then President of the Gambia, a trained vet called Jawara. He was having a holiday at his home in Haywards Heath. The following morning I was told that there had been a coup overnight in the Gambia. Immediately I rang the President and got him off the neighbouring golf course to tell him the news by telephone. His first question was, 'I have one wife here. What has happened to the others?' During the morning I had several conversations with him. Four hours later I persuaded him to ask me for assistance in restoring democracy. I agreed with Peter Blaker, Minister for the Armed Forces, that two available SAS men should be sent in to try and unravel it. One of them was already in the Gambia in remote country far up the main river. I asked that, whatever they did, they should not be seen by the press doing it.

Very soon there was a counter-coup and the President was restored to office while he sat in Sussex. The papers showed photographs of two white men leading a charge up the High Street of the capital. I turned a blind eye to this since they had succeeded in fulfilling our objective.

In 1981 I flew to Uganda as the first European minister to visit the country following the downfall of Amin. After nine years in exile in Tanzania, Obote returned once more as President. I had met him in London. He and Mrs Obote were very friendly, hosting a lunch at State House with a pianist playing music on an out of tune piano, rather like a provincial tea room in the 1900s. We had very lengthy discussions on how he would like to rebuild Uganda and what help he would need from us. At one point he sat me on a sofa and asked me to look at the ceiling. He pointed to many bullet holes and explained that Amin used to fire into the ceiling above him if he was irritated by the advice from his civil servants. At other times he would just shoot an advisor. I told the President that I felt sorry for anyone who might be in bed in the room above us.

I had a whole day in helicopters and small planes in Karamoja in North East Uganda, seeing the relief work of various organisations like Save the Children Fund. Amin had left a devastated country but it has a very rich soil. Any number of bananas can be grown on small plantations. I have an impression that this might have saved many Ugandans from even more severe starvation.

It was in our interests to help Uganda to recover. But Obote turned out to be disappointing. I met his Minister for Defence, Museveni, who was sharp and impressive. Later he led a rebellion and became a strong President.

Ugandans have the usual African infectious sense of humour. I watched a new television service with a news programme. Bored at reporting my visit they put up a notice saying, 'Have gone for tea.' Later another notice went up saying, 'We'll be with you in a moment.' Eventually a newsreader read out a Government message, which said, 'If anyone is having anti-Government feelings, they should stop it immediately!'

It was an experience to visit Swaziland just before the death of the former King. He reigned almost as long as Queen Victoria and is alleged to have had a very large number of wives and about 600 children. When I called on him, the High Commission had failed to tell me that Swazis must remain below knee level in the presence of the King. As we entered the audience room it looked as though a bomb had gone off. There were about twenty-five people lying prostrate on the floor. At the far end was the King, seated between two elephant tusks. I made my way over the bodies and was told to sit beside His Majesty. While he and I were having a very pleasant conversation, the Prime Minister entered the room in a dark suit on all fours and slithered quietly on to a sofa like a newt.

The Indian Ocean area was also my responsibility. On arrival in Mauritius I was met by the flustered High Commissioner who whisked me away in his car through crowds of people. I asked him why there were so many people when there was only one plane at the airport. Looking embarrassed, he said it was a demonstration against me by the Ilois who were resettled in Mauritius after they were turned out of the Chagos Islands by Harold Wilson to enable the Americans to use Diego Garcia for military purposes. I was concerned that we had shunned them and said they should be allowed to demonstrate again in front of the High Commission. A few days later I arrived at the High Commission to be surrounded by the same people. I asked that the main leaders be invited into the office to meet us for a cup of tea. They turned out to be rather formidable ladies who explained that they were treated as second class citizens by Mauritians and that they wanted to return to their islands. I managed to arrange for them to receive a sum of money from HMG to improve their conditions. It is interesting that they have now received the backing of the courts to return to their islands.

Of course I kept in touch with Kenya, seeing Arap Moi and the ministers. In 1993 Rose and I toured the country on behalf of Booker Tate and the Commonwealth Foundation. We visited our former districts of Embu and Isiolo before flying on to see Wilfred Thesiger in Maralal. Returning to Africa always excited me, but I was sad to see the decline in democracy, the corruption and the mismanaged economies.

THE CARIBBEAN

I got to know the Caribbean from the 1970s onwards. A colourful and attractive but rather explosive region, it has a fascinating mixture of people – from those of Indian origin, their forebears being indentured labour to the original Caribs, the Creole of mixed race, and of course Europeans. While much of the area became a British responsibility, today the US influence is strong. In the '70s the threat to stability was considerable with Castro and Che Guevara stirring up revolutionary activity while Guatemala laid claim to British Honduras (now called Belize), and some of the smaller islands were potentially unstable.

In 1976 I accompanied an all-party delegation led by Lena Jeger, the Labour MP, to Trinidad, Belize and Jamaica. This was my first introduction to the region and I loved the atmosphere. In Trinidad Dr Williams presided over a country with oil but heavy unemployment, a decline in agriculture and a drift to towns. Jamaica faced similar problems in the decline in agriculture, acute poverty and violence. In Belize sugar, fish and bananas kept the country viable but fragile, with a commitment of British troops to deter a Guatemalan invasion. The smaller islands tended towards fragmentation. I led for the Government in getting the St Kitts-Nevis independence legislation through Parliament though Nevis never wanted to be associated with St Kitts. The Bahamas, which Rose and I visited in the '90s, attracted many tourists with its 700 or so islands and strong American influence.

In January 1979 I accompanied an all-party delegation to Cuba. Malcolm Rifkind was the other Tory and the two Labour left-wingers were Martin Flannery and Stan Newens. First of all it caused a problem for me. Francis Pym, the Shadow Foreign Secretary, agreed that I should go on the mission in my capacity as Shadow Spokesman for non-European affairs. I was wrong to assume that he had cleared it with Margaret Thatcher who was not happy with my visit. But I learnt much from the tour. We had a good two-hour meeting with Castro. He was celebrating twenty years of power in 1979 and was dominating and charismatic. He said that Malcolm and I were the first Tory MPs he had met and he found us 'tall and charming' and a big improvement on Republican Congressmen! He boasted about the revolutionary role of Cuba in Africa, particularly Ethiopia and Angola. There was a stale smell of dictatorship. Our rooms were bugged, the truth was distorted, there were many political prisoners, food was rationed and freedom curtailed. It brought home to me how foolish successive American Administrations had been to adopt a permanent blockade of Cuba. It gave ammunition to Castro to rally his people behind him just as David fought against Goliath. A more relaxed American policy and plenty of contact might have produced a different story.

The Caribbean certainly produced characters as leaders. Dr Williams in Trinidad was a reserved academic, always wearing dark glasses and uncharismatic. Jamaica had the Manleys. I got to know the son quite well; a likeable, charming but snake-like character with distinctly leftist views. Then there was the PM of Belize (formerly British Honduras), an austere intellectual Jesuit called George Price who had little humour. When he asked my assistant private secretary what university he attended, he could not believe that he had never been to one and was totally bemused when I told him that the Foreign Secretary, Lord Carrington, hadn't been to one either. In Antigua there was the rather controversial Bird family in charge, and Dominica had the powerful Eugenia Charles as Premier.

I once made an unfortunate error when I failed to recognise the Governor General of St Kitts-Nevis on meeting him for the second time. This small man entered the room very modestly and went on his own rather shyly into the corner of the room. Very quickly I realised that he was in fact the Governor General and I sought to recover the situation as quickly as possible. But I think I had slightly punctured his self-esteem; and the pressure wasn't that high in the first place.

Belize was the biggest political problem and as Minister of State I paid two visits. On one occasion my luggage had been packed by Rose who mistakenly included her underclothes. My case was sent ahead to the residence of the commander of the British Forces while I toured the country by helicopter. When I got there in the evening the corporal, who was my batman, refused to come anywhere near me. Only later did I realise that I had Rose's underclothes! They therefore accompanied me to the embassy in Washington where the head butler swept them away and repacked for London – including as well the underclothes of Lady Henderson, wife of the ambassador. This caused great amusement with ministerial colleagues on my return.

Grenada featured briefly in my life. One Saturday there was a communist-led coup. The Foreign Secretary was abroad. I asked the Ministry of Defence to tell me where the nearest British warship was and I was told that one was visiting Venezuela and that the ship's company were playing a local football match. I asked that the ship should sail immediately for Grenada as our first duty was to ensure the safety of British citizens. That evening I was happily watching the final shoot-out of a traditional Western when the Prime Minister rang from Chequers to discuss the situation. I reassured her that the ship was not sailing into battle and she accepted my decision. Her concern was that Grenada had been a British responsibility and that Reagan's decision to intervene to impose democracy was against international law. I told her that I would be in Washington on the Monday and could discuss this with the Secretary of State. To my surprise I was never asked to follow up. As we know, the Americans restored democracy.

LATIN AMERICA

It is an exciting continent. I wish I knew it better. It was as long ago as the 1820s that Canning said that the New World should be brought in to redress the Old. Of course in the nineteenth century Britain played a leading role in building their railways and notable British individuals played their part in fighting for their independence from their European Imperial powers. But the twentieth century was very different. Britain left it to the USA, Spain, Portugal and Italy to develop relations with Latin America and watched the turmoil of revolutions, dictatorships, brief attempts at democracy, economic crises. The musical *Evita*, which I saw five times, brought out the character of the Perons.

I only had a few months as Minister of State responsible for Latin America and no time to tour. The Falklands resignation took place when I was on the verge of doing a visit to Mexico and Ecuador. My sole experience was in 1971 when I visited Argentina, Uruguay and Brazil on either side of my voyage to the Falklands, a story that features elsewhere.

More recently Rose and I had been to Ecuador and the Galapagos. There is something very romantic about the mountains, the haciendas, the Incas, the volcanoes, the wildlife, the Pacific Ocean and the afforested jungles. More British tourists are enjoying the continent now.

There are some valiant politicians, such as Lord Montgomery, who keep up the contact and promote the British interest. But we could be working much harder at our relations, trading more and exchanging views and experiences on democracy. We should not leave it all to the Americans.

NORTH AMERICA

I visited both Canada and the United States quite often between 1971 and 2000. But in each country Rose and I did two remarkable and very different tours. In the autumn of 1973 Peter Walker, the Secretary of State for Trade, asked the four Parliamentary Private Secretaries to Trade Ministers in that department to undertake a tour of all the Provinces of Canada. The purpose was clear. Britain had voted to enter the European Union. Leading members of the Commonwealth felt that we were turning our backs on them, Canada especially so. Our task was to tour Canada to reassure them that we were committed to retaining strong relations with them. I was PPS to Geoffrey Howe (Minister for Trade and Consumer Affairs in the Cabinet). The others were Tom King, Cecil Parkinson and John Hannam. Our wives were invited to accompany us. We threw ourselves into it, working together at the beginning and the end of the tours in Toronto and Vancouver with seminars and then touring on our own to selected Provinces. I was allocated Ontario, Alberta and British Colombia.

The programme was intensive, exhausting but exhilarating, with an immense amount of media work counterbalanced by seminars, visits to businesses, factories and universities. I made the concluding speech in Vancouver and I think by the end we had made an impact and given a clear message. The programme had been arranged by the High Commissioner, Sir Peter Heyman, who was full of energy. I met for the first time Jean Chrétien, then Minister for Indian and Native Affairs. In 1982 I helped Humphrey Atkins (Lord Privy Seal) to take the Canada Bill, which cut all final colonial ties with Canada, through Parliament. Chrétien was then Minister for Justice. He insisted on watching the debates from the gallery, thus egging on backbenchers like Bernard Braine who were filibustering over Quebec and the treatment of minorities. I took Chrétien out to supper and persuaded him that he must return home and leave it to us to deal with the trouble-makers if he wanted the legislation to succeed. He took this advice and left the following morning. During supper he told me that he wanted to be PM. Later he succeeded and remained so for many years. I saw him only once more, in 1995, when I chatted to him at the Commonwealth Heads of Government Meeting in Auckland. He managed to hold a fragile Canada together which is an achievement in itself. But he never struck me as being in the same league as Pearson or Trudeau.

Probably our visit to British Columbia was the most exciting part of the tour. In fact I was the first British MP to visit places like Kamloops and Fort George in an official capacity. Some Canadians struck me as being chippy and believed that we in Britain were not interested in them, or that we were irrelevant to them. But generally there was immense friendliness and the wide-open spaces excited me. In the '80s I toured Canada as Arts Minister. Again I was struck by the dynamic expansion of British Columbia. By then there were thousands of Hong Kong Chinese settled there, including their Lieutenant Governor. The saddest sight was the Native Indian community who seemed to have lost their soul and their purpose. I was struck by the individual strength of the provincial premiers, particularly Mr Davis of Ontario, who always had a large cigar in his mouth, and the long-serving Mr Barrett of British Columbia, son of a fruit merchant, a rugby player and keen to demonstrate that he was more in favour of private enterprise than us, even though he professed to be a socialist. Victoria, by contrast, was more like Bournemouth in 1900. I was watching a cricket match in a park when an American asked me to explain the game of cricket to him.

Canadians are keen to avoid domination by their US neighbour. Hence our close friendship is important to them. They are equally important to us, not just for the historical and cultural reasons. The United States by contrast is quite different. The Canadians are rather quiet and unshowy. The Americans are noisy and self-confident. Our most notable tour was in the autumn of 1982 following my resignation over the Falklands. The American State Department asked me to do a tour of the country to lecture on British foreign policy and to explain the background to the Falklands War. In Washington we had the usual complaints that Europe was not doing enough to share the defence burden. In Chicago we witnessed the efficiency of the police in reducing crime. In the rest of Illinois we learnt of the importance of agriculture and the strength of the Bible Belt. In Colorado we witnessed the strength of the American defences, visiting an underground bunker called NORAD. In California we learnt of the unusual nature of their democracy with proposition 13 which involved tax measures being put to a referendum, and took in the sheer beauty of San Francisco, where Rose had once worked.

In New Mexico we witnessed the Hispanic infuence in Santa Fé, and in New Orleans we soaked in the best jazz in the world in Preservation Hall. The lecture audiences were generally polite and supportive, notwithstanding some rather rude remarks as to how we got ourselves in the Falklands War, or how they saved us in the First and Second World Wars. But on the whole we were struck by their friendliness, though there was often a high level of immaturity and ignorance of world affairs. The people were most hospitable in putting us up and mostly they seemed besotted by our monarchy. In one house there were sixty books on the subject.

As a minister I became a regular visitor to Washington and the UN in New York. Over time I met people like Schultz, Bush Snr, Weinberger, Perle, Eagleberger, Tom Enders, Crocker and Cy Vance. Schultz won me over when, after a long discussion, he left to take his granddaughter to the cinema. Perle was a warning of things to come with neo-conservative views about using the big stick around the world whenever possible. Much later on during the State Visit in 2003, I met Bush Jnr, Powell and Condoleezza Rice. The latter was charming and keen to learn; Powell was measured, having worked his way from a humble Jamaican background.

Canada and the United States are very different and vast expansive countries. We need the friendship of both for different reasons but it is all made easier by our strong cultural ties with them.

THE SOVIET UNION

I have never had direct responsibility for policy towards the Soviet Union, but I have learnt something about the country, and the soul-destroying nature of an all-embracing dictatorship. In my teens and early twenties I followed very closely events in the country firstly under Stalin and then Khrushchev. My aunt Priscilla Napier's brother, William Hayter, was ambassador in Moscow in the '50s. I remember my cousin Vin Robinson coming back from Moscow saying that she met Khrushchev at a reception and he called her a 'NATO cherry'. Clearly he was less grim than Stalin, but mercurial.

But my expedition with three other undergraduates at Cambridge by land-rover behind the Iron Curtain in 1957 opened my eyes to the oppressiveness of tyranny, both in Poland and in Hungary. In Budapest we were detained, marched in front of the Minister of the Interior and given until midnight to drive out of the country. We drove into Yugoslavia, but with only a few minutes to spare. Driving through Poland on a Sunday the churches were overflowing, which bears out my view that people only tend to go to church when times are hard and tough. The reason for our detention in Hungary was due to our meeting students in secret in Warsaw, which made the authorities suspicious. The very fact that we had to meet like that was an indication of the measure of the dictatorship.

Gromyko was the first Soviet leader whom I met. As secretary to the Conservative Foreign Affairs Committee I accompanied Reggie Maudling, the Shadow Foreign Secretary, to the Soviet Embassy in the early '70s. Reggie handled the discussions with charm and panache. Much of the conversation was about human rights and how they treated their dissidents. As a long-standing Foreign Minister Gromyko fended us off with his usual skill. But we were living in two different worlds.

In the spring of 1977 I accompanied an inter-Parliamentary Union delegation to the Soviet Union. We were led by the delightful Welsh Labour MP and former Agricultural Minister, Cledwyn Hughes. The delegation included Mervyn Stockwood, the Bishop of Southwark, Bryan Magee, Niall Drumalbyn and two Tory colleagues, Robert Hicks and Bob Boscawen. We visited Armenia, Moscow and Leningrad. The highlight was our meeting with Mr Podgorny, the President of the Praesidium. I rather liked him. In response to my question on his recent visit to Africa, he undid his tie and said that it was too hot there, and that I, as a former District Officer, ought to know that it is easy to go in and almost impossible to pull out. My diaries indicate that I was depressed by the sombre mood and condition of the people, who looked pale and worn out. I was struck by the fact that the Soviet Union was an empire, half of it made up of non-Russian republics like Armenia with 150 nationalities. By visiting their memorials in Leningrad and Moscow I was reminded that they lost no less than 20 million people in the Second World War, in addition to the many millions who were killed by Stalin's purges in the 1930s. This, coupled with the fact that they have a long border with China, let alone NATO to contend with, meant that they spent enormous resources on their defences and the regime was extremely conservative and cautious. The class system was developed through the privileges of being an active member of the Party.

I concluded that those 240 million Russians without privileges sought comfort in the Church and accepted that, throughout their history, they had been used to authoritarian rule. They knew nothing else. But by then it was clear that, to maintain their empire and be ready to defend their country, it would absorb resources that the country could ill afford and that it would be at the expense of the people. I did not get the feeling then of a country wanting war, but it was equally obvious that we needed to maintain our guard in the West.

The leaders of the regime, led by Podgorny and Brezhnev, were elderly and cautious. I speculated on who might take over from them. Soon after this Gorbachev emerged as a leader. In the early '80s I sat next to him at the Speaker's dinner for him. That day he had been meeting Margaret Thatcher at Chequers. I asked him how he had got on. He said that she was tough but felt he could do business with her. It was a turning point. His discussions with Reagan and Thatcher made him realise that the West would never give up their guard and that the Soviet Union could not afford to maintain an empire and large armed forces. Indeed in 1983 I had announced to the House of Commons, in the absence of Geoffrey Howe, that we were to deploy cruise missiles in Europe. That was further evidence of the West's resolve. Gorbachev is a hero in the West and dismissed in Russia. We owe him, as well as Reagan and Margaret Thatcher, a great deal for the end of the Cold War.

From 1983 to 1985 I had ministerial responsibilities for arms control and became involved in policy formulation, conferences and meetings on the many aspects of the issue. The subject required real Foreign Office experts who could understand the technical issues. The most controversial issue was the Star Wars where Reagan would have extended our defences to outer space, but there was much debate about the deployment of the cruise missiles in Europe. By contrast some steady progress was made on reducing the threat of chemicals in warfare. I find it a difficult subject to grapple with but our policy was of course much affected by the strength of the Soviet forces and the need to maintain a balance.

I did pay another visit to the Soviet Union in the later '80s as Minister for the Arts, accompanied by Rose. We visited Moscow, Leningrad and Georgia. In the latter we could see again the difference and character of the Caucasus area, though of course Stalin came from there. We visited monasteries and the theatre and had endless toasts with the Culture Minister. The Royal Shakespeare Company did a brilliant performance of *The Winter's Tale* in English and they were rapturously received. In the capital, Tbilisi, there was the usual oppressive domination by the State. What we didn't realise on our visit was that the communist Soviet Union only had a very short time before it would collapse.

I had no link with Russia after the Cold War had ended until 2003 when Mr Putin did a state visit to the UK. As always it went smoothly and the Putins appeared to enjoy it. He showed more humour than the impression of him gives. At the airport when I saw him off on behalf of the Queen I praised his ambassador. Through an interpreter he said, 'Don't say that. It will go to his head, and then he will be impossible!' Later the ambassador was promoted. But Putin gave the impression that democracy did not mean much to him. Since then his hold on his country has strengthened and he appears to be an authoritarian ruler. Russia seems to swing between anarchy and authoritarianism. But we must maintain a vigorous dialogue and business with Russia. Perhaps over time some form of democracy which suits them will take hold. They are a great people and have suffered too much.

BRUNEI

I am proud to have negotiated the final stages leading to independence for Brunei, a responsibility which I was given on returning to Government in 1983. John Belstead had been handling it up until then. I had a clear framework for the negotiations and was glad that an able diplomat, Francis Cornish, had been sent as the High Commissioner to handle this critical stage. On my first visit I found the Sultan of Brunei almost unable to converse at all. He had a puzzling relationship with his father Sir Omah who had abdicated some years before. Sir Omah resolutely sat through our negotiations in the Palace which may have been an embarrassment to the Sultan. On one occasion the Sultan invited me to join him in watching a football match from his new air-conditioned stadium. During the match his father fell off the sofa onto the floor while attendants undid his tie and tried to revive him. The Sultan took no notice. I decided to draw his attention to the fact that his father appeared to be dying. He replied, 'Don't worry about that, he's always doing it.' Negotiations covered a broad agenda, not least the position of the Gurkha battalion, which came under his control and would remain there after independence.

I was not over-impressed by all of the Sultan's family, especially the Foreign Minister Prince Mohammed, and I was worried that the lack of any process for consulting the people might lead to trouble later on with his population of 200,000. At that stage he was keeping them happy with material benefits. For example, they were given television sets so that all the houseboats on the river had television aerials sticking out. I was very pleased however that my friend John Friedberger was to be retained after independence as commander of all their forces. He was the last British commander in Brunei. I accompanied the Prince of Wales for the independence celebrations which were attended by about twenty Heads of State and involved lavish entertainment in the Sultan's new vast marble palace. Thus ended 135 years of British association with Brunei, a country with a substantial empire a few centuries ago.

I was always grateful to Lee Kwan Yew, Prime Minister of Singapore, for his help and advice in handling the negotiations. He had a good feel for the situation in South East Asia and in Brunei. In more recent years I have occasionally kept in touch with Brunei. When calling on the Sultan in the '90s I told him I was off to climb Mount Kinabalu. He asked me how I would get to the summit. I replied that I hoped to do so by foot. He said he preferred to get there by helicopter.

SINGAPORE

Singapore was a remarkable contrast to the sleepy monarchy of Brunei. Lee Kwan Yew was one of the Far East's most dynamic leaders. I felt that he had outgrown Singapore and should be Secretary-General of the UN, but he seemed content and remained a lively and highly intelligent observer and indeed advisor on South East Asia and the Far East. He was grateful for Britain's skilful handling of their independence negotiations in the 1960s. When I met him in 1993 in Singapore, he was then no longer PM but Senior Minister, creating an awkward situation for his successor. Singapore is a model for a City State. Lee was the benevolent authoritarian leader who, through firm dominating leadership, led his country to a stable condition with a modest amount of democracy, strong law and order and a dynamic economy. Lee is a true Commonwealth statesman.

THE COMMONWEALTH

In my lifetime I have been fortunate enough to witness a transformation from Empire to Commonwealth and to have played a very small part in both.

In that short period of seven months in 1981/2 I had ministerial responsibilities for policy towards the Commonwealth. It was only a small proportion of my role. There was no great enthusiasm for the Commonwealth in the Tory Party and certainly Margaret Thatcher regularly found herself a target for criticism over sanctions on South Africa, which she disliked. Throughout all this period it was the Queen who kept the light shining on the Commonwealth and helped to steer the emerging independent nations towards an association of equally important countries with no predominant partner and with Britain no longer playing an imperial role.

Just as I was about to leave Parliament in 1992, Lynda Chalker, Minister for Overseas Development, asked me whether I would accept the nomination of HMG as a candidate for chairmanship of the Commonwealth Foundation. It was set up in the 1960s to oversee the non-governmental side of the Commonwealth, in particular to encourage the professional bodies looking after the interests of, for example, doctors, foresters, teachers and vets in the Commonwealth. The Governors of the Board comprised High Commissioners in London. The idea appealed to me, and I accepted.

In due course, during the Commonwealth Heads of Government meeting in Harare, I received a telephone call one Sunday from John Major, the Prime Minister, to tell me that the Heads of Government had selected me for the job. It had never occurred to me that I would be appointed to a job by fifty-three Heads of Government. I was to be the first British Chairman of the Foundation, and I was glad to take up this challenge. Its Director was Enoki Faletau, a Pacific Islander. He was delightful, but exceptionally laid back. On his retirement I chose Dr Humayun Khan, a former Foreign Secretary of Pakistan, as the next Director. He proved a good choice and was very diplomatic with a broad approach to the job.

With a limited annual budget of about £2 million, contributed by Commonwealth Governments, we had many calls on our funds. We gave grants to facilitate the work of the professional bodies, to finance a Commonwealth Writers' Prize and to fund Commonwealth fellowships to potential high flyers to study the Commonwealth. The Queen took a strong personal interest and we would take the winners of the prize to see her. On one such occasion I took Vikram Seth, the Writers' Prize winner of that year. On the way to the Palace, he told me that he would bathe each morning before breakfast in the Serpentine. At one point there was a lull in the conversation with the Queen which I decided to fill by remarking, 'Mr Seth likes bathing before breakfast.' Her perhaps understandable reaction 'He must be mad!' had me moving the subject hastily on to something else. On a later occasion we entertained the Queen at Marlborough House where various artists from different countries sang to us. The Eskimo women from Canada sang through their noses with their cheeks full of air, causing enormous hilarity, not least from the Queen.

The Commonwealth Foundation stands alone in linking together a cross-section of cultures comprising a quarter of the globe. There are some who are inclined to write it off as a meaningless association. I don't agree. It is wonderfully effective in drawing together people of so many different cultures and religions. It acts as a lubricant in an intolerant world and is highly relevant to the massive immigration to the UK and other countries such as Canada and Australia of people of Asian, African and Caribbean backgrounds. It is difficult to tell how the Commonwealth will evolve, particularly after the Queen has died. I hope that its inherent values will survive in some way.

13

The Arts, the British Library and the Civil Service

Expecting the unexpected has often stood me in good stead. It happened again in early September 1985, when I was summoned to Number 10 on the day of a reshuffle. The PM informed me that she wanted me to be the political head of a department, but one outside the Cabinet. I was therefore to be Minister for the Arts and, by the way, also the Minister under the PM for the Civil Service. As an extra throwaway I was also made Minister of State Privy Council Office, which is a titular office. I told her that I had no idea where the Arts Office was. She said that she didn't know either, so we set off to discover its location from the private secretary. It turned out to be in the Treasury building overlooking St James's Park and it was enormous, probably the largest ministerial one in existence. I could hardly have imagined that I would become the supremo for the arts – either in this world or the next. My knowledge was limited, and all that I could claim was that my mother was a playwright and that I played the piano very badly.

My predecessor was Grey Gowrie who had served for two years in the job and was turning out to be a most imaginative and knowledgeable minister. He told the press that he couldn't afford to continue working as a minister, in so doing reflecting the problem of the poor pay of Lords ministers. For several weeks after my appointment, the press asked me if I was sure I could afford to be a minister.

It was Harold Wilson who had created the first Minister for the Arts, Jennie Lee, Aneurin Bevan's widow. I had some distinguished Conservative predecessors in David Eccles and Norman St John Stevas, but the latter did the job alongside being the Leader of the House of Commons, and could not give enough time to the arts.

I faced a tough start as the arts world was bemused by my appointment and thought that I had been given the job as a philistine to reduce taxpayers' support still further. My leading critic was Peter Hall, who regularly attacked me in public, describing me as a 'nerd', which was then an unfamiliar word to me!

In the event I became the longest-serving Arts Minister, staying for five years, and eventually much enjoyed the challenge and the chance to achieve a few things. I was extremely fortunate to have a bird's-eye view of the arts in Britain and to learn so much about every facet of the country's artistic achievements. I felt that, paradoxically, there were actually some advantages in not knowing too much about it all and in having no particular hang-ups or prejudices: at least I could approach the job with a fresh and open mind.

The press were very hostile. Melanie Phillips wrote an article in the *Guardian* saying: 'The best thing to do with Richard Luce is to have him stuffed and tucked away in the Natural History Museum.' I lived on that for some time, noting in my speeches that whilst in 200 years' time the names of Churchill and Thatcher may be long forgotten, people will queue up to pay in order to see me on display. Nonetheless, press criticism became relentless and the first eighteen months were in that respect grim.

I was lucky to have Richard Wilding as my permanent secretary. A Wykehamist with an excellent brain, he was always able to get to the key point. In the first week there was an inclination on his part to try to tell me what to do, probably a 'Yes, Minister' way of testing out whether I was capable of taking charge. Just one sharp exchange was necessary to make it clear that as minister I would be taking the decisions. He accepted my rebuke with good grace and thereafter gave me clear dispassionate advice, without being dismayed if I did not always take it. His career was damaged when he said in a lecture that civil servants should withhold two per cent of their loyalty to an elected Government. Margaret Thatcher, to her discredit, ensured that he was not promoted beyond this job. On Richard's retirement Charles Henderson took his place. A pleasant man from the Department of Trade and Industry, he was not so coherent and clear in his advice. He later left the Service for the private sector. I felt sorry for my second cousin Tom Luce, who wanted the job of permanent secretary as a move from the Treasury, but who could not do so while I was minister.

I was equally fortunate in the PPSs and Whips who were appointed to look after me. Tristan Garel-Jones, who later became an FCO Minister of State and Deputy Chief Whip, was the Whip allocated to my Ministry. He loved the subject, knew a lot about painters and had a creative mind. Michael Colvin was my first PPS in that Ministry. He was a painter and dedicated supporter of the arts who worked conscientiously in Parliament to gain support for my policies. I lobbied for him to become a junior minister, but the Whips were hostile to him for consistently voting against the Industrial Relations Bill. Michael's judgement was not always good, but he would have been excellent under the supervision of any Secretary of State in areas like defence. Rose and I became good friends with him and his wife Nichola. In later years they stayed with us in Gibraltar. A few weeks after their visit we heard on the news that two people were missing after a disastrous fire at the large Hampshire house of the Colvins. We were soon told that Michael and Nichola had been burnt to death. Rose and I were in tears at this tragedy and attended their memorial service in Romsey Abbey.

Jeremy Hanley, son of the comedian Jimmy Hanley, took over from Michael as my PPS. His mother was Dinah Sheridan, who was a delightful actress. Jeremy had inherited a keen sense of humour from his father and could be exceptionally funny. He knew and loved the arts world, particularly the performing arts, and was an immense help. He later became a successful Minister of State at the FCO and for the Armed Forces, but had an unhappy time as Chairman of the Party, for which he was not suited.

I had two good special advisers: first Andrew Tyrie, who had a sharp mind and moved on to advise Nigel Lawson. Later he became MP for Chichester and a very constructive and active one too. Elizabeth Cottrell succeeded him. She, like Andrew, acted as my political eyes and ears and antennae. She was excellent and particularly skilled in portraying the political dimension to any difficult decisions, and in the drafting of speeches. I am sorry that she was never selected for a constituency.

Early on I had to decide what to do about the general hostility from both the arts world and the media. They were right in believing that on the whole ministers were not sympathetic to the arts, but wrong to think that I was uninterested. My two allies in Cabinet were Nicholas Edwards (now Lord Crickhowell) and Kenneth Baker, then Secretaries of State for Wales and for Education. They gave me some helpful support and advice.

Peter Hall had done considerable harm to his own cause by implying that the taxpayer owed the arts world a living, while insisting that the arts had to be free from Government interference. This stance lost the arts world the sympathy of both the Prime Minister and the Chancellor. I decided to tackle the problem head on. The arts world could not have it both ways: freedom from Governmental interference meant that the arts could flourish in a free society, but financial dependence on the Government would directly contradict this principle. The only future for the arts must be to diversify their sources of funding. Grey Gowrie had most sensibly set up a new funding scheme for business sponsors. I developed this new concept into a successful scheme which attracted a huge number of businesses to become enthusiastically involved with the arts, bringing in more money, expertise and the involvement of employees. I believed that the paying public needed to be the main source of finance and said that we were all capable of enjoying opera, theatre, ballet or music. My initial tactic of attacking élitism in the arts proved mistaken since it failed to acknowledge that it is precisely the élite, in the form of the very best artists and knowledgeable audiences, who set the standards of excellence. I adjusted my stance to say that we needed both public support and the involvement of arts practitioners. It was gratifying to witness the resultant increase in public attendance and the expansion of new museums at the rate of one every fortnight. I watched the Royal Ballet perform in a big top tent in the Isle of Wight, and the Royal Shakespeare Company in Hull – both, you might snootily think, artistic away matches. But on both occasions you could hear a pin drop.

I was able to demonstrate to Nigel Lawson, the Chancellor, that for every £1 of taxpayers' money £5 could be raised through private sources. This, not unnaturally, appealed to him, and led to some modest increases in taxpayers' support.

After the 1987 election I decided to persuade those in the arts to help me develop this partnership, at the same time securing three years' funding from the Treasury so that arts institutions could plan their future in more stable circumstances. Many did not like the move away from State support and towards plurality of funding but accepted the challenge. The Prime Minister congratulated me on a speech I made in Newcastle which set out this new theme and which received considerable press coverage.

To counteract the hostility of both the media and arts, I toured the country each week to visit the arts and learn as much as I could. I very quickly saw the huge disparity between London, with all its hot air and cynicism from the national media and the arts, and the real world outside the capital where arts workers did their jobs without too much fuss and where the quality of their work was frequently impressive. I would like to think that these regional visits helped to convince the arts that I was genuinely interested in them and enthusiastic about creating a more positive climate for them.

It was fun getting to know some of our outstanding artists. I gave lunches for many of them. Certainly my lunch at Admiralty House for actors and actresses had never been done before and I invited some Cabinet ministers to help me entertain people like Gielgud and Judi Dench. In my first week I arranged for Dame Ninette de Valois, the doyenne of ballet, to tell me about dance. In her nineties, she was frighteningly stern and was no doubt terrifying to young ballet dancers being taught under her in her earlier years. I came into contact, too, with luminaries like Roy Strong, the Director of the V&A and Tim Clifford, the Director of the National Gallery in Edinburgh. They were brilliant, but the price of brilliance is often vanity and emotion. This was difficult to handle. On the other hand I admired Dicky Attenborough who was always so warmhearted. On one occasion the Prime Minister convened a seminar to discuss the problems of the film industry. She asked why we had not arranged this earlier since she was enjoying it, to which Dicky replied, 'Because you haven't asked me, darling.' There was a tense pause and she laughed.

There were some (George Melly was one) who were liable to be snarky at my expense on public occasions. But I had the wonderful luxury of being able to see such a full cross-section of art and heritage and to learn more about our country houses, our museums, theatres, opera, painters, crafts and dance. The days were often hard going, but the evenings an eye-opener for Rose and me. I reckoned that, contrary to the Jeremiahs, art in Britain was flourishing and that, given the opportunity, the British public were not philistines and were capable of enjoying all forms of our arts and heritage whatever their background.

I was gratified to be able to help diversify funding but realised that Governments of any complexion would never contribute sufficient funds for capital investment and the refurbishment, for example, of theatres, museums and churches. I had a rather cool and stiff meeting with Nigel Lawson on this subject, where I told him that the only viable alternative to Government funding was the creation of a national lottery. His response was that this was not feasible because Margaret Thatcher was against the encouragement of gambling. Indeed she confirmed that to me. My view was that the British are gamblers anyway, so why not channel funds constructively into the arts, and perhaps the sports? But it was no use: she wouldn't budge. Later, after I retired as minister I joined the Lottery Campaign led by a composer, Denis Vaughan. John Major was more receptive than Margaret Thatcher had been and it was duly launched.

One warning I would give to any Arts minister is not to surrender to blackmail. This was something the Royal Opera House at Covent Garden attempted when it deliberately ran up a deficit of £3 million in order to pressure me to bail it out. I had a difficult meeting with John Sainsbury, the Chairman, and the Director, Jeremy Isaacs. On another occasion the Royal Shakespeare Company closed their stage in the Barbican Centre for four winter months, persuading Neil Kinnock to hold an emergency debate in Parliament where I maintained the line that this kind of pressure was completely unacceptable. If I had given both organisations what they wanted, the whole arts world would have tried the same tactic.

The most consistently difficult issue in the House of Commons was the charging of entry fees by national museums and galleries. I had to face many a stormy debate and make the point that almost every other country in the world charged an entry fee, including communist ones like East Germany; I also stressed that other types of art, including theatres, charge to see a play. Exemptions could be given to students and pensioners and I argued that charging often enhanced the appreciation of seeing the objects. But it was an ideological fixation with the Labour Party.

I decided to devolve more of the decision-making and funding to the regions, leaving the Arts Council with the strategy and responsibilities for the large arts bodies. The Regional Arts Associations were in a better position to know about the arts in their own cities and towns, and I felt that the taxpayers' money would be better spent that way. I was sorry that the Labour Government later weakened this arrangement, claiming, possibly rightly, that too much money was being spent on administrative costs in the regions.

At the end of the 1980s I helped to launch the Voluntary Arts Network, of which I later became president. By offering information to the amateur arts about how they could best further their interests, VAN was a useful and important interaction with the professional arts. I later helped to sponsor another new body called Adapt, which gave grants to theatres and other arts bodies to facilitate access for disabled people.

Historic houses were an endless fascination for me, and I was always pleased to discover houses that were still lived in by the owners. Since my family had, from time to time, lived in Rockingham Castle, I had some understanding of owners' problems. Questions arose about the export of works of arts and I would be given recommendations as to whether to release an object, or to put a temporary halt on its export while attempts were made to find resources to save it for this country. Such recommendations came from the Review Committee on the Export of Works of Art under the so-called Waverley Criteria. Our objective was to save only objects of singular connection and special value to this country. Canova's sculpture, *The Three Graces*, caused endless controversy but was eventually saved. Martin Charteris, chairman of the National Heritage Memorial Fund, said jokingly the real reason for this was that they were soft porn! The Mappa Mundi also remained in Hereford Cathedral, thanks to Paul Getty. In my first few weeks as Arts Minister I had to release a Mantegna, which I saw later being well viewed and looked after in the Getty Museum in Los Angeles.

To counteract the Socialist claim that only they were friends of the art world, I established a Conservative Group for the Arts under the chairmanship of Patrick Cormack. He did the job wonderfully and large audiences attended meetings in cities around the country. Patrick badly wanted to be Arts Minister himself. Indeed he became a distinguished parliamentarian, but never a minister. He could have been a very good Speaker too, and all this must have been disappointing to him. I appreciated all the more his loyalty to me.

The Labour Party produced two Shadow Ministers during my time. Norman Buchan, the MP for Paisley, was a Glaswegian and a courteous and decent man, but not particularly articulate or broad in his approach. Sadly he died young. Mark Fisher, who followed him, was a different proposition. Son of Nigel Fisher, the Tory MP, he didn't seem to fit easily into the Labour Party. He was always charming to me but in public he expressed his views rather aggressively. He was Shadow Minister for a long time, and was eventually rewarded with the job of Minister for the Arts in 1997, only to be removed very soon after by Tony Blair. He was disappointed and has since written a book about British museums which received good reviews.

The overseas aspect to the job consisted of routine meetings of the European Union Ministers, which really achieved very little and were singularly boring. Belgium had to be represented by three ministers to cover the Walloons, the Flemings and the Federal Government. We met each year in different countries. Jorge Semprun, the former communist exiled writer, became the Spanish Minister for Culture and hosted an enjoyable meeting in Santiago de Compostela. Mr Solana followed him and proved a friendly, rather quiet man. To my surprise he later became Secretary General of NATO and the Co-ordinator for Foreign and the Defence Policy for the EU. Jack Lang was the Socialist Culture Minister for France and very close to Mitterrand. This explained why he was given so much money up front for big arts projects in Paris. He was also Mayor of Blois and became very excited when he discovered that I first met Rose in Blois. When all the European ministers met there, he took us all out to dinner and proposed a toast to Rose and me. Quite a showman, I rather liked him.

Unquestionably, the most colourful European minister was Melina Mercouri of Greece. A famous actress, married to a French film producer, she was ambitious to be President of Greece. She had a dynamic charm and every other word was 'darling'. She invented the idea of having a European City of Culture which would be held by rotation for one year at a time. It was our turn in 1990. Several British cities bid for the role, including Bath, Leeds, Edinburgh and Glasgow. After an intense competition I chose Glasgow, much to the annoyance of Edinburgh who felt that they deserved it by right. Glasgow showed the greatest enterprise in a united bid from the City Council and private businesses. Melina said, 'Darling, you don't mean Glasgow, you mean Edinburgh.' I invited her to the opening, by which time she was accompanied by a nurse as she was dying of cancer of the throat. When I introduced her to the Queen, she immediately announced, 'He is right, you know.' The Queen looked startled, since she had not been privy to our discussion of the merits of the two Scottish cities. Glasgow took full advantage of its newly acquired status and built a new concert hall. I am proud of this achievement – and of working with a Socialist council. The fact that my grandfather commanded HMS *Glasgow* gave a special flavour to the link.

Melina had a long-running dispute with me over the Parthenon Elgin Marbles which she wanted the British Museum to arrange to return to Athens. She used this as her campaigning platform to rally Greece behind her and planned to build a museum, below the Parthenon, where they could be housed. David Wilson, the director of the British Museum, was unnecessarily rude to her on television though he rightly pointed out that Parliament would have to pass legislation to allow the Marbles to be returned. I decided to continue the discussions in a friendlier way, and invited Melina to the UK on an official visit, when I hosted a lunch for her at Lancaster House. In front of the assembled guests I asked, 'What will you give me in return for the Marbles?' 'Greece?' she replied. When I laughed, she added, 'Me?' She was an engaging character whose company I enjoyed, but the issue was a serious one. If we are to return the Marbles, it is easy to foresee an unstoppable one-way flow of objects of art across the oceans, emptying our museums of objects acquired over centuries. However some countries are happy to exhibit replicas of such objects. Rajiv Gandhi approached the problem very sensibly: during the opening of a Henry Moore exhibition in Delhi he told me that Indians were putting intense pressure on him to force the return of Indian objects in the V&A and elsewhere to Delhi. But he stressed that they could not look after them properly there – so could I do him a favour by getting the objects at the V&A out of the vaults and putting them on regular display? He could then tell Indians that 'their' artefacts could always be seen in London. On my return to the UK I spoke to Peter Carrington, chairman of the V&A. The Nehru Gallery was then established and all can now indeed see these Indian objects on display at any time.

Another overseas visit included attendance at the British Country Houses Exhibition in Washington, where various house-owners were taken round the exhibition by bus, rather won over by this novel form of travelling. In Berlin I was struck by the large number of young people in the audience when I opened a Francis Bacon exhibition. It seems to me that in central Europe art is a feature of everyday life.

Britain's approach to the arts is somewhere between the United

States and Europe. In America there is virtually no taxpayers' support, but a positive atmosphere for giving, whereas in Europe there is a heavy dependence on State support. Britain has managed to strike a balance between the two.

It turned out that I was one of the last Arts Ministers in control of a department. Later the job was swallowed up under the Secretary of State for Heritage and with Labour, for Culture and the Media.

THE BRITISH LIBRARY

I have long concluded that the British are not very clever at handling large arts projects. The French are better. They have built, for example, the Pompidou Centre and refurbished the Louvre successfully. In France Ministers of Culture tend to have the full support and enthusiasm for the arts from their Presidents for whom it is a matter of prestige to have their large arts projects, particularly in the capital city. As a consequence ministers are given all the necessary resources to achieve their projects quickly. Mitterand and Pompidou were good examples of this. In our country it is always difficult to achieve the necessary support and resources from a Prime Minister preoccupied by other matters. This means that ministers have prolonged battles each year with the Treasury and the project can be easily fragmented or delayed, thus becoming more and more expensive, as can be seen with the Millennium Dome and the new Scottish Parliament.

On first becoming Arts Minister I had asked for a summary of the main issues facing me. The new British Library project was high on the list. Within a few days the Prime Minister, Margaret Thatcher, asked me to come and discuss its future. I therefore concentrated on briefing myself urgently with the help of Richard Wilding, my admirable permanent secretary. It was immediately clear that the PM was going to try and persuade me to drop the plan to complete the new building, on the grounds that it would be a white elephant. In September 1985 it consisted of a deep hole in the ground adjacent to King's Cross Station. If it was to be terminated, now was the time to do so.

Before my meeting with the PM I examined the history and the purpose of the new Library. The person who had campaigned for the project was Lord Eccles, one of my predecessors who had served in the early1970s in the Heath Government. He felt it was important to

LEFT The author's father when Political Resident in the Persian Gulf, 1964
RIGHT Katharine and Godfrey Nicholson at home in Berkshire, 1960

Sudan, early 1950s: the author (in Bombay bowler), with his sister D and his mother

LEFT Rose on becoming engaged to the author, 1960 RIGHT Godfrey Nicholson and Alexander Luce at D's wedding, 8 July 1967, at Salisbury Cathedral

Family at Dragon's Farm, Sussex, mid 1970s: the author, Edward, Rose, Alexander

The author, as Minister of State, Foreign Office, in discussion with
the Sultan of Oman in his desert tent, 1981

Rose, the author and Sally Merrick: General Election campaign 1983

An evening with the arts: the author and Rose, late 1980s

Visit to Wilfred Thesiger, Maralal, Kenya, 1993

The author, with Rose, receiving Honours degree at University of Buckingham
from the Chancellor, Lady Thatcher

Ready for the Queen's Birthday Parade, Gibraltar June 1998: the author with Rose and Port Sergeant holding keys of the city

Leaving Gibraltar on HMS *Northumberland*. ADC Colin Risso on right.

The author's introduction to the House of Lords, 2000, with Rose and two sponsors, Lord Weatherill and Lord Fellowes

Visit to Chartwell, 2005: the Carringtons, Mary Soames, Rose and the author

Leading the Queen in procession in St Paul's Cathedral for the Golden Jubilee
Thanksgiving Service, June 2002

establish one new prestigious building to replace the thirteen or so scattered over London, housing various parts of the British Library. Such a building would provide a modern twenty-first century facility with space for readers, for research, and a growing number of books. Modern technology would help to make it operate efficiently. Lord Eccles was strongly backed by Lord Dainton, who later became the British Library's chairman. David Eccles himself became chairman after the Conservatives lost office in 1974. In a typically British way, discussions and planning took an interminable time: Shirley Williams in the Labour government had begun to develop the plans in the late 1970s; then Norman St John Stevas became the minister in 1979 and was followed by Lord Gowrie soon after, who was in charge when construction began.

I concluded that the arguments were strongly in favour of completing the project, rather than abandoning it. We had already developed an outstanding public library system throughout the twentieth century. It would have been a pity if a country of our size and reputation should not have a central library to compete with the best in the world, such as the Library of Congress in Washington.

I met the PM alone in her room in Parliament for an hour or so. Because no one else was there, we were able to have quite a sensible discussion, but she put to me a series of probing questions to test whether I had really thought it through. I think she was rather hoping that I would want us to pull out. In the end she reluctantly accepted that we should go ahead, but in carefully planned stages.

I had taken responsibility for this project at a critical stage – having done so it would have been impossible, once I ceased to be minister, for my successor to pull out. However I faced endless problems. Project management was poor and there were many delays and miscalculations by the Property Services Agency. Richard Wilding tightened up the management and decision making process. Meanwhile I battled with successive Chief Secretaries for adequate sums to enable us to progress to the next stage. Breaking the project down into stages was the Treasury's way of trying to control the costs. In fact by so doing they delayed the project by years and caused endless adjustments, which led to managerial difficulties. The lack of an even and proper flow of funds not only caused inefficiencies and delays but also inevitably led to the constant escalation of costs to the taxpayer.

In addition there was growing controversy over the designs of the building drawn up by the architect, Colin St John Wilson, a nice man who was unfairly vilified. The Prince of Wales, who had been shown and approved the designs earlier, began to change his mind and expressed his reservations in public. I very much valued the interest, support and encouragement which the Prince showed in the arts. I met him to explain that the Library project was developing rapidly and that it was too late to make any changes to the design, which he reluctantly accepted. David Mellor, one of my successors as Arts Minister, described the design as 'vile'. It is undeniable that the outside of the building is not a work of great beauty, but the courtyard and interior are graceful, spacious and imposing.

A more politically controversial proposal arising from the project was the planned closure of the Round Reading Room in the British Museum, where many notable writers, amongst them Karl Marx, had worked, written and researched. A campaign against the closure led by academics and writers sparked me to invite Roy Jenkins to chair a small committee to study the matter and to make recommendations. Roy handled this task with commendable skill and care, bursting the bubble of political discontent by explaining the issues and by ensuring that the Reading Room would still be stocked with books belonging to the British Museum. The reading rooms of the new Library are better and more spacious. I was very grateful to Roy for taking on this task.

Lord Quinton, a delightful academic, was chairman of the Library Board when I first came into the job. When he retired, I decided that Micky Saunders Watson, who had already been chairman of the Historic Houses Association, was the right person to give managerial leadership and direction to this controversial construction. I didn't want a bookish academic at that stage. That need would come later. The only difficulty was that Micky was my second cousin. In view of this I decided to clear the matter with the PM, to whom I explained the situation, and she approved. Micky did an excellent job, giving time and effort to the detail of the project and working closely with all the people involved, including Brian Lang, the chief executive.

On one occasion I made an official visit to Paris as the guest of the French Minister of Culture, and Mayor of Blois, Jack Lang. He showed me the rather rusty old national Bibliothèque and said that he wanted to build a new national library in Paris. He asked if he could come and inspect our project. He did so and told me he would go back and complete a new library before we could build one. He got the resources from Mitterand and built it in no time. But it has not been that much of a success, and has faced many problems. Perhaps this is an argument for proceeding with a little more care. But we must never again do a project like this without learning the lessons, managing it efficiently and ensuring that the necessary resources are secured from the beginning.

The new British Library was eventually opened in the late 1990s, whilst I was in Gibraltar. Eventually, in 2002, the permanent secretary at the Department of Culture arranged for me to visit the building. I was impressed by the space, effectiveness of the technology and atmosphere. The building may not be the most beautiful in Britain, but it is something of which we should be proud. It was worth all the sweat, tears and aggravation of my early years to see the result but I never want to be responsible for a big project like that again!

THE CIVIL SERVICE

Ministerial responsibility for the Civil Service offered a sharp contrast to the high public profile of the arts. The Prime Minister always takes overall responsibility for the Civil Service, but the minister in effect carries out all day-to-day duties and the implementation of strategic decisions.

I was fortunate in my two principal advisors as Secretary to the Cabinet and Head of the Home Civil Service, Robert Armstrong followed by Robin Butler. Both later became life peers. Robert possessed an outstanding intellect and always gave clear advice, while Robin was a strong leader. At weekly meetings we would review current issues relating to the Civil Service. On one such occasion I was suggesting to Robert that there were not enough ethnic minorities in the Service. At that moment a military band marched by below the window. We paused to watch them. They were the Gurkhas.

Peter Kemp was my permanent secretary; a late entrant to the Civil Service who had been in the Navy. He was a tough character, but exactly what I needed in order to achieve significant reforms. Margaret Thatcher was clear in her view that we needed to modernise the Service which in the 1980s was made up of about 5,000 policy advisors to ministers. The remainder, some half a million, were involved in the operational side; that is to say in the implementation of decisions. The Service's image was one of passing the buck, with no one being clearly accountable for such decisions as were made. While that may be an unfair reflection on the performance of many, it is true that there were certainly no clear lines of responsibility. The decision was therefore taken to establish discrete organisations which would be directly accountable to the permanent secretary, and ultimately the Secretary of State, for their performance. Agencies were set up to take charge and account annually to Parliament for their performances, including HMSO, the Government Meteorological Office, the Driving Licence Agency, the Social Security Benefit Offices and the Sunningdale Civil Service Centre. Each agency was given a chief executive and operational instructions. MPs were initially suspicious that they would no longer be able to challenge the responsible Secretary of State in Parliament. I allayed their concerns by pointing out that any chief executive could be summoned before the appropriate select committee, though this in itself presented a new challenge for officials. Since their inception these agencies have created a diverse range of systems of accountability according to the scale of financial viability, and I think that these were important reforms that have led to a more effective and responsible Civil Service.

I used to visit the Sunningdale Civil Service Centre to lecture and to take part in discussions. I decided to modernise the accommodation so that we could compete with the private sector in the provision of conference facilities. I put the case to the Chief Secretary that we needed one million pounds to provide en suite facilities. An official interjected 'They don't need baths.' I said, 'Speak for yourself.' We got them.

During this time the television series *Yes, Minister* attracted a large audience and caused much amusement. My own experiences made me realise how well the series writers did their research. One day my ministerial driver, Dave Draper, said as we drove through Whitehall at about 6 pm, 'By the way, sir, the PM is doing a ministerial reshuffle today.' I replied, 'What? We must get to a telephone as quickly as possible in case she needs me.' Dave quietly murmured 'Don't worry, sir, you are not being moved', thus proving that the Government drivers' network knew more than anyone else what was going on.

One day the man who played the role of Minister and later Prime

Minister, Paul Eddington, asked to see me to lobby against tobacco sponsorship for the arts. During the conversation I asked him if I had understood his point properly. With a delighted smile on his face he replied, 'Yes, Minister.'

Many delegates from overseas came to Britain to study the Service, whose calibre and the impartiality commanded much respect. My own feeling was that the best of our civil servants were in the Foreign Office and the Treasury; for my part I was very lucky to have three excellent private secretaries in the Foreign Office in Peter Westmacott, Haydon Warren-Gash and Jeremy Cresswell, all of whom became distinguished ambassadors. In other branches of the Service the level of competence varied very widely and there was a tendency towards mutual protection and a closing of ranks when someone performed badly. Nevertheless I remain an admirer of our Civil Service and its adherence to the principle of providing dispassionate and impartial advice to elected Governments.

14

The Falklands

My first awareness of the Falklands dates from the late 1960s, when I was the Conservative Parliamentary candidate for Hitchin constituency. The Labour Government appeared to be attempting to hand over the Falkland Islands to the Argentine, whereupon a sudden instinctive public sympathy for the 2,000 British islanders in the far-off South Atlantic led to spontaneous feelings of support in Britain. 'Save the Falklands' car stickers were everywhere, and in our family too. The plan was stopped in its tracks, but it must been an indication to the Argentinians that there was in principle a lack of resolve in Government to hold on to the islands. As it was, all Argentinians had been educated at school to believe that the Malvinas, as they called the Falklands, were theirs by right.

The British, French and Spanish had occupied the Falklands at various times during the eighteenth century. In the 1820s the Argentinians achieved independence from Spain and automatically assumed that they had inherited the Falklands. But in the early 1830s the British Navy, under the leadership of my forebear, Admiral Seymour, asserted their authority and ever since that time the islands had been under British sovereignty.

My early family connection with the islands was strengthened in 1914 when HMS *Glasgow*, under the command of my grandfather, Captain John Luce, played a prominent role in the Battle of the Falkland Islands. It was the first naval victory of the First World War and delighted Winston Churchill who was then First Lord of the Admiralty. John Luce was awarded a CB for his part in it. When I visited the Falklands in 1971, a Falklands kelper told me how, at the age of six, he had watched the battle from nearby hills and had seen HMS *Glasgow* sailing by at thirty knots.

I actually visited the Falklands after I won the Arundel and Shoreham by-election in April 1971. I received a telephone call from an old Sudan family friend, Colonel Peter Molloy, who was then secretary of the Commonwealth Parliamentary Association. He asked me whether I would be prepared to visit the islands in the autumn as a member of a two-man Parliamentary delegation. I readily agreed. My decision marked the beginning of my involvement with the Falklands, which later led to the dramatic events of 1982 and my resignation as a Minister of State, with Peter Carrington, then Foreign Secretary.

Bernard Conlan, a very likeable Labour MP with an excellent sense of humour, was the other delegate. At the time there was a strong body of opinion in Parliament that those colonies who wished to remain British should be able to do so. There was no direct British interest in the Falklands, but a responsibility for the 2,000 subjects who were mainly of British origin. However even a Conservative Government was anxious not to allow the issue to overstrain relations with the Argentine and the Foreign Secretary, Alec Douglas-Home, encouraged practical cooperation to develop between the Argentine and the Falklands which led to a Communications Agreement made in July 1971, which allowed, amongst other things, more direct flights and sea journeys to the Argentine.

The Falklands are 600 miles from the Argentine and 8,000 miles from Britain. In those days it took nearly a week to get there. We flew to Montevideo in Uruguay and then travelled by sea for about four days – a service which was to be superseded in the light of the new Communications Agreement. Bernard and I were part of the penultimate sailing expedition from Montevideo, departing one evening on RM *Darwin*, which was fifteen years old and took up to forty passengers. It was the roughest sea crossing I have ever experienced. But I enjoyed my visit, not least because I love islands and I loved the remoteness; and I enjoyed, too, the prospect of grappling with a foreign policy problem arising from the end of the Empire.

The islands were like the Outer Hebrides, though much more distant from civilisation, and the islanders fiercely British and deeply suspicious of the Argentine, though anxious for better communications and hoping for help in developing their economy. Wool was their main product and of premium quality; but prices were not good. They wanted to develop a fishing industry, a seaweed alginates business and to have a proper airfield. They were defended by thirty-five Marines, a naval hovercraft team of twelve and a volunteer force of sixty. The Argentinians would have observed that it would not be too difficult to capture the Falklands. They tried to strengthen their hold on the islands by buying farmland using an Italian company as their cover. HMG decided not to permit this.

We travelled by small aircraft over the two main islands of West and East Falklands, visiting the various small settlements such as Darwin and Chartres, and spent one glorious day on West Point Island, populated by about twelve inhabitants and thousands of birds. The mountains, though not high, were snow-capped. The wild open spaces were covered with tussac grass and diddle-dee, a heather-like shrub. The rivers were full of fish. There were cosy warm peat fires in the houses, which were mainly painted white with red roofs. The pollution-free skies revealed at night the yellow glow of the sun on the Antarctic to the south. But the islanders seemed lonely people; marriages tended to break up and drinking was heavy. Moreover at that time they had no automatic right to settle in the UK and were suspicious of the Foreign Office and anxious about their future.

We held discussions with the rather inarticulate members of the Executive and Legislative Councils, and stayed with the Governor, Toby Lewis. He was a delightful New Zealander who each morning put on a beret and fed his ducks and chickens.

When the time came for our departure, the Argentinians arranged a special flight using their Air Force flying boat to take us the 600 miles back to Commodoro Rivadavia in Argentina. This was intended as a symbolic demonstration of the value of the new Communications Agreement. The flight was not enjoyable, about five and a half hours in stormy weather at 2,000 feet. When we arrived at our destination we saw the issue from a broader perspective through meetings with the British ambassador, Sir Michael Hadow, who repeatedly stressed the need to establish trust between the islanders and the Argentine. He employed the rather unfortunate analogy of persuading a girl to go to bed with you by building up trust through the provision of chocolates and other kindnesses. I can think of a better one, such as the process of trying to persuade someone to marry you, which I was to use later about Gibraltar. In any event the hope was that the Communications Agreement would enable trust to develop, followed by some kind of agreement on sovereignty. At the same time the more impatient Argentinians were suggesting that HMG hand over the Falklands in return for their support for Britain over Rhodesia. As we now know, the girl was keener on the chocolates than on intimate relations: tensions increased on both sides.

Throughout the 1970s, as a backbench MP and later Conservative spokesman on Non-European affairs, I maintained a keen interest in the Falklands. I raised questions in Parliament, met island councillors and representatives and launched an adjournment debate on the Shackleton Report. This was a report drawn up, under the aegis of Lord Shackleton (son of the famous explorer), at the request of the Government, on the future development of the Falklands. I criticised the Labour Government for not implementing many of the report's recommendations, including that of an airfield. The growing criticism made by myself and my Parliamentary colleagues was that the Government were neglecting the interests of the islanders and falsely signalling to the Argentine that we were not interested in the Falklands' future.

In the spring of 1979 Margaret Thatcher formed her first Conservative Government and I was made Minister for Africa. On 15 September 1981 I was with Rose on an official visit to the Cameroons, in a place called Victoria just south of Mount Cameroon. An urgent message arrived asking me to get access to a secure telephone as soon as possible to talk to the Prime Minister. We drove furiously to the British Consulate in Douala. My private secretary, Jeremy Cresswell, felt sure that I was about to be sacked and made a provisional booking on the flight home that evening. Eventually the familiar strong voice came on the line to say that she was undertaking a ministerial reshuffle and had decided to promote me to Minister of State at the FCO. The line was not absolutely clear as she asked, 'Where are you?' I said, 'The Cameroons.' This seemed to baffle her.

My ministerial promotion added the Americas to my Africa responsibilities. I had therefore to concentrate on a number of new issues and areas, amongst which the Falklands loomed as a growing political issue. I had taken over from Nick Ridley, who had courageously and with perhaps some foolhardiness tried to unlock the dispute with the Argentine by proposing a leaseback scheme under which sovereignty would be conceded to the Argentine, but Britain would continue to administer and govern on their behalf. Unfortunately Ridley failed to persuade the Cabinet, and indeed was badly mauled in Parliament. He had simply failed to prepare the ground first. By the time I took over, the impasse was serious and officials such as John Ure and Robin Fearn could only propose stalling talks with the Argentinians. Our respective positions had polarised: the Argentinians were losing patience while islanders and

Parliamentarians were adamantly opposed to any changes. We had reassured the islanders that there would be no changes without their consent but at the same time we were not showing them much practical support. We had announced the withdrawal of HMS *Endurance*; disbursement of aid was slow; we were not implementing the Shackleton Report's recommendations and there were 400 islanders without any right of abode in Britain. It was all too easy to understand how the Argentinian dictator, General Viola, might gain the impression that Britain was not interested in retaining the Falklands.

I agreed to a proposal from the Argentine Government that we should meet in Geneva in December 1981. General Galtieri's rise to power resulted in the postponement of talks until the end of February, in New York. The Foreign Secretary, Peter Carrington, and I agreed that we were bound to face a rough ride through 1982 with pressure building up through the United Nations, the imposition of Argentinian sanctions and possibly some kind of military action as we approached the 150th anniversary of British sovereignty in January 1983. There was however no evidence or advice that we would be likely to face actual aggression in the foreseeable future.

Before the talks in New York took place, the Argentine Government proposed that we agree to establish a Negotiating Commission which would meet monthly, with a clear timetable to agree sovereignty and related issues by the end of 1982. For the New York talks – the last any minister held before the invasion – I received excellent advice and support from Tony Parsons, our ambassador at the UN. My team included Anthony Williams, our ambassador to the Argentine, and two sensible Island councillors, Blake and Cheek. My opposite number was Deputy Foreign Minister Señor Ros who was supported by Ortiz de Rosas, the Argentine ambassador in London. We had a full day in each embassy. Señor Ros was a decent, civilised man who was a diplomat by profession and whose wife was English. He negotiated in good faith but constantly rang the Argentine Foreign Minister, Costa Mendez, and even President Galtieri for instructions. I agreed that a Negotiating Commission could be established, but was not prepared to be bounced into an agreement to hold regular monthly talks. In the end we agreed a communiqué and Ros believed that he had the consent of the President to move forward on this compromise. Ambassador Williams did not forecast any major problems with the Argentinians.

In the middle of all this a Tanzanian aircraft was hijacked at Stansted airport. David Trefgarne took my place on the emergency committee meeting in London, but the news programmes showed an old film of me talking to Julius Nyerere in Tanzania. The PM rang me to ask what I was doing in Dar es Salaam. I told her that I was in New York, a statement she found baffling, as she had just seen me in Africa! Rose had also been wondering whether I had gone to Tanzania by mistake.

Before returning home I briefed Javier Perez de Cuellar, the UN Secretary General, and flew to Washington for similar discussions with Tom Enders, the US Assistant Secretary of State for Latin America. At this time the Americans attached great importance to an anti-Soviet strategic alliance with Latin America. Knowing that he was about to visit Galtieri to discuss this, I decided that Enders must be asked to intervene on our behalf to warn Galtieri not to be so provocative over the Falklands. The problem was that the Falklands meant virtually nothing to Enders and, though he said he would raise the matter, he was hardly in persuasive mode. The truth is that the Americans, whether Reagan, Haig, Kirkpatrick or Enders, collectively failed to take this sufficiently seriously or to put pressure on Galtieri during the period before the invasion.

I flew home by Concorde to wind up a debate on El Salvador. In the Commons lobby that evening I spoke to the PM. When I said that we must restore HMS *Endurance* to the Falklands she commented, 'That's no good; it only goes "Pop, pop, pop". We should send aircraft carriers instead.' The following day Peter Carrington advised against this, as the Cabinet would not have been convinced that a case for deployment could be made at that stage.

Peter Carrington and I met on 3 March to assess the situation. John Ure told us that a nuclear-powered submarine had been sent in 1977 by Prime Minister Jim Callaghan, but that the present situation was not nearly so serious as that. (As it turned out, Callaghan later boasted that sending a submarine in 1977 had pre-empted any conflict. In fact it never surfaced, and the Argentinians never knew that it was in the South Atlantic.) We concluded that in the absence of any evidence of impending military action, we could not go to Cabinet to get agreement to send a deterrent force. The New York talks had bought us time, and we concentrated on diplomatic efforts to restore the dialogue. In fact what had happened was that Ros had been disowned by Galtieri and no communiqué had been published. We were told that the reasons for this abrupt change of attitude may have been because the Argentine press was becoming aggressive and Galtieri was facing serious economic problems and trade union strikes.

The spark that lit the flames of the Falklands conflict was the landing in Leith Harbour, South Georgia, of an Argentinian group led by one Constantino Davidoff claiming that they were fulfilling a contract with Christian Salvesen to dispose of scrap metal. On Saturday 20 March I was telephoned at home by John Ure who told me of this incident and said that the group had landed without permission. Thirteen days later the invasion of the Falkland Islands took place. During that fortnight we were increasingly boxed in: on the one hand HMG was trying hard to defuse tensions but Costa Mendez was not prepared to work to normalise the situation. If we had not sent HMS *Endurance* to South Georgia we would have been accused of pusillanimity by both Parliament and the islanders.

By the following weekend I realised that we were in deep trouble. By Monday 29 March we had the first evidence of troops embarking on naval ships in the Argentine, but we were told that his could well be to do with their routine naval training exercises. We received agreement from John Nott, the Defence Secretary, to send two submarines in secret, knowing they would take fourteen days to reach the Falklands. The House of Commons and the Back Bench Foreign Affairs Committee were growing increasingly anxious and irritable. I informed them that we would defend the islands to the best of our ability and were taking precautionary measures, which was the least I could say without provoking even more anxiety. In the Foreign Affairs Committee, the mischievous Alan Clark asked me whether we were sending three Hunter-Killer submarines. I refused to announce details of the measures we had taken, for fear that this would provoke precisely the reaction we wanted to avoid from Galtieri. If he was considering invasion, any details of this kind would have led him to bring forward his plans. Putting his vanity before the national interest, Clark told the media that I had said we were sending submarines to the Falklands. Simultaneously an *Express* correspondent saw a submarine sailing from Gibraltar, and wrongly assumed that it was on its way to the Falklands. That night and in the next morning's papers the headlines announced that submarines had been dispatched. It was my worst moment, and proved to me the weakness of a free press in such dangerous circumstances. Galtieri would now have every reason to move fast.

Meanwhile the machinery of Government was unable to change gear. On Wednesday 31 March officials poured cold water on intelligence reports that the Argentinian forces had the capacity to attack within two days. That evening I went straight to Margaret Thatcher's office in the Commons. John Nott was with her, and later we were joined by Peter Blaker, Minister of State for Defence, Antony Acland, Permanent Under Secretary at the Foreign Office, and Admiral Leach, First Sea Lord. We met from 7.30 pm to 11 pm that night. The Prime Minister was inevitably confused and trying to absorb the fast-moving situation. John Nott told her that we did not have the capacity to recover the Falklands. When the First Sea Lord arrived, however, he replied to the PM's inquiry, 'Prime Minister, if you instruct us to recover the Falklands, we will do so.' On that note the PM took the decision to mobilise and dispatch a task force based on the assumption that the Argentinians were about to invade.

The next day, 1 April, we were still receiving advice from the Cabinet Office that there was no definitive evidence of an invasion. Indeed, my private secretary was told to prevent his minister from raising such alarms. Peter Carrington returned from a visit to Israel that day, and we were with the PM until the early hours of the morning, talking, but realising that there was nothing more we could do. In our presence, Margaret talked to Reagan who agreed to ring Galtieri. His call had no effect.

By Friday morning Humphrey Atkins, Lord Privy Seal, announced to the Commons that the invasion had taken place. Afterwards I came straight back to see Peter Carrington. As I came through the door he said firmly, 'You're not going to resign.' I rehearsed with him the arguments for doing so, but he told me it was my duty to stick in there with him and to do our best to recover the situation. That evening the PM rang me about her draft speech for the emergency debate the next day, a Saturday. I offered to come over and help redraft it. She declined, worked all night on it and summoned me to come and join her on Saturday morning with Ian Gow and officials. At one point Robin Fearn was asked to go out and redraft a paragraph. Clearly he hadn't heard, no doubt due to exhaustion. A few minutes later, Margaret said, 'Oh good, you're back, can I have the paragraph?' He looked stunned: she immediately became very angry with the Foreign Office in general. At that point I intervened sharply to defend officials who had been up every night of the week during the crisis. Most creditably, she immediately apologised and said that she was rather strained herself.

In the midst of this drama my mother insisted on talking to me on the telephone. She said that she had an idea as to how to solve the problem. I should immediately arrange a football match between the two countries. Patiently I pointed out that the Argentinians had already invaded.

Saturday's debate was the most agonising affair of my Commons career, even though I was not speaking. Parliament had to let off steam; the Lords were kinder to Peter Carrington, but we had a rough meeting upstairs of the Conservative Foreign Affairs Committee. No one asked Peter to resign, but I could see his morale slipping sharply. I passed him a note to say that whatever he decided to do, I would do it with him. Later he put me in charge of mobilising the vote in the Security Council in our favour. I spoke to a number of Heads of Government and Foreign Ministers and asked Margaret Thatcher to intervene directly with King Hussein. She agreed immediately, saying 'God bless you.' We won the vote.

Peter then mysteriously disappeared to the country. I was unable to get hold of him all Sunday while I defended our action to the media, but I knew by now that he must be contemplating resignation. The PM had also been told that I had been thinking of going, and rang me to order me not to. But I said that it was a matter of honour. She replied, 'I can't quarrel with honour.' Peter was told that Charles Douglas-Home, editor of *The Times*, was contemplating a major attack on him on Monday. If this materialised, Peter said he would resign.

On Monday morning I flew up to Brize Norton from Northolt to welcome back the Governor of the Falklands, Rex Hunt, and the Marines who had been released by the Argentinians. As the aircraft landed, Peter rang to say he was resigning. *The Times*'s editorial pretty much described us as traitors for not preventing the invasion. I said immediately that I would do the same, and please would he wait until I had returned to London. He told me, 'You'd better hurry, as mine is being announced at 12.30 and you must first see me and the PM.' I hurriedly drafted my resignation letter and whisked Rex Hunt into the plane with me to fly to Northolt. From Northolt we raced with a police escort through all the red lights to No 10. Rex Hunt inquired with some surprise, 'Do you always travel like this?' I replied, 'Only when I am resigning.' The PM was generous and kind and insisted that I must return to Government in a few weeks. I thanked her but said that life was not quite as simple as that.

I lunched at the Athenaeum with my father-in-law. He was immensely patient, listening to me letting off steam. We walked together to Rab Butler's memorial service, where ironically Peter Carrington gave the address, and Enoch Powell sent his wife over to me with a message saying that he knew what I was going through. My private office staff were charming. Led by Jeremy Cresswell, they gave me two bunches of flowers – one for me and the other for me to give to Rose because, they reminded me, it was our twenty-first wedding anniversary! That evening Peter gave a farewell drinks party. Rose had by then joined me in London and gave me all possible support. The next morning I woke exhausted and said, 'How do I get to Parliament?' Rose replied, 'Take a tube.' I staggered to Sloane Square tube station. When a train arrived, I hadn't realised that with the new system you pressed buttons to open doors, and got exceedingly angry. A fellow passenger stepped forward and did it for me. I'd returned to normal life.

Resignation is a traumatic experience. For as long as the Falklands war continued, I felt a sense of agony and often asked myself whether I should have handled my responsibilities in a different way. With hindsight I would of course have done so, and in particular would have recommended naval deployment in secret at a much earlier stage.

Why did I resign? The invasion was a foreign policy disaster. In those circumstances it was essential for the appropriate ministers to do the honourable thing and carry the can for the invasion, even though we were not able to prevent it. Moreover it was important for the Prime Minister at that stage to have a ministerial team at the Foreign Office whom Parliament and the country could trust, especially as there were to be negotiations with the Argentine Government. The new Foreign Secretary and Minister of State could carry responsibility untainted by the experience of the previous weeks.

I made my traditional personal resignation statement to the House of Commons and tried to present it in as factual and balanced a way as was possible. I had many very kind letters and words from MPs of all parties, and from many other people too. I have been gratified in recent years to hear it said that Peter Carrington's and my resignations are remembered as honourable ones.

I was anxious that the public should know the circumstances that led to the war. For that reason I asked the Prime Minister to establish an inquiry once the war was over. She did so, and asked Lord Franks to chair it. Distinguished privy counsellors from all parties joined him on the Committee: they were Lord Barber, Lord Watkinson, Lord Lever, Lord Merlyn-Rees and Sir Patrick Nairne. The proceedings were held *in camera* and it was left to the Committee to divulge confidential information, providing that it was judged not to be contrary to the national interest to do so. It was a model of how to carry out an inquiry of this kind.

The Franks Report was published in January 1983 and concluded unequivocally that there was no justification for attaching any criticism or blame to the Government for the Argentine Junta's decision to invade the Falklands. Moreover there was no clear reason or evidence to believe, before 31 March, that an invasion of the islands would take place at the beginning of April. The Report praised my skill in handling the negotiations in New York.

There are inevitably some who, even to this day, maintain that the Report was a whitewash. The Opposition were naturally disappointed that the Government was not blamed for the disastrous invasion and others, including journalists, failed to understand that most of life in Government involves making difficult judgements from a complex grey area of issues, rather than simple choices. But I think that at the very least Peter's and my resignation demonstrated that we took responsibility for the calamity, irrespective of who was to blame. Moreover our actions released the PM from the team of ministers who were facing strong Parliamentary criticism for what had happened, and enabled her to appoint Francis Pym as the new Foreign Secretary and Cranley Onslow as my successor. They could negotiate afresh with the United States and Argentine Governments, untainted by mistrust from Parliament and the country. For however difficult the decision had been, we had misjudged.

The Report was critical of the failure of officials to gather together all the evidence of the growing animosity of the Argentine Government, let alone drawing it to ministers' attention, and expressed the opinion that the MOD and the FCO should have liaised more effectively. My own views are more critical than those of Franks concerning the failure of officials at home and in the British embassy in

Buenos Aires to provide any coherent warning of the growing aggression of the Argentinian press, for example, or to explain the context of the incidents in South Georgia. I would also point to the naivety of some Cabinet ministers, and John Nott's obsession with reducing the Navy and ignoring our warnings over the impact of withdrawing HMS *Endurance*. In later years John Nott has more than once asked me why Peter Carrington and I resigned, which to my mind says rather more about him that it does about us. If he was suffering from a feeling of guilt that he should have resigned too, then I don't think that he needed to do so. On the other hand I think that I was a little unfair to the PM concerning her prevarication and confusion before she finally took the decision to recover the Falklands. She had enough other problems to preoccupy her, and the behaviour of the Junta was probably the last thing that would have occurred to her. Finally, I think the American performance before the invasion was lamentable.

The strength of the Report was that it looked at the invasion against the perspective of the previous seventeen years. Here we have the story of two irreconcilable interests – the Argentinians who were determined to acquire sovereignty and the islanders who had understandably refused to live under that dictatorship. From that time in 1966 when the British Government said that it was willing to discuss sovereignty, the British position steadily weakened and negotiations became increasingly tricky with growing Argentinian frustration and mistrust. The story is also one of misjudging each other's position and the misreading of each other's minds. We do frequently make the mistake of thinking that other Governments behave and act like us, and we often pay a heavy price for it. In the Argentine the first repressive Junta took over in 1976, increased their military strength led by a hawkish navy, were frustrated that the geographical Beagle Dispute with Chile had gone against them, faced increasingly serious economic problems and strikes and were looking for something to divert attention.

Meanwhile the actions of the Labour and Conservative Governments over this timespan must have given a pretty clear impression, however false, that Britain was not going to make too much of a fuss over the Falkland Islanders. One could cite the lack of a permanent credible military deterrent in the Falklands, leading to the announced withdrawal of HMS *Endurance*; Britain's naval withdrawal from the South Atlantic region; the failure of the British Government to remove an Argentinian force which occupied a part of Southern Thule in the Sandwich Islands in the mid 1970s, the failure to implement the main Shackleton Report recommendations, for example to build an airfield and to allow all the residents British citizenship; the apparent regular stalling by British Governments during negotiations; and the hardening resistance of the island inhabitants and Parliament to the ceding of sovereignty. With this picture built up over time it is perhaps not surprising that, with hindsight, the Argentine military dictatorship took the risk that they might be able to invade and get away with it.

In the light of the recent Iraq experience and the focus on the quality of available intelligence, it is fair to question whether the intelligence services failed ministers over the Falklands. Certainly I would have expected to have been told that the Argentine newspaper *La Prensa* gave warnings of military action in January and February that year; that HMS *Endurance* had an unusually hostile reception when she called at an Argentine port in January; that the Argentine naval chief was making bellicose noises; and that at the end of February it had been reported that a Uruguayan official had told our ambassador in Montevideo that he thought the Argentine was contemplating military action. This is not to suggest that ministers would have taken different decisions in the light of this information but it does indicate that the intelligence flow on the Argentine was not being given adequate priority or being properly coordinated. Even senior officials were not getting the fuller picture. Perhaps they saw the danger of crying wolf. There had been several invasions in previous years which had come to nothing. What is probably more striking is that our embassy in Buenos Aires did not appear to believe that any invasion was imminent, as was indicated by the attitude of Ambassador Williams during the New York talks. The Argentine Government was clearly frustrated that we were not wanting to move as fast as it was in getting the Negotiating Commission operating and meeting regularly, but at no time did our ambassador warn us that this disparity in approach could so frustrate the Argentinians that they would contemplate military action.

Britain was, as with Gibraltar, torn between fulfilling her responsibilities to the remnants of the old British Empire and pursuing her national interests which might involve compromise. Perhaps one day both sides might be able to find a peaceful and satisfactory way of cooperating to the mutual benefit of all the parties.

When she stayed with us in Gibraltar I discussed our resignations with Margaret Thatcher and asked her what she really felt about it. She said that her first reaction was one of loneliness and isolation. I can quite understand that she was devastated by the loss of Peter Carrington. But she did accept the argument of an honourable resignation in that it cleared the way for a new team of ministers in the Foreign Office.

As for Peter his departure, never to return to Government, was desperately sad for the Government and the country. My own account gives the impression that he was not in clear charge of the Falklands. He was. He had set the policy framework for handling the Falklands when I took over as Minister of State. He was a marvellous delegator. He left me to get on with it, but always kept his finger on the pulse. He had the whole world to cope with, but wherever he was travelling he kept in touch. He was an outstanding Foreign Secretary. It was a privilege to serve under him. Ever since those days Rose and I have appreciated and enjoyed the Carringtons' friendship.

The Falklands conflict led to another family involvement in that my sister D's husband, David Hart Dyke, was at that time captain of HMS *Coventry*. As the naval armada sailed towards the Falklands, and after my resignation, I received a letter from David saying that all the naval captains in the expedition were ready to do what was required of them but that they were very concerned as to whether the Government realised the danger and in particular the need for much stronger air support. I passed this straight on to the Prime Minister.

At the same time he sent me a letter for D which I was to safeguard carefully in case he never returned. I realised, after the sinking of HMS *Sheffield* and the other setbacks, how real the danger was of losing HMS *Coventry*. It was therefore with the worst foreboding that I heard John Nott announce one evening in late May that another ship had been sunk, without naming it. I just knew it was the *Coventry* and I kept in touch with D. It wasn't until the afternoon of the next day that we knew that David was alive and the last off the ship.

D showed immense courage during this crisis and spent as much time as she could supporting the wives of those whose husbands had been killed or wounded. The experience is recounted most movingly by David in his book *Four Weeks in May* in which he describes what war is like for both servicemen and their families.

15

The University of Buckingham

It had never occurred to me that I might one day return to university after I left Cambridge. I was neither academic nor intellectual. But in 1991, when I had voluntarily returned to the backbenches and was expecting a further decade or so in Parliament, John Fairbairn, a friend, telephoned me at home to say that the University of Buckingham – he was a member of its Council – was looking for a vice-chancellor to succeed Dr Michael Barrett. He asked me if I was prepared for my name to be added to the short list for the job. I went to find Rose, who was in the garden, and told her that I thought John had gone mad and that I couldn't be less suitable.

However I took the suggestion seriously and consulted a number of Parliamentary colleagues. Geoffrey Howe thought it was a good idea, as did Terence Higgins, MP for Worthing, who felt that I was not so wedded to Parliament as others were. There was a precedent, too, for a Tory MP taking on a vice-chancellorship: Edward Boyle had been appointed to the University of Leeds in the 1970s.

I decided to have a go. I was only fifty-five or so, and was ready for a different challenge. I was duly put on the short list, which was eventually narrowed down to Professor Peter Watson, the acting vice-chancellor, and me. I travelled to Buckingham for half a day to be interviewed by the Council, under the chairmanship of Sir Nigel Mobbs, and this was followed by discussions with individual academics. I liked the atmosphere of the whole place and had no hesitation in accepting the offer of vice-chancellor, with Peter Watson as my deputy. Chris Patten said on hearing of my appointment, 'This shows that there is life after death.'

I left Parliament in April 1992 and took up the job immediately, excited at being in charge of the only independent university in the UK, founded by Vice-Chancellor Max Beloff and others in the early 1970s. I was free to take on some extra tasks and became chairman of the Commonwealth Foundation and of the Atlantic Council of the UK, as well as being on the board of Booker Tate. This meant spending weekends in Sussex, three or four days in Buckingham and one or two days in London each week. At Buckingham we were given an attractive house named Willowbank on the campus, originally the University's first common room. It had a nice garden, dominated by a lovely beech tree, and was quiet, being at the end of a cul-de-sac.

It turned out to be a gruelling five years, the term for which I had agreed to serve, (rather than seven). It was particularly tiring for Rose because of the thrice-weekly moving, with her having to do all the packing and carrying. She is a saint to have done it, and helped me enormously with all the entertaining of a wide variety of outsiders and insiders, and especially the students.

In the late 1960s Max Beloff and other academics had decided that it was time to challenge the postwar pattern of the State university system. It was a courageous undertaking in such a State-oriented environment. When I mentioned Buckingham to people, they would invariably react by saying 'Beloff' – he was the inspiration and driving force, and had left Oxford to take it on. He was therefore the father of the university and, I have to say, quite difficult to handle, often interfering or disagreeing on policy matters while I was there.

The first few months at Buckingham were quite a culture shock. I felt rather as though I had been appointed captain of a ship without having been in the Navy. It must have been equally difficult for the academics: of the fifty universities at that time there were only two or three that had non-academic vice-chancellors. My former tutor Jack Plumb suggested (I hope jokingly) that of all his former students I was the least likely to become a vice-chancellor. I was subjected to a barrage of advice.

The majority of academics were very committed to their teaching, giving students one-to-one tuition and personal attention. This was one of the keys to Buckingham's success. But many of them did not like being involved in the decision-making of the university, preferring to criticise the administrators. I made it clear from the beginning that this was not acceptable and Peter Watson, an accountant by background, agreed that for the university to succeed, academics had to share responsibility and be part of the decision-making process. We decided to appoint deans to manage each of the four schools: Law, Humanities, Science and Business Studies. Under my chairmanship a committee was formed consisting of the deans and Peter Watson. I would rely on Peter to give the academic lead while I concentrated on promoting the university at home and abroad. Peter handled the finances extremely cautiously and well, if not a little secretively.

Margaret Thatcher followed Lord Hailsham as my Chancellor and Sir Nigel Mobbs, chairman of Slough Estates, was chairman of the Council. Nigel gave strong support, always encouraging, especially in difficult times, steady and full of common sense. Other members of the Council such as Gillian Miscampbell, Timothy Raison, Professor David Myddelton, Steve Shirley, John Daniel and Ian Beer were generally helpful and supportive. With Rose's help I entertained every week on a large scale in order to gain fuller recognition for the university.

The intrinsic strength of the university lay in its independence of Government, the personal attention and tuition given to each student, the sense of a real community derived from its small size, the motivation of the students – arising partly from the payment of full cost fees – and the pleasant campus, mainly on the south side of the town, not subject to the distractions of nightlife. Its strong distinguishing feature was having four terms a year: this meant the degree period could be two years, with students putting in the same amount of term-time study as they would in three years at other universities. The commitment and self-discipline required tended to suit mature students better. During my time as vice-chancellor about 70% of the students came from abroad, drawn from about seventy countries, mainly Commonwealth. It pleased me that our son Alexander had been a student at Buckingham in the mid-1980s.

I found my job much like managing a business: hair-raising, but stimulating. I lost sleep from time to time. We admitted 1,000 students for the first time in the university's history but numbers then began to decline, principally because of competition from the new universities and the decline in the Asian economies.

My policy of devolving responsibilities to deans had slightly mixed success: some deans were stimulated by responsibility while others responded badly. I recruited a marketing specialist to help us promote at home and abroad and put academics in charge of different countries so that they could encourage new students to apply through personal contact. I accompanied them on visits to Pakistan, Malaysia, Hong Kong, Taiwan, Bermuda and the Bahamas.

Rose and I were helped in our entertaining at Willowbank by

Margaret and Denis Thatcher who came to stay for graduation cere-
monies and around whom we arranged special parties. On one occasion Vaclav Klaus came to receive an honorary degree. He was then
Prime Minister of the Czech Republic. After dinner, at about ten
o'clock, Margaret told Vaclav that it was time for him to go to bed! He
didn't want to go but she persuaded me to walk him to his hotel. On
another occasion Caspar Weinberger, American Secretary of State for
Defence during the Falklands War, received an honorary degree and
spoke so warmly of the mutual support during the war that he was
given a standing ovation. By contrast, David Dilks told me that when
'Cap' – as he was known – received an honorary degree at Leeds
University (where David was a leading academic), the students rioted
and shouted during the drive to the station. Cap had said to David,
'Don't worry. I find that if students shout, they generally don't shoot.'

Towards the end of my five years at Buckingham, I managed to persuade Sir Evelyn de Rothschild to donate a million pounds to help
finance a new Business School building, behind my offices by the river.
His then wife Victoria, over a lunch party for four, had said, 'My husband may shoot me, but I think he should support the Business
School.' We both laughed nervously and changed the subject. A few
days afterwards he wrote to ask for proposals. A fortnight later, most
generously, he produced a million pounds.

I decided that the best way to get this project completed on time and
to promote it would be to invite the Queen to unveil the building and
tour the university. She and the Duke of Edinburgh came one sunny
day in 1996, reinforced by the Thatchers. The schoolchildren of
Buckingham lined the streets leading to the main campus. After the
unveiling ceremony Rose and I gave all four lunch at Willowbank. The
catering staff were presented after lunch but were too paralysed to
curtsey. Towards the end of the lunch Margaret said that if she were
still Prime Minister she would expand the Armed Forces. At that point
the Queen said it was time to go. The visit did much to promote the
prestige of Buckingham.

I was a member of the Committee of Vice-Chancellors, whose size
suddenly expanded from around fifty to a hundred when the polytechnics became universities in 1992. I found the group rather a gloomy
gathering, forever complaining about and mocking Government
policy, but doing nothing constructive. Originally the British academic

world feared and despised Buckingham. But once they discovered that the university was not a threat to them, they became more relaxed and friendly.

The expansion of university places overall and the mistaken policy of granting polytechnics university status posed a threat to Buckingham. In my last few months as vice-chancellor, when numbers began to decline from the peak of 1,000 students, we were compelled to retrench after some agonising within the Deans Committee about priorities. It seemed me to that the academic staff had lost something of the pioneering spirit.

My successor, Professor Bob Taylor, deputy head of SOAS at the University of London, reversed my policy for devolving authority to deans. Meanwhile, student numbers continued to decline and Margaret Thatcher retired as Chancellor. Dr Terence Kealey has taken up the cudgels valiantly and provides the best hope for recovery. Whatever the outcome, Buckingham has blazed a trail.

A few years later Rose and I returned to the university when I received an honorary degree from Margaret Thatcher. The polite applause increased significantly when Margaret summoned Rose to join me on the platform. It really pleased me to see how well appreciated by the university Rose was. In 2003 she joined the University Council, thus giving us both a continuing link with a unique institution.

My Buckingham experience crystallised my views on universities. A good university should follow the concept of the nineteenth-century institutions. As Cardinal Newman established, they are there to enable the students to search for the truth. Personal tuition is at the heart of this process and should help the students train their minds to think issues through, consistently, rigorously and coherently. But it is also an opportunity to broaden experience as well as the mind, by enabling the students to participate in a wide range of activities and to learn to live with their contemporaries. If we are to have more rounded graduates, then there needs to be less emphasis on examination and more on the broader experience of life. I am encouraged to learn that employers are looking for all-round experience. The qualities of integrity, initiative, determination and unselfishness are as important as intellectual achievement in examination.

The Buckingham venture gives a few helpful pointers to universities in the twenty-first century. Throughout the nineteenth century until well after the Second World War, universities catered for only a small proportion of school leavers and were relatively free from Government intervention and bureaucracy. Today nearly 50% of all eighteen-year-olds go to university. This positive development means, however, that universities rely on taxpayers' support, but at a level which, in most universities, means that there are insufficient resources to allow the kind of personal attention which I used to have in my day. The Buckingham experience has demonstrated the true cost of a good university education, that fee-paying students can be highly motivated as they are at Buckingham, that their independence makes it possible to innovate where it has been proved that students can achieve a proper degree in two years and that freedom from Government bureaucracy is a strength. The Labour Government's decision to introduce a measure of fee-paying for students together with the introduction of pilot surveys of two-year degrees in some universities shows that the independent university has already served a useful purpose.

16

Gibraltar

In July 1995 Rose and I stayed with the Rifkinds for Malcolm's first weekend at Chevening as Foreign Secretary. We went prepared for a relaxed weekend with old friends. But on the Friday evening I was having a drink alone with Malcolm when he asked me if I would consider the job of Governor and Commander-in-Chief of Gibraltar. I must have looked startled, and he assured me that it was a politically important task. I explained that I was only three years through a five-year contract with the University of Buckingham and that I couldn't let them down. He had anticipated this and told me that he could send one more military Governor for a short period – Admiral Sir Hugo White – who was earmarked to become First Sea Lord.

During the weekend my mind began to turn towards the possibilities arising from yet another unexpected turn of events. My experiences in Kenya as a District Officer and life as a Foreign Office minister lent considerable appeal to the idea of being a Governor in a complex political scene. I agreed to consider it seriously a year or so later, when I had completed my contract at Buckingham. I felt elated by the challenge of being the first civilian Governor in 300 years of British rule.

And so began the next stage in my unpredictable life. In autumn 1996 I confirmed to Malcolm Rifkind that I would be prepared to succeed Sir Hugo White. One precondition, which was subsequently satisfied, was that Malcolm should seek the support of Robin Cook, Shadow Foreign Secretary, in view of the pending general election. The announcement was a little controversial. *The Times*'s editorial suggested that my Falklands experience did not augur well. Former Governors, led by General Sir William Jackson, wrote letters to the *Daily Telegraph* criticising the appointment and suggesting that this was the beginning of a sell-out. Rose and I were both very sharp with him on the telephone and asked how he thought it helped Gibraltar publicly to run down the new Governor. He apologised. But the criticisms had already sown anxiety in the minds of Gibraltarians as to why I was being sent.

The answer was that Gibraltar was no longer a purely military base. Whereas in the past defence had constituted about three-quarters of the economy, it was by then much reduced and the territory needed to adjust to a new age and new sources of income. Malcolm wanted me to help make the transition as smooth as possible. Clearly it would also be helpful if I could recommend ways forward for the longer term.

I was very conscious that my resignation over the Falklands in 1982 might lead Gibraltarians to draw the wrong conclusion. The parallels between the two territories were close. I was therefore both pleased and relieved when during my arrival ceremony in the Assembly Chief Minister Caruana said that my resignation had been an honourable one.

After a few weeks of intense preparation, including meetings with ministers such as David Davis, Minister of State, and the Chief of the Defence Staff, Sir Peter Inge, we left home on 21 February 1997 to spend the weekend with Roger Westbrook, ambassador to Lisbon, before sailing to Gibraltar. Our ambassador to Spain, David Brighty, joined us so that he could brief me on the Spanish aspect and Nick Diggle, my ADC, came up from Gibraltar notwithstanding the death that weekend of his father who had said on his deathbed that, whatever happened, Nick must accompany me when I arrived.

On Sunday morning we walked down through cobbled streets to the harbour to board HMS *York*, a type 42 frigate captained by Commander Moll. We sailed slowly down the broad River Tagus out into the Atlantic and past Cape St Vincent. At dawn on 24 February the ship was stationary ten miles off Gibraltar, preparing for the arrival ceremony. Through the mist I saw in the distance the solid grey-blue Rock emerging. I felt nervous, despite having been taken through arrival procedures by Nick Diggle on a video, and wondered how, not being military, I would cope. A few days earlier the Queen Mother's private secretary, Sir Alistair Aird, had said to me, 'I must be the first to shake the hand of the only person I know who has jumped from being a subaltern to a commander-in-chief!'

Above all, as the ship sailed slowly into harbour escorted by small ships and tugs, I thought of my father who had commanded the entrance of the Indian Ocean to the Red Sea as Governor of Aden; now I was doing the same thing for the entrance of the Atlantic into the Mediterranean. For all his high standards I must do my best to follow him. Not for the first time I reflected that I was lucky to have Rose at my side.

As I was piped off the ship, accompanied by a seventeen-gun salute and the fly-past of a Nimrod, I was greeted by the Acting Governor, Michael Robinson, the Chief Justice, Derek Schofield, Chief Minister Caruana, Opposition Leader Joe Bossano, Mr Speaker Alcantara and the Commander of the British Forces, General Pack. There was also a police and regimental guard of honour outside the Assembly. Getting out of a car with a sword is a dangerous and delicate operation but I emerged complete. The Speaker presided over the oath-taking ceremony, with friendly speeches from Caruana and Bossano. In my response I spoke of the sense of privilege I felt in taking up this responsibility and I drew attention to the coincidence that an ancestor of mine, Lord Napier of Magdala, had been Governor in the 1870s and had built the west wing of the Convent, the Governor's Residence.

As we left the ceremony Rose and I were met by crowds four or five rows deep all the way down the Main Street. We walked along slowly, shaking hands with as many people as possible, and eventually arrived at a reception in the Convent for 200 leaders of the community, after which we had the rest of the day to contemplate the Convent and garden.

Thus began an eventful three years as Governor. I had left Kenya in late 1962 as one of the three last British District Officers in East Africa during the final stages of the Empire. Now, thirty-five years later, I was becoming a Colonial Governor.

Since our residence was in the Convent many at home assumed that we lived with nuns. Five hundred years ago the building had been a Franciscan monastery or '*convento*' and it was certainly the most historic and attractive house and garden of all overseas embassies and Government houses. The garden was lush with vegetation and trees, some of them rare, like the imposing but rather ugly dragon-tree which came originally from the Canaries, and a large and ancient carob tree outside my office. A swimming pool kept me fit and a tennis court was popular with visitors. We chose to sleep in the Napier wing added by my ancestor. The old part of the house had a Spanish-style courtyard, and a fountain which we installed, with the official offices surrounding it. Upstairs were the banqueting room with the coats of arms of all the previous Governors, a dining room and a good-sized drawing room which Rose redecorated colourfully. She also refurbished an old ball-room after the Foreign Office came up with a grant and was accorded six pages in *Country Life* describing her efforts. It was a dream of a place for entertaining and hundreds of Gibraltarians flowed through each year, as well as constant visitors coming to stay. Something like 5,000 people a year were shown around the main part of the building.

The Ministry of Defence did their best to persuade us to move into the official accommodation of former Commanders of British Forces, called The Mount. It was built higher up on the sharp slope on the side of the Rock with a stunning view across the Bay of Gibraltar and towards Morocco. The Commander of British Forces was no longer going to live there as the job had been downgraded. I realised that living in The Mount would send completely the wrong sort of signal to Gibraltar: it would look as though the first civilian Governor was detaching himself from a central role in the affairs of Gibraltar, perhaps indicating that this was part of a pull-back by the British which might lead to the creation of a Channel Islands status. I decided not to move.

At the end of the twentieth century the role of a colonial governor was not fully understood, certainly not – in my view – by the Foreign Office. There is a world of difference between the job of an ambassador and that of a governor: a former advisor to my father in Aden once described the contrast between my father and his successor in Aden, Sir Charles Johnston, a former ambassador, explaining that if riots took place in the colony Sir Charles would telegram immediately to the Colonial Secretary asking for instructions, whereas my father would deal with the crisis and inform the Colonial Secretary several days later of the action he had taken. In Gibraltar my staff in the Convent comprised about twelve diplomats, including a Deputy Governor, whose job it was to liaise with the Foreign Office, while I was responsible for governing – though of course our duties often over-lapped. There was far too much nannying from London because the Foreign Office was inclined to treat governors in the same way as ambassadors. I tried to ignore all this as best I could.

It was, as Malcolm Rifkind had told me, a highly political job. Gibraltar's population of 30,000 was roughly the same as that of the Adur district council area in Sussex but the range of tasks and respon-sibilities of both the Governor and the elected Chief Minister were those of a mini-state, ranging from foreign policy, defence and security issues for the Governor, to education, refuse collection, hospitals and old people's homes for the Chief Minister, though in fact he was always strongly interested in all issues. Walking down the main street one soon discovered that each Gibraltarian was his own foreign secretary, whereas on a stroll through the high street of Shoreham-by-Sea you just had to field complaints about local prices or the behaviour of a neighbour.

The Rock of Gibraltar has layers of history. The discovery of the skull of a Neanderthal woman in Gibraltar predates the discovery of Neanderthal man in Germany. The importance of the research in Gibraltar was to ascertain whether there was a link between Neanderthal man and modern man over a timespan of 30,000 years.

In AD 701 Tarik led an Islamic force from North Africa, first occupying Gibraltar and thus launching the 700-year Islamic Empire of the Iberian Peninsula. In the fifteenth century the Spanish Empire under the leadership of Ferdinand and Isabella occupied Gibraltar until Spain, weakened by the Wars of the Spanish Succession, was defeated off Gibraltar by a British-Dutch naval force under Admiral Rooke in 1704. The 1713 Treaty of Utrecht then sealed the future of Gibraltar under the British until today, ruling that Gibraltar was under British sovereignty in perpetuity but that Spain had the first right of refusal should Britain opt out.

The identity and mentality of the Gibraltarians are explained by their geography and history. They have faced fifteen sieges – of which the most famous was in 1783 under General Elliott, the then Governor. In more recent history we should never forget the sacrifices the Gibraltarians made for the British and Allied forces in the Second World War, when to enable over 30,000 British servicemen to be based on Gibraltar, all Gibraltarian wives and children emigrated for five years to Madeira, Tangiers, London and Northern Ireland, while their husbands stayed at home to help the war effort.

During the war Gibraltar became the last remaining territory on the Continent in Allied hands. Eisenhower, the Supreme Allied Commander in North Africa, stayed in Gibraltar with the Governor for eighteen days in the autumn of 1940, preparing the final stages of the plan to eject Rommel from North Africa. Earlier that year Hitler had tried to persuade Franco to allow German forces through Spain to occupy Gibraltar. Churchill got wind of this and sent a message to Franco which said, 'If you allow Germany to occupy Gibraltar I will take the Canaries.' It worked. While I was Governor I gave a banquet to mark the occasion, attended by Eisenhower's granddaughter, young Winston Churchill and Roosevelt's daughter-in-law.

On her world tour in 1954 the Queen and the Duke of Edinburgh visited Gibraltar. There are some who feel that this provoked Franco into putting increasing pressure on the British to hand Gibraltar over to Spain. Indeed, when the Spanish royal family learnt that the Prince and Princess of Wales were to join the Royal Yacht in Gibraltar for their honeymoon in 1981, there was a stormy reaction from King Carlos and the Spanish Government. The Spanish royal family cancelled their plans to attend the wedding and relations between the two royal families were strained. Sir Richard Parsons, then ambassador in Madrid, told me that his maid came into the drawing room saying, 'There is someone on the telephone who says he is the King of Spain.' This turned out to be the first salvo from King Carlos, one of whose many titles was Sovereign of Gibraltar. Franco's closure of the frontier in 1969 had led to a sixteen-year siege, and it was only when Spain joined NATO and later the European Union that the frontier was reopened. Until very recently the Spanish have been at pains to harass Gibraltarians, delaying them on the frontier and isolating them from EU Directives.

The siege mentality has produced a fiercely independent and rather obstinate people. The Gibraltarians are ardently loyal to the monarchy and deeply suspicious of every British Government, who they believe will make every effort to sell them out to Spain. Indeed successive British Governmental tactics over decades have sometimes been so questionable that this is not the least bit surprising. Spanish tactics have been equally crass and counter-productive. Bullying the Gibraltarians will never win them over, nor will attempts to settle their future behind their backs. Ironically the attempts made by the British and Spanish Governments after 2001 to agree a joint sovereignty deal for Gibraltar without consulting them have unintentionally created conditions in which both Gibraltarians and Spanish are talking directly to each other, working to build confidence through economic cooperation in the region and by promoting the joint use of the airport.

Gibraltar's 1969 Constitution made it clear that the Governor had responsibility for the overall welfare of the territory, foreign policy, defence and internal security matters, together with authority to make appointments to senior positions like those of the Chief Justice, Attorney General and Police Commissioner. There is no doubt that previous military Governors had allowed the authority of the Governor to decline and had sometimes turned a blind eye to attempts by Chief Ministers to encroach onto their territory. This was the case with Caruana, the present Chief Minister. There were times when I had to intervene to prevent him from legislating in areas under my control. However I was sympathetic to Caruana's desire to achieve maximum autonomy in a post-colonial age, though independence would not be possible without Spanish consent – a most unlikely proposition. I emphasised to him that this must be achieved through negotiations with HMG to amend the constitution, not by sowing discord and undermining the Governor's constitutional obligations. I felt enormously pleased when his Government, six years later, put an all-party case for reform and which led to an adapted constitution. In the meantime my job was to establish a working relationship with the Chief Minister which would enable us to help stabilise Gibraltar. Whilst Joe Bossano was Chief Minister in the 1990s the territory faced many problems, and his slowness in tackling drug crime and allegations of money-laundering caused considerable tension with HMG.

When I arrived in Gibraltar Peter Caruana was a relatively new Chief Minister and my relationship with him was key. He was very suspicious that, as a former minister, my motive in accepting the job could only have been to establish more control and possibly even to encourage a deal with Spain. I therefore instituted weekly lunches in the Convent with him for up to two hours when we talked alone and frankly about many issues. Peter had the forensic mind of a lawyer: he could grasp often rather tedious detailed problems very quickly and act as an excellent advocate for Gibraltar. In so doing he has benefited Gibraltar over the years. What did not help was his suspicion that HMG, the Governor and others were always plotting to do him down. He believed that my efforts to get to know the people and institutions of Gibraltar were intended to undermine him, rather than a case of the Governor doing his duty. Our weekly meetings enabled me to at least try to clear the air on issues and to give the Foreign Secretary an idea of what was necessary in order to help Gibraltar. Bossano, by contrast, was engaging and amusing and had an unusual brain, but he did not always use his talents to good effect.

I should have liked to have the opportunity to work with Sir Joshua Hassan, the former Chief Minister. He lived for only a few months after I arrived and was the elder statesman of the territory, giving me good advice during our occasional chats. His Jewish family came from Morocco and he had established his own legal practice in Gibraltar, which he continued even as Chief Minister. He was given a State funeral on his death. Rose and I followed the coffin through Gibraltar's main street in a military ceremony, and I poured soil over his body at his Jewish burial in the cemetery.

Dominic Searle, the young editor of the *Chronicle*, was a refreshing person to talk to in a very claustrophobic atmosphere; I also established links with the leading businessmen of the territory, such as Joe and James Gaggero who ran GB Airways. Back home I had Malcolm Rifkind as Foreign Secretary for my first three months. He was refreshingly robust in dealing with the Spanish Foreign Minister, pointing out in public that Ceuta and Melilla, Spanish territories in North Africa, were similar to Gibraltar and that Spain was hypocritical on this issue by accusing us of doing in Gibraltar exactly what they were doing in Africa. Robin Cook then succeeded Malcolm on the election of a new Labour Government. I always found him perfectly reasonable to deal with but his priorities lay elsewhere. During a meeting at Carlton Gardens with the Spanish Foreign Minister he asked me to attend and speak. I said that I had no speech to make, but would like to ask Matutes a question: what would his wife have said to him if he had said to her, 'Will you marry me – I shall bully and harass you until you accept?' Matutes smiled and said, 'She would not have liked that.' I replied, 'And nor does Gibraltar.' I'm not sure Cook was happy, but I had made the point. I was the first official appointment for him after he became Foreign Secretary and I congratulated him. 'That must have taken some effort to say,' he replied. Later at a meeting Gordon Brown rang him but Robin said he would not talk now as he had a more important meeting with the Governor of Gibraltar! When I later came to see the Prime Minister, Tony Blair, I thought the body language was not good; it seemed that Cook was treated rather as a minion.

There were a number of law and order issues to deal with, of which the most difficult was the growing incursion of Spanish fishing boats into Gibraltarian waters. This was clearly a deliberate attempt to demonstrate Spain's claims to Gibraltar. Some of their vessels were large and armed. There had been a previous understanding that some vessels could come in a certain distance, but this was nothing less than a massive invasion. I decided that we had to assert our authority. Our own naval patrol ships on their own did not have the capacity to do so, and I was forced to ask HMG for a fishery protection vessel to enable me to enforce the law. The Foreign Office did everything they could to block my request. I eventually told Robin Cook that he would have to find another Governor unless he promised the vessel. Finally a commitment was given by Blair but, before any further ado, our existing forces managed to detain a large Spanish vessel and arrest fourteen fishermen. This burst the bubble of tension and the Spanish fishermen were invited by Caruana to negotiate a local agreement. Notwithstanding a weekend of some disturbances, the agreement was successfully reached and I praised Caruana for taking control and preventing the Foreign Office and the Spanish Government from undermining us. The episode made me see exactly why Gibraltarians had never trusted the Foreign Office.

The territory's defence role, though much reduced, remained important to the Government and many British and American ships passed through. I took a keen interest in the Gibraltar Regiment, formed in the 1950s and made up of around 400 regulars and territorials. The regiment was extremely well trained and I chose Andrew Bonfante and Colin Risso successively to be the first ever Gibraltarian ADCs. I watched the regiment train in the UK, Gibraltar and Morocco and had many dealings with them, especially on ceremonial occasions, such as the Queen's Birthday Parades, the Ceremony of the Keys and the guard mount on Saturday mornings. To the accompaniment of their excellent band it gave me great pleasure to review them, escorted by the Port Sergeant who held the keys of the city on my behalf. At banquets in the Convent he would march in with a drum beating and report to me, 'The gates of the city are locked. All is well, sir.' I would thank him and he would march off. I decided that they deserved to have royal status and obtained the Queen's agreement to make them the Royal Gibraltar Regiment in a ceremony outside the Convent, accompanied by Caruana. On one occasion, during the Duke of Kent's visit, the ceremony to renew their colours in a magnificent setting led to my accompanying the Duke in his field marshal's uniform to review the veterans. One veteran was decked out with medals. When the Duke asked him about them, he said: 'The thing is, sir, the top row is mine and the bottom row is my father's award for his part in the Battle of Tel el Kebir in Egypt.'

Rose and I loved the Gibraltarian children. A party of them would arrive each year on my birthday to sing 'Happy Birthday to You' in the Convent garden. We visited all the schools. One boy who couldn't pronounce 'Your Excellency' said, unruffled, 'Oh well, good morning Your Majesty!' When I asked one girl how long her Christmas play lasted, she said, 'For as long as it takes, of course.' When visiting young Scouts, I found a group practising first aid and looking anxiously at a boy pretending to be a casualty. I asked them what was wrong with the boy. No one answered until suddenly the boy's head popped up and he said reassuringly, 'It's all right, sir. I'm only pretending.' Our affection for them led Rose and me to establish the Luce Foundation on our departure, enabling deprived children to take part in adventure training outside Gibraltar, including a week on a tall ship. It has been ably run by Colonel Guerrero and Andrew Bonfante.

We had many visitors, including Royals. Princess Alexandra and Angus Ogilvy, the Gloucesters and the Duke of Kent all made very successful visits, much appreciated by the Gibraltarians. Margaret and Denis Thatcher came on their first ever visit, which was treated on a par with a royal visit by the Gibraltarians. While they were staying with us we were all woken early one morning by a bomb scare. We sat in the thick-walled bomb shelter of the Convent, once used by General Elliott. As we were drinking coffee the acting Commander of British Forces, Colonel Sankey, came in to say that HMS *Nottingham* was shadowing a Spanish naval ship which had entered our waters. Margaret, delighted to be caught up in this atmosphere, said, 'Let's bomb Madrid.' I responded that I thought we ought to wait a little.

Gibraltar has many different religions. Three-quarters of the population are Roman Catholics, there are a small number of Anglicans and the remainder are Jewish, the Asian Hindus and Moroccan Muslims. The Saudi Government paid for a large mosque to be built by the lighthouse, and looking towards Africa, which was felt to be a little provocative. A gathering of cardinals arrived to rededicate the church of Our Lady of Europe on the promontory. Cardinal Hume came to install the new Bishop of Gibraltar, Charles Caruana. During his address he said 'Some of you may regard a cardinal as a perfect human being. If so, you can think again.' When Cardinal Winning of Glasgow visited, we were discussing the levanter which is similar to a sirocco and which makes you feel quite unwell and depressed and he said, 'Yes. You can't commit a cardinal sin in a sirocco.' The Archbishop of Canterbury, George Carey, and Eileen, came for the weekend and were excellent company. In his sermon he noted, 'I'm glad the media did not see me high on the Gibraltar Rock today because they would have seen one primate talking to a whole lot of other primates.' Overall there was an impressive measure of harmony between the religions, a little more than mere tolerance. Each religion or denomination was strongly rooted.

Gibraltar certainly creates a claustrophobic atmosphere, due partly to its smallness but also to continual Spanish harassment. We were pleased, therefore, to be able to drive quite easily across the frontier into Andalusia and to spend some weekends away from the territory. A visit to Cota Donana just south of Seville provided a wonderful display of birds, including flamingos and eagles. There was also an ever-present sense of deep and positive influence of 700 years of Arab presence. Andalusia, particularly Donana, reminds me always of North Africa. Indeed the geographic link is seldom far from one's sight as you look across the Straits to the Moroccan mountains.

Being Governor in the old days was a form of benign dictatorship. But in the UK overseas territory of today your powers are limited even though you carry ultimate responsibility. Much of my work required taking a keen interest in their diverse lives and using my powers of tact and persuasion to move things forward. Nevertheless in one way or another I was involved in a wide range of issues from the police, drugs, prisons and the environment, to the law and tourism. Peter Caruana did much to strengthen the non-defence economy and I worked with him to ensure high standards of regulation of the offshore business and generally to encourage the visits of cruise ships and tourists as well as the traditional bunkering in the harbour. In my role representing the Queen, I had to do a Christmas broadcast from the Convent, and visit with Rose the hospitals and the old people's homes on Christmas Day. Gibraltarians are great money raisers and Rose became heavily involved in working with charities. For her, playing bridge in Gibraltar and Sotogrande was a good way of making friends with Gibraltarians.

I was very glad to have the help of distinguished judges like John Waite and Brian Neill on the Court of Appeal and of British Attorney General Ricky Rhoda and Police Commissioner Alan Castree.

Looking back now, I am so glad that I took this job, notwithstanding the considerable strains and intensity of relationships with the elected Administration and the British and Spanish Governments. Gibraltarians are the salt of the earth and deserve a more harmonious future with their Spanish neighbours. They have now adjusted to having civilian Governors and to a more diverse economy. There is an Anglo-Spanish interest in encouraging economic cooperation in the region and who knows what could emerge from a more harmonious atmosphere in the future. The alternative is a hiding to nothing for all parties. It is in Britain's interest to develop strong ties with Spain, but her responsibility towards Gibraltarians must never be forgotten.

Rose and I felt very moved and sad as we sailed away in HMS *Northumberland* on 20 March 2000 with the band striking up the National Anthem, surrounded by tugs and ships making a great cacophony of noise and farewell. The Queen Mother told us that when she and Prince Albert sailed out of Gibraltar in 1927 the band played the hymn 'Now Thank We All Our God'. They weren't sure whether they were thanking God for their presence or departure. But, for our part, Rose and I thank God that we had an opportunity to serve the valiant Gibraltarians. They remain much in our thoughts and the Luce Foundation gives us a permanent link with the younger generation.

Late in the afternoon of the day of departure a Lynx helicopter took off from the rear deck of HMS *Northumberland* and flew us to Faro airport in South Portugal where the ADC and others had brought our car to the villa of Asa and Susan Briggs. After a few days' rest we travelled north to the UK.

17

The Monarchy

On leaving Gibraltar in March 2000 at the age of sixty-three I had not planned on taking up another job. We spent much of the summer sorting out our house and garden and seeing friends.

Towards the end of July David Airlie rang me and asked me whether I would allow my name to be considered for Lord Chamberlain. I hadn't seen David for years and was startled by his approach. I formed the impression that it was a very part-time job and had little idea what it involved. Discussions with David and Robin Janvrin (Private Secretary) helped me to clear my mind. It was a substantial job and I began to realise that I was excited to be offered a new challenge and that probably I was not yet ready for full retirement. The job, although bigger than I realised, did however allow me long weekends at home, which I much valued.

The appointment is made by the Prime Minister but at the Queen's request. Until 1924 the Lord Chamberlain was appointed by the Prime Minister after each general election. It was more of a political appointment, but of course the Bedchamber crisis of 1839 demonstrated the dangers of linking Royal Household appointments to political parties. By early August Blair was on holiday in Italy but he eventually approved and announced the appointment. I agreed to take up the post on 1 October and, in the meantime, the Queen invited us to Balmoral in early September for a relaxed short visit and made us feel very welcome. Princess Margaret was also staying there.

Since I was hazy about the job, I can only imagine readers will be too. I will therefore try to summarise it as best I can. It has evolved even in recent times. The Lord Chamberlain is head of Her Majesty's Household. To that end he works with five heads of department who constitute the Lord Chamberlain's Committee and who are responsible for the effectiveness of all aspects of the Royal Household. They are the Queen's Private Secretary, Sir Robin Janvrin, who is the principal advisor to the Queen and who also handles the press; the

Comptroller, now Colonel Ford and mainly Sir Malcolm Ross in my time, who is responsible for all the ceremonial aspects of the monarchy, including investitures; the Master, now Air Vice Marshal David Walker and earlier Vice Admiral Sir Tom Blackburn, who looks after all the hosting of events and functions on behalf of the Queen; the Keeper of the Privy Purse, Alan Reid and before that Sir Michael Peat, who looks after all the financial management of the Household including the Civil List and the Privy Purse; and the Director of the Royal Collection, Sir Hugh Roberts, who is responsible for the supervision of the vast collection and for making it as accessible as possible to the public.

The Lord Chamberlain acts as a kind of part-time chairman of the Royal Household with the Committee setting the strategy and policy for the Household under the overall direction of the Queen. It is this last aspect that makes the job unique. In my view the job requires a sensitive touch for, apart from the ultimate accountability to the Queen for the performance of the Household, the Lord Chamberlain's real value is to act as a facilitator of decision-making. This means that he must not act as a chief executive; that he must help the Queen to appoint really competent heads of department and then delegate maximum responsibility to them. At the same time he must be available to give advice or to consult the Queen whenever necessary and to be ready to step in if a problem develops. It is essential to establish a good working relationship with the Monarch and to develop a natural chemistry. It takes a little time to discover on what issues the Queen likes to be consulted, to decide or to be informed and where she would prefer the Lord Chamberlain to take a decision and to get on with it. The system also works best if all heads of department have direct access to the Queen and can consult her when necessary. It is the Private Secretary who must act as the main daily link and adviser to the Queen. It is also important to keep in touch with other members of the Royal Family and where necessary to give advice on any problem.

The Lord Chamberlain also has a number of other duties. He is Chancellor of the Royal Victorian Order and as such recommends to the Queen appointments to that Order. Every four years or so there is a service in Windsor Chapel for the Order which the Queen attends, and an annual service in the Savoy Chapel. The Lord Chamberlain is also the link between the Sovereign and the House of Lords; his job is to communicate messages both ways. For example, after each State Opening of Parliament the House of Lords sends a message of thanks to the Queen in response to the Queen's Speech. I would then reply on her behalf by reading out her message at the Government despatch box and then handing it to the Lord Chancellor, now the Lord Speaker. I replied on Her Majesty's behalf to the Lords' message of sympathy on the deaths of the Queen Mother and Princess Margaret. More unusually I read out a statement of approval from the Queen on the election and appointment of the first Lord Speaker, Baroness Hayman, in early July 2006. On that occasion I sat between the Lord Chancellor, Lord Falconer, and the Leader, Lady Amos, and remained on the front bench while other speeches followed my statement.

The Vice Chamberlain is always a Government Whip, and therefore during my time a Labour MP, and provides a link with the Queen by writing a brief daily report of the House of Commons proceedings. No such equivalent exists for the Lords though I regarded it as my job to keep her posted of any major developments. I should also stress that there is a Lord Great Chamberlain, as this sometimes causes confusion. He is responsible for the conduct of royal affairs at the Palace of Westminster. His role is limited nowadays to a ceremonial one. It is a hereditary job which involves only three families. In the Queen's reign it is the Cholmondeley family. The Carringtons will take the role for the next Monarch.

The job also includes being Deputy Chairman of the Trustees of the Royal Collection. It is chaired by the Prince of Wales and meets three times a year. To demonstrate the Prince's commitment, not once did I have to take his place in six years doing the job. The collection has about a million objects of art, mostly owned by the Queen in her capacity as Monarch, and a good deal of effort is made to show interesting objects to the public through exhibitions and loans. During the Golden Jubilee in 2002 two new Queen's Galleries were opened in Buckingham Palace and the Palace of Holyroodhouse, thus giving much more scope for public access and exhibitions.

Of all the great offices of State, the Lord Chamberlain is the one job which remains today one of substance. The title stems from the Middle Ages. Even in the time of Edward the Confessor Monarchs had a chamber in which the King's jewels, funds, papers and other valuables were kept. The Household official in charge of this chamber came to be called the King's Chamberlain and later other duties were added. From the twelfth century onwards the Lord Chamberlain's role developed. He became an important political figure as the King's spokesman in Council and in Parliament.

My impression is that in postwar years the role of the Lord Chamberlain has acquired more responsibilities and was developed more fully under Lord Airlie. One task, however, was fortunately dropped in 1968. My then predecessor Lord Cobbold and the Home Secretary, Roy Jenkins, agreed that the Lord Chamberlain would no longer have the role as licenser of stage plays produced anywhere in Great Britain, a position which gave him absolute control. This was a relief, because I would not have been able to take the job had I been given such powers of censorship. Having advocated the need for the arts to be as independent as possible from Government when I was Arts Minister, it would have been hypocritical for me to take the job with these powers. Moreover, it seemed to be that this historical role going back to the seventeenth century would have increasingly brought the Monarch into unnecessary and often embarrassing controversy.

I was the seventh Lord Chamberlain during the Queen's reign. In his thirteen distinguished years David Airlie modernised the job as well as the Queen's finances and the management of the Royal Household. Tom Camoys succeeded him as the first Roman Catholic Lord Chamberlain since the sixteenth century. Sadly he was unwell and had to retire early.

The long history of the office explains the nature of my appointment. In August 2000 the Queen made me a life peer, an appointment for which I took the oath in mid-October with Jack Weatherill (former Speaker) and Robert Fellowes (former Private Secretary to the Queen) as my sponsors. To maintain the need for impartiality in the office, I became a crossbencher but, as I have explained, with no right by convention to speak or vote until after retirement. On the Queen's return to Buckingham Palace from Balmoral in early October, during an audience, she officially installed me as Lord Chamberlain. The symbols of office included a white stave, a light strip of willow, which appears to have been carried in previous centuries by senior courtiers and which indicates status and authority. On the death of a Monarch, that stave is broken over the Monarch's coffin to indicate the end of a reign. I was present in 2002 when Robin Crawford, as the Queen Mother's Lord

Chamberlain, unscrewed his stave in two halves (but he was later allowed to retain it). The Queen also presented me with a sizeable key which is worn on State occasions on the coat tail of the morning coat or tails. This is supposedly the key which unlocks the door to the Monarch's private belongings in the chamber. On every State occasion such as a State banquet or the arrival of a Head of State, I carried the stave and wore the key. I was also awarded the GCVO in my capacity as Chancellor of the Royal Victorian Order.

There are two other great offices of State worth mentioning: the Lord Steward and the Earl Marshal. The Lord Steward was Lord Ridley when I arrived and the Duke of Abercorn for most of my time. It used to be a powerful job but today it is more titular. At a State banquet he receives all the guests and introduces them to the Queen and the Duke of Edinburgh. He then accompanies me in leading the Queen and the guest Head of State with other Royals and guests to the banquet. James Abercorn has been a wonderful friendly support and encouragement, as was Matthew Ridley.

Eddie Norfolk took over as Earl Marshal after his father's death during my time. He has taken a serious grip on the job, which is to be responsible for the State funeral of the Monarch and the Coronation of the new Monarch. To fulfil that task he would have the support of the Lord Chamberlain and all the relevant Household staff – we would all be at his disposal.

My six years in the job were quite eventful. When I first arrived both the Earl of Wessex and the Duke of York were on the verge of a change of direction in their lives. The Duke of York was leaving the Navy and wanting to establish a new role in his life. He agreed to head the promotion of trade and investment overseas on behalf of the country, working closely and in coordination with the Department of Trade and Industry. He has thrown himself into the job vigorously and has been tireless in promoting business in all parts of the world from the Gulf to Russia and China. The Earl of Wessex had a more difficult decision. In view of his interest in the arts, television and cinema he had established a business called Ardent, to do with the production of films for television and cinema. Meanwhile, the Countess was fairly busy with a PR firm which she had established before her marriage. I was sympathetic to the view that modern Royals should want to prove that they can achieve their ambitions like others. But in reality it is not really tenable to balance being a Royal on the one hand and a businessman on the other. I much admired the Wessexes for their bold decision to cut their losses and concentrate wholly on fulfilling their royal duties, which they do admirably. I was only too sorry that they had to face so much media attention while they made up their minds.

Our main challenge when I arrived was to plan for the 2002 Golden Jubilee celebrations. Robin Janvrin and Michael Peat took the lead in this although we invited Lord Sterling to coordinate many of the plans for the Jubilee weekend itself, in particular the pageant and the organisation for the huge crowds in the Mall.

Just before the celebrations began in the spring we saw the deaths of Princess Margaret and, some weeks later, the Queen Mother. The Princess's funeral service took place in St George's Chapel at Windsor. My role was to lead the coffin procession, accompanied by my wand, down the steps and then accompany the Dean of Windsor, David Connor, for the final burial. Earlier I was present for the arrival of the coffin at Queen's Chapel where it lay for a few days. It was sad that the Princess died first, with the brave Queen Mother wheeled into the service looking worn but courageous.

The timing of the Queen Mother's death was impeccable – over Easter, and just before the beginning of the celebrations. Her State funeral was deeply moving. I accompanied the Queen and the Duke of Edinburgh at Westminster Hall for a short ceremony for the lying-in-state. The most striking and moving part of the proceedings was the large number of people queuing to view the coffin, and most remarkable of all was my experience driving from the Abbey to Windsor Chapel, following the coffin some twenty-four miles, with the whole route lined by people. I drove with the Dean of Windsor behind the Prince of Wales's car. Through Parliament Square, Whitehall and the Mall there was a stunning silence where thousands of people watched quietly and paid their respects. As we got towards Gloucester Road people began to clap. Later, on the outskirts of London, cars stopped on the far side of the dual carriageway and people stood with their heads bowed and sometimes their hats off. It was a true cross-representation of the British population: men, women, children, Asians, Caribbeans of all ages. Later that day there was a service in the Chapel and the Queen Mother was buried next to King George VI in a side chapel. There was only room there for the Dean, Robin Crawford, to break the wand, and me. The Queen and immediate family watched through the bars of the chapel; the end of a remarkable life.

All through those early months of 2002 the media were exceedingly gloomy and pessimistic about the forthcoming celebrations, rather assuming that the public was not interested. But the team ploughed on with their plans and, as is now known, the summer was an outstanding success. Above all the Thanksgiving Service at St Paul's where James Abercorn and I led the Queen and Duke up the aisle to a moving service, lunch at the Guildhall with the Lord Mayor and a truly successful weekend with a classics concert one day and a pop concert to follow, with a pageant down the Mall to Buckingham Palace over the weekend. Thousands upon thousands turned up in the Mall, young and old. Meanwhile the country celebrated in towns and villages. As the Queen hoped, it got people together as a community.

The decision of the Prince of Wales and Camilla Parker Bowles to marry in April 2005 was broadly welcomed by the public. Notwithstanding all the difficulties in the weeks prior to the wedding, the day itself was a happy occasion and the marriage seems subsequently to have been widely welcomed by the public. The Monarchy is all the stronger for it.

Alice Duchess of Gloucester died aged over 100, followed shortly after by Angus Ogilvy after a long illness. I played the same role for them at a Windsor Chapel funeral and final burial in the Frogmore grounds.

In my last few months, the summer of 2006, there were most successful celebrations of the Queen's eightieth birthday, including public and private celebrations at Windsor Castle, a special fly past after the Queen's birthday celebrations, an appropriate thanksgiving service in St Paul's and a lunch at Mansion House, a children's literature occasion in the Palace gardens and many other special events. We also marked the Duke of Edinburgh's eighty-fifth birthday in June and they both sailed off on a private cruise at the end of July. Although tiring, it was an exceedingly happy summer in the knowledge that the public and media were at one in supporting the Queen. To see a relatively benign media was almost beyond belief. More important than anything else was to see the Queen embark upon her eighties looking happy, strong and self-confident and knowing that the nation was behind her and hugely appreciative of the quiet leadership and continuity that she had provided over the fifty-five years of her reign. It was a satisfactory time for me to take my leave aged seventy and to hand over to Lord Peel as my successor.

Through this relatively happy period for the Monarchy, my job was to work closely with all the heads of department and the staff to ensure that we gave the Queen and the Royal Family the most professional support possible to enable her to do her job. There were all the many routine annual events from the opening of Parliament and investitures to garden parties and State visits. During my time State visits included King Abdullah of Jordan, President Mbeki of South Africa, President Bush, President Lula of Brazil, President Chirac, the President of Poland, President Hu of China and the King and Queen of Norway. All these occasions or functions need to be performed at the highest level of competence by the staff. I felt very proud of them. We all sensed the privilege of serving the Queen and responded to her leadership.

The Lord Chamberlain's Committee, consisting of the five heads of department and the private secretaries to the Prince of Wales and Duke of Edinburgh, met under my chairmanship twice a month to give a sense of direction to the Household and to discuss any problems. Because the range of jobs in the Household is so wide-ranging, the five heads of department are talented people with very varying backgrounds and experience. Unlike a business or Government, it was crucial to channel all the talent available into working for one single cause – support of the Queen. As a team, those five heads of department were the most versatile range of people I have ever worked with. Importantly, too, they managed to create a pleasant atmosphere within the organisation, something on which the Queen sets the greatest store.

Of course there were many problems to tackle in my time, ranging from lapses in security, to strengthening leadership in middle management, to opening up wider career prospects for the staff, to improving the management of departments and coordination between the different Royal Households. Certainly the Household is more of a bureaucracy today and less of a personal family business – which I regret, but professionalism requires specialist teams in areas like security, personnel and health and safety.

I think also that the mechanism for the Royal Family to work efficiently together is improving. Regular meetings each year take place between the Queen and the Prince of Wales, while once a year before

Christmas all the active members of the Royal Family meet under the leadership of the Queen and the Duke with senior staff to air any outstanding issues.

The Lord Chamberlain's office is in the corridor on the north side of the Palace on the first floor. It is a very quiet area as my only other neighbours were the Duke of Edinburgh next door with his considerable library and office and the Queen's private quarters and study at the far end of the passage. My excellent PA, Elizabeth Ash, was surrounded by a remarkable collection of Indian swords, jewellery and ivory, presented to the Prince of Wales, later King Edward VII, in 1875 on his visit to India, given mainly by the princes of that country. There was no typical day in the office as the work was very varied. The most active period was for eight months when the Queen was resident in Buckingham Palace during the week and Windsor at weekends. Ceremonial work would include investitures of which there are about twenty-six every year. I accompanied the Queen and stood just to the right of her and a little behind to read all the citations of those receiving awards. Although the actual ceremony is about an hour, the whole process took up most of the morning and usually ended with my having a meeting with the Queen in her private study to discuss any business that I needed to raise with her. It would also provide an opportunity for her to raise matters with me on family affairs, national matters or in particular about Household policy or staffing.

Garden parties in the summer would involve my introducing the Queen to small groups of people organised by the Gentlemen Ushers and last about an hour before having tea in the royal tent and meeting distinguished VIPs. State visits were always busy on the first day when the Queen would introduce the Head of State to senior members of the Household, led by me, to be followed by drinks and a relaxed round table lunch. In the evening the State banquet for 170 guests would involve all guests first meeting the Queen and the Head of State, followed by a banquet in the Ballroom or St George's Hall at Windsor. After leading out the Queen and Head of State I would then introduce some guests to the Queen while the Lord Steward would do the same for the Head of State. I was glad to have a bedroom and bathroom where I could change in the Palace.

Visiting staff in their offices in Buckingham Palace, Windsor Castle, St James's and Holyrood was always important for it enabled me to see how the various offices were working and to get to know the staff. I hosted drinks parties, often helped by Rose, to try to get the staff to mix together more as a team.

Paperwork involved a wide range of issues but might include signing royal warrants, reviewing the Queen's programme for the forthcoming six-month period, considering security issues, approving changes in staff, looking at policy for motivating the staff, considering a particular problem involving a member of the Royal Family or how to respond to a particular national crisis or a media criticism. The range of issues was endless but usually interesting. It was always helpful to have individual meetings with heads of department and other senior staff to discuss policy and issues.

When the Queen was working from Sandringham at Christmas or Balmoral in the summer or Windsor Castle over Easter, it was occasionally necessary for me to visit her to discuss various issues. In early September 2005 we both stayed with her at Balmoral for the weekend when the Prime Minister and Mrs Blair were guests. On a fine evening she and the Duke would entertain in one of their small bothies with casual clothes. If it rained we would change for dinner. Although she continued to do paperwork and some official engagements, it was a chance for the Queen and Duke to relax happily in a more homely setting.

Although I believe that the Queen is strongly supported by the British public who appreciate her dedicated service and sense of duty, there is a lack of knowledge, especially among the younger generation, of the role of a Monarch. I made a point of making a few speeches to specially chosen audiences to test this out. It is important I think to get across her role as Head of State and Head of the Nation as well as her task as Head of the Commonwealth and as Supreme Governor of the Church of England. Most striking of all is the sense of continuity and stability that she has provided over fifty-five years with a rapidly changing country. It is a reassuring achievement.

Epilogue

I count myself supremely fortunate to have led such a varied and interesting life. Looking back over seventy years I feel I owe everything first to my parents for providing a secure framework and giving me the support and courage to climb the mountain, and secondly to Rose. I cannot describe adequately in words what her support, love and companionship through our nearly fifty years of marriage have meant to me. I could not have managed my work in Africa, the struggle to get into Parliament, politics, being a Minister, a Vice-Chancellor, a Governor or Lord Chamberlain without her.

A secure and happy family life is a foundation which I could not have done without. Nowadays, with the welcome arrival of equal opportunity for men and women, we see husbands and wives pursuing different careers. But Rose has managed to demonstrate that it is possible to continue successfully with the tradition of former generations by giving two for the price of one in so many of the jobs that I have done. Much of course depends on the nature of the job but in my case it has worked and my roles have been helped immeasurably by Rose, thus making our family life even more stimulating and fun.

Despite all her support for me in the constituency, as a Minister and in my other jobs, Rose carved out a life for herself, working for the English-Speaking Union and becoming its acting chairman, supporting the Fairbridge and Venture Trusts for adventure training and getting heavily involved as president of many charities in Gibraltar. She did not go to university but made up for it by successfully doing a course in English literature at Birkbeck College. Later she joined the council of the University of Buckingham and became involved in particular with alumni since she had played a major role in entertaining students while at the university. Music has also given her great pleasure, singing alto in the Bach Choir, the St Paul's Knightsbridge Choir and the Parliamentary Choir.

Rose and I have two sons, Alexander and Edward, who have made a break from the traditions of our family in recent generations. Alexander is a fully qualified and committed nutritionist, demonstrating to patients how this form of specialism can improve their health and quality of life. Edward became a journalist and has worked for the *Financial Times* in the Philippines, India and the United States. His Indian wife, Priya Basu, works for the World Bank and no doubt inspired Edward to write a book about contemporary India entitled *In Spite of the Gods: The Strange Rise of Modern India*.

Two things, then, above all have buttressed me through exciting but often difficult times: the first, a happy, loving family fulfilling themselves and supporting each other when necessary; the second, a home that has been a haven of peace in contrast to the outside world and has enabled me to recharge batteries, to relax and to reflect. Privacy is important to me.

But, in a very material age, how important is religion? For my part I draw strength and comfort not only in the compelling story of Christ but in the belief that there is some kind of God, a supreme intelligence of some form. No power of reason alone can tell us what form it takes; only faith and belief can guide us. I find it hard to believe that we as humans disappear into an empty nothingness but it is equally hard to imagine, if we have souls, what form it takes and how we make contact with all our relatives and friends. When told that his grandmother had died Edward came to life with the remark 'Lucky Granny. Even now she will be having tea with Admiral Lord Nelson.' This was an unlikely set of circumstances to imagine, especially those who knew Katharine Nicholson. Equally I loved my cousin Lennox Napier's advice. When asked by a six-year-old contemporary how you know where to go when you die, he said 'Ask at the information desk.'

My mother once awoke from a dream about her brother Trevie who died in the war, and told me later that she knew he was all right but could not describe in what way. Like her mother, she too was spiritual though not particularly fussed about going to church. She had a simple guideline in life. We should always be sure that none of our decisions and actions hurt other people unnecessarily or deliberately. To translate this into action is not always easy. It is a good benchmark for our private and family life but creates a more complex challenge in our public life. For sometimes it is necessary to persuade people that their talents are not being fulfilled in their current job and that they should move on. That is painful but it may be kinder in the long term.

There are from time to time experiences in this world that have led me to believe that something supreme quite beyond us must have created these circumstances. We have all no doubt met some people with a kind of saintliness in them which is inspiring. Sitting on a bench in a garden on a fine summer's day watching the dragonflies dancing round a pond, the swallows dive bombing for water, the many colours of the flowers, the fruit trees, listening to the one-noted buzz of the bees, it is strange if we don't ask ourselves who can have created such utter beauty and peace.

But then by contrast to see the utter evil that exists in the world from violence between individuals to genocide in the Balkans or Africa. Mankind has the ability to distinguish good from evil. It is true, as Lord Hailsham once said, that 'those who try to create Heaven on earth end up by creating Hell on earth'. But there must be some reason why we believe it is an important ambition to live a good life behaving decently and understandingly towards our fellow human beings and where possible doing our little bit to leave a better world. I was struck by a notice above a carpenter in his shop in the city of Belize which said, 'Some carve out a career for themselves. Others just chip away.' Each of us can contribute to a better world by just chipping away.

The qualities that I most admire and which I believe are most needed are humility, self-discipline, humour, a sense of responsibility and service, and showing real interest in our fellow human beings. There is much truth in Bonhoeffer's saying 'Only through discipline may a man learn to be free'. Dependence on drugs, alcohol, self-centredness will immediately imprison you in that practice. At the end of the day I feel that we must be able to laugh at ourselves and allow humour to get us through adversity. The assistant private secretary who said to me 'Minister, there is something that is worrying you because you have been cracking jokes all day' was most perceptive.

I wonder if the reader would agree that one of the most serious contemporary problems is the prevalence of self-centredness and that we would be a much happier society if more of us could look outwards rather than inwards. I am conscious of my own failings in this. It goes back to my mother telling me, when I was thirteen, that my shyness was really a kind of self-centredness and that, in shaking hands with someone, it was best to look at the person and wonder what made them tick rather than look at the ground and think of oneself.

Our strengths and weaknesses are influenced by genes and our upbringing. My own real failure at school has probably brought out four characteristics in me: a pessimism which enables me to expect difficulties but relief when it turns out better than expected; a fragile confidence in myself or my abilities; a contempt for vanity; and an admiration for achievement and leadership. On this latter point it is certainly true that I respect those who fight their way to the pinnacle of their ambitions – whether to be a Prime Minister, a chairman of a big company or a Service chief. But, in recent times, I have come to admire even more those who cope with personal adversity. I have friends and relations who have faced every kind of difficulty and handicap in life but who, instead of bitterness and envy, have shown courage and generosity towards others. They won't accept failure. They fall down. They get up again. These are the real winners.

The truth is that we don't know how we can cope with adversity unless and until we are confronted by it. One modest experience of mine has been a bad back since the age of thirty-four. This is nothing compared to the suffering of others, but it has given me an interest in the subject of pain. My old friend Phyllis Pearsall, the inventor of the A to Z maps, was written off as dead in an air crash after the war. She recovered and lived for another fifty years, but with a most painful back. I asked her how she coped with it. In a nutshell, she said you must divert the pain's attentions. I told her that was easier during the day when you are occupied but what about the night? 'My dear,' she said, 'I read the Bible all night.' The Carthusian Father Prior in our neighbouring monastery takes an opposite view – that you must not fight against pain but accept the suffering. Perhaps the answer is both. Certainly when the pain is relieved it sharpens one's understanding and interest in others' suffering.

Many of us are conscious that religion has been, throughout the ages, one of the greatest causes of bloodshed and conflict. It never ceases to amaze me that people can believe that God treats them as chosen people or looks only after those who support a specific religion. What about the billions who belong to other religions all over the world? Why should God apply to us and not to them? The Prince of

Wales has done a valuable service by drawing attention to the fact that Christians, Jews and Mohammedans share the same roots of faith in one God, the God of Abraham. The Holy Koran has a verse 'O Mankind! We created you from a single pair of a male and female, and made you into nations and tribes, that ye may know each other.' It doesn't say that 'ye may despise each other'. What we should be seeking, he stresses, is unity through diversity. From the strength of our own faith, we should be seeking to understand each other's religions. For example, why on earth cannot all Christians share the same Communion? And why need the Sunni and Shia be so divided simply through a dispute about the line of succession from Mohammed? There are big differences that need to be understood and discussed; for example, how to reconcile the Shia view that integrates religion, politics and society, with the Lutheranism of Europe where the individual is free to make his own political choice. The starting point must be respect for each other's religions and a conscious effort to create more mutual understanding. Tolerance is the key.

A visit to the Galapagos in January 2003 helped Rose and me to think more about Darwin and evolution as against the creationists. I think the problem only arises if you take the Old Testament of the Bible literally. Add to this a subject which causes me wonder and fascination – astronomy – and we really have to think hard. The Astronomer Royal recently wrote a book which suggested that there is more than one universe. I have always thought that space must be infinite. If not, then what happens on the other side of the wall? It is a matter of unbelievable wonder to look at the stars on a clear night and contemplate how this has come about, what life exists on other planets or galaxies and how we are but an infinitesimal part of the whole. Look back at ourselves from outer space and we look in awe at our earth, its beauty but its intense vulnerability. With that perspective, it should unite the infinite variety of people in the world to respect and improve our environment, to live in peace with each other and to work for a better and more just life. There are some who are frightened by outer space. I would like to know and discover so much more. Over the centuries modern technology will enable us to do just that. In that way, we may learn more about ourselves, about mankind and about God.

It is encouraging that so many people still respect Remembrance Sunday. For I remain conscious that my parents' and grandparents' generations faced unthinkable horror through two World Wars and that the twentieth century produced human monsters like Hitler, Stalin, Mao and Pol Pot. So many died to save civilisation. It is perhaps our memory of their sacrifice that should spur us on to fight for a better way of life and international peace.

Today we face different kinds of difficulties ranging from international terrorism, the failure of States, the drugs trade, a collapse in values and faith and a threat to our planet through climate change. More inspired leadership should face us with the truth and give us hope that there is light at the end of the tunnel. Moreover the reassuring thing is that each of us can contribute in our own way, for everyone has something to give.

Appendix

You will have seen inside the service paper the picture of the memorial plaque in the Abbey Cloisters which was unveiled by Her Majesty on 23 March 1966. The tablet is dedicated to all those who served the Crown in the colonial territories and the inscription reads 'Whosoever will be chief among you let him be your servant'.

This inscription refers of course to the great sense of service and duty given by the many thousands of members of HM Colonial Service, later HM Overseas Civil Service, over 160 years. As the Union Jack came down on 30 June 1997 in Hong Kong, so that Service came to an end. Today there are over 25,000 overseas Service officers and widows, many of whom are here this morning.

We are here today to commemorate the dedicated work of such people.

This is not the time, in recalling the work of former colonial servants, to discuss the merits or demerits of the Empire. Suffice it to say that these men and women worked in the largest territorial empire the world has ever seen though in relative historical terms it was very short, compared for example with the Roman Empire.

For much of the time there was surprising ignorance in Britain about our Colonial Empire. Many people will have heard great tales of military exploits. But very few would have heard of the unsung heroes who quietly got on with the practical job of building roads and railways, running schools and hospitals or of creating courts where justice was dispensed.

Her Majesty's Colonial Service, which can be traced back to the introduction of Standard Colonial Regulations in 1837, was the oldest of all the overseas services. The Indian Civil Service and the Sudan Civil Service followed later.

Throughout the nineteenth century it was a surprisingly small service, made up principally of administrative officers and supported by medical and legal officers. Nonetheless, the Colonial Service at its height in the 1920s covered forty territories, principally in Africa, the Caribbean, Asia and the Pacific. By 1937 the unified Service was responsible for over sixty million people in two million square miles of territory.

After the Second World War the Service expanded dramatically to embrace a wide range of professional services, as British financial support was introduced for development. To mark the rapid transition to independence of many countries the Service was in 1954 renamed Her Majesty's Overseas Civil Service. The newly published book *On Crown Service* by Anthony Kirk-Greene provides an excellent history of the Service.

The heart of the Empire was the District Officer supported by the professional services. Reading the diaries of former administrators brings home the nature and significance of their work and the kind of people who set off to run the Empire. The most striking thing is the scale of responsibility given to young people in the then remote regions of the world. I was the last of three British District Officers to join the Kenya Civil Service. At the age of twenty-four I was second in command of Isiolo District with a population of 70,000.

There was no such thing as a typical day for an administrator. Let them speak for themselves. Leonard Woolf was administrator of Hambautoto District in Ceylon in the early 1900s – 100,000 people in 1,000 square miles – any day he could have been involved in customs, collecting revenue, authorising expenditure, police, prisons, local government, roads, irrigation, Crown lands, welfare, law and order, fisheries, wildlife, and court cases. He wrote: 'I worked all day from the moment I got up in the morning until I went to bed at night, for I rarely thought of anything else except the District and the people, to increase their prosperity, diminish poverty and disease, start irrigation works, open schools... I did not idealise or romanticise the people or the country; I just like them aesthetically and humanly and socially.'

Then there was Vincent Glenday in Northern Kenya, who, in

response to an idealisation of the District Officer, said 'Cut all that out and what is left: my job; and that is as clear as the day – to maintain law and order, to keep the wells open and to improve the condition of the people – it is enough for me.'

Then there is Mr Cairns who was a District Commissioner in Tanganyika in the 1950s. He records: 'All day people spill into these offices, like water over a dam, and when their problems are finished they are replaced by others...' As an afterthought, he says 'Bush living, like olives, is an acquired taste.' Mr Cairns was a Canadian. By the 1930s quite a few administrators were recruited from the Dominions.

In my own district in Northern Kenya in the early '60s I recall with pleasure the sheer human warmth and humour of the Africans. Two tribes were fighting and killing each other over a precious water hole. Imperiously I summoned the headmen and their followers to sit under a baobab tree while I lectured them angrily and probably pompously in Swahili about the need to stop fighting and to share the water. At the end an African at the back asked a question. 'Bwana,' he said, 'you tell us to stop fighting. Can you explain how it is that in Europe you have fought two world wars this century?' The game was up. I said 'You win' and they all went off in peals of laughter to share the water in peace. Perhaps I realised in my subconscious at that moment that the Empire was coming to a close.

I have given the picture of the District Officer as the hub of the Empire. But the administrator could not have done his job without the support of the men and women professionals in the Service – agriculturalists, engineers, foresters, doctors, surveyors, lawyers, geologists, architects, school teachers, prison and police officers to give just a few examples.

Nor should we forget today two other supporting services: first the Corona Club whose closure we mark this month after a centenary of existence, set up in 1900 to provide a dining club and meeting place for existing and former members of the Service; and secondly Corona Worldwide whose Jubilee we mark and which was established to support wives and children living in overseas colonial territories and which now offers a service in over 100 countries.

Who were these people who went out to serve the Empire? What motivated them? The late Sir Ralph Furse was the architect of the recruitment policies for the Colonial Service this century. Personal qualities were the key – examination results were less important than character. The personal interview was the means of selection. Sir Ralph describes the type they were looking for 'the challenge of adventure, the urge to prove himself in the face of hardship and risk to health, of loneliness often and not infrequently danger; the chance of dedicating himself to the service of his fellow men and the responsibility at an early age on a scale life at home could scarcely ever offer'.

Most of these officers, supported valiantly by their wives, set off for some remote region of Africa, South East Asia, the Caribbean or the Pacific to serve the people most of them came to love. I recall visiting a carpenter's shop in Belize and an inscription above the carpenter read 'Some carve out a career for themselves; others just chip away.' All of us in our different ways just chipped away. We tried to leave something for the future. Above all we wanted to be remembered for justice, fairness and incorruptibility. It is against those standards that the Service would wish to be judged.

I was therefore struck by the tribute of the then Prime Minister of Nigeria, Sir Abubakar Tafawa Balewa, in his speech at Independence. He expressed gratitude 'to the British officers whom we have known, first as masters and then as leaders and finally as partners but always as friends'. That tribute speaks for itself.

But it was the transformation of an Empire into a Commonwealth of equal partners which can perhaps be seen as the Service's greatest legacy. Arnold Smith, the first Secretary General of the Commonwealth, wrote in his book *Stitches in Time*, published in 1981: '100 years from now, I suggest, historians will consider the Commonwealth the greatest of all Britain's contributions to man's social and political history.'

If that prognosis is anywhere near the truth, then the foundations were laid by the thousands of officers of Her Majesty's Overseas Civil Service. It is entirely appropriate that we should remember them today with respect, pride and thankfulness.

Index

Abdullah of Jordan, King, 173
Abercorn, James, 5th Duke of, 170, 172
Acheson, Dean, 42–3
Ackroyd, Dame Elizabeth, 71
Acland, Sir Antony, 141
Adamson, Terence, 55
Aden, 16, 38–40
Ahtisaari, Martti, 104
Aird, Sir Alistair, 155
Airlie, David, 13th Earl of, 166, 169
Ake, Simeon, 86
Alcantara, Judge John E., 156
Alexandra, HRH Princess, 163
Amery, John, 81
Amery, Julian, Baron, 81, 96
Amin, Idi, 105
Amos, Valerie, Baroness, 168
Andrews, Eamonn, 69
Angola, 90–1
Arafat, Yasser, 97–8
Arap Moi, Daniel, 107
Armstrong, Robert, Baron, 131
Arundel and Shoreham constituency,
    adoption and campaign, 72–3
Ash, Elizabeth, 174
Atkins, Humphrey, Baron Colnbrook, 77,
    110, 141
Attenborough, Richard, Baron, 123
Attlee, Clement, 1st Earl, 48
Azhari, Prime Minister Ismail, 38

Baker, Kenneth, Baron, 121
Baldwin, Stanley, 1st Earl Baldwin of
    Bewdley, 44, 47
Balewa, Sir Abubakar Tafawa, 185
Balniel, see Crawford
Banda, Dr Hastings, 49
Barber, Anthony, Baron, 144
Barker, Noel, 72, 79
Barrett, Dave, British Columbia, 111
Barrett, Dr Michael, 148

Beamish, Sir Tufton, 74
Beloff, Max, Baron, 148–9
Belstead, John, 2nd Baron, 115
Bevan, Aneurin, 43, 119
Blackburn, Vice Admiral Sir Tom, 167
Blair, Tony, 126, 161, 162, 166, 175; and
    Cherie Blair, 175
Blaker, Peter, Baron, 105, 141
Blundell, Sir Michael, 54, 55
Bonfante, Major Andrew, 162, 163
Boscawen, Robert, 77, 113
Bossano, Joe, 156, 160, 161
Botha, Pik, 84–5
Botswana, 90
Boyd-Carpenter, John, Baron, 74
Boynton, Sir John, 91
Braine, Bernard, Baron, 111
Brezhnev, Leonid, 114
Briggs, Asa, Baron, 71; and wife Susan,
    165
Brighty, David, 155
British Library, 128–31
Brooks, Andrew and wife Helen, 57
Brown, Gordon, 161
Brown, Greta, 79
Brunei, 115–16
Brunei, Sultan of, 115–16; and father Sir
    Omah, 116
Buchan, Norman, 125
Buckingham, University of, 148–53
Bush, President George, Snr, 98, 112
Bush, President George W., Jnr, 112, 173
Butler, Matthew, 93
Butler, R. A., Baron, 49, 143
Butler, Robin, Baron, 131

Cairns, J. C., 184
Callaghan, James, Baron, 77, 80, 139
Cambridge, author at, 42–3
Camoys, Tom, 7th Baron, 169
Carden, D.C. ('Bill'), 87

Carey, Archbishop George and wife
    Eileen, 164
Carlos, King, of Spain, 159
Caribbean, author in, 107–9
Carrington, Peter, 6th Baron, 67, 80, 81,
    83–94 *passim*, 104, 108, 127, 135,
    138–43, 144, 145, 146
Caruana, Bishop Charles, 163
Caruana, Peter, (Gibraltar) Chief Minister,
    155, 156, 160–1, 164
Castree, Commissioner Alan, 165
Castro, Fidel, 107, 108
Chakulya, Minister, 84
Chalker, Lynda, Baroness, 117
Chamberlain, Neville, 47–8
Charles, Eugenia, 108
Charteris, Martin, Baron, 125
Chataway, Sir Christopher, 76
Chissano, Joaquim, 90–1
Chrétien, Jean, 110–11
Chung, Sir S. Y., 100–1
Churchill, Sir Winston, 15, 47, 48, 159
Churchill, Winston, 83, 159
Civil Service, 131–3
Clark, Alan, 140
Clarke, Kenneth, 74
Clements, Sir John, 19, 21
Clifford, Sir Timothy, 123
Coad, Major General B. A., 34
Cobbold, Cameron, 1st Baron, 169
Coe, Mark, 39
Colnbrook, *see* Atkins
Colquhoun, Maureen, 72
Colvin, Sir Michael and Lady, 121
Conlan, Bernard, 135–6
Connor, Rt Revd David, 171
Cook, Robin, 154, 161, 162
Cooper, Albert, 96
Cope, Sir John, 22
Cormack, Sir Patrick, 125
Cornish, Francis, 115
Cottrell, Elizabeth, 121
Coward, Sir Noël, 14
Cradock, Sir Percy, 103
Crawford, 28th Earl of, 45
Crawford, 29th Earl of, as Lord Balniel
    MP, 44–5; 169–70, 171–2
Cresswell, Jeremy, 137, 143
Crichton-Miller, Neil, 65
Crickhowell, *see* Edwards

Cuba, 107–8
Cuckney, John, Baron, 63
Culme-Seymour, Mary, later Napier,
    author's grandmother, 12
Cumber, Sir John, 91
Cyprus, 32–5

Dainton, Fred, Baron, 129
Davies, John, 78
Davis, David, 155
Davis, William, Ontario, 111
de Valera, Eamon, 43
Dench, Dame Judi, 123
Deng Xiaoping, 102
Dennis, C. C., Liberia, 86–7, 90, 91
Diggle, Nick, 155
Dilhorne, *see* Manningham-Buller
Dilks, David, 151
Dodds-Parker, Sir Douglas, 16
Donald, Sir Alan, 85
dos Santos, José Eduardo, Angola, 91
Douglas Home, Sir Alec, Lord Home of
    The Hirsel, 17, 20, 74–5, 77, 135
Douglas-Home, Charles, 142
Douglas-Home, Elizabeth, Lady, 74
Downey, Janis, 79
Dowson, John, 55–6
Draper, Dave, 132
Drumalbyn, Niall, 1st Baron, 113
du Cann, Sir Edward, 77
Duff, Sir Anthony, 88, 94
Dunn, Lydia, Baroness, 101
Durrell, Lawrence, 35

Eccles, David, 1st Viscount, 119, 128–9
Eden, Anthony, 1st Earl of Avon, 15, 62
Eddington, Paul, 133
Edinburgh, HRH Duke of, 151, 159, 170,
    171, 172, 173, 175
Edwards, Nicholas, Baron Crickhowell,
    121
Eisenhower, President Dwight D., 158–9
Elizabeth, HM The Queen Mother, 44,
    56, 165, 168, 169, 171–2
Elizabeth II, HM Queen, 98, 118, 126,
    151, 159, 166ff, 182
Elliott, Ian, 79
Emery, Sir Peter, 76
Enders, Tom, 112, 139
Eoka, 32–5

Fahd, King, of Saudi Arabia, 99
Fairbairn, John, 148
Falconer, Charles, Baron, 168
Faletau, Enoki, 118
Falklands, The, 134ff
Fearn, Sir Robin, 137, 141
Fellowes, Robert, Baron, 78, 169
Fifoot, Paul, 93
Fisher, Mark, 125–6
Fisher, Sir Nigel, 59, 125
Flannery, Martin, 107
Foot, Sir Hugh (later Baron Caradon), 35
Ford, Colonel Andrew, 167
Forster, E. M., 43
Fourie, Brand, 104
Franco, General Francisco, 158–9
Franks, Oliver, Baron, 144
Franks Report, 144, 145
Friedberger, Major General John, 28, 39, 44, 116
Furse, Sir Ralph, 184

Gaggero, Joe and James, 161
Galtieri, General Leopoldo, 138, 139, 140, 141
Gandhi, Rajiv, 127
Garel-Jones, Tristan, Baron, 120–1
Gibbs, Sir Humphrey, 80
Gibraltar, 154–65
Gielgud, Sir John, 123
Gilmour, Ian, Baron, 80, 88, 89, 93, 96
Glenday, Vincent, 183–4
Gloucester, HRH Princess Alice, Duchess of, 172
Gloucester, HRH Duke of (Prince Henry), 15
Gloucester, HRH Duke (Prince Richard) and Duchess of, 163
Gorbachev, Mikhail, 114
Gow, Ian, 141
Gowrie, Grey, 2nd Earl of, 119, 122, 129
Graham, Sir Richard, Bt, and Lady (Beatrice), 24
Grimond, Jo, Baron, 42
Grivas, Colonel George, 32
Greenwood, Arthur, 48
Gromyko, Andrei, 113
Guerrero, Lieutenant Colonel Eddie, 163
Gulf States, 40
Gummer, John, 74

Hadow, Sir Michael, 136
Haggard, Victor, 25
Haig, General Alexander, 139
Hailsham, 2nd Viscount, 28–9, 150
Hall, Sir Peter, 119–20, 121–2
Hanley, Sir Jeremy, 121
Hannam, Sir John, 110
Harding, Field Marshal 1st Baron, 33, 35
Harlech, David, 5th Baron, 85
Hart Dyke, David, 147
Hart Dyke, Diana, 'D', author's sister, 14, 23; in Sudan, 36–8; 147
Hassan, Sir Joshua, 161
Hastings, Sir Stephen, 81
Havers, Michael, Baron, 94
Hawley, Sir Donald, 41
Hayhoe, Barney, Baron, 74
Hayman, Baroness, 168
Hayter, Sir William, 19, 113
Helm, Sir Knox, 16
Heath, Sir Edward, 66, 67, 72, 76, 77, 80
Henderson, Charles, 120
Henderson, Mary, Lady, 109
Heseltine, Michael, Baron, 77, 98
Heyman, Sir Peter, 110
Hicks, Sir Robert, 113
Higgins, Terence, Baron, 148
Hitchin constituency, 64ff
Hitler, Adolf, 158
Hodson, Denys, 63
Hong Kong, 100–3
Houphouet-Boigny, Felix, 86
Howe, Geoffrey, Baron, 75–6, 97, 98, 100, 101–2, 110, 114, 148
Howe, Sir Robert, 15; and Lady Howe, 38
Howick, Evelyn (Baring),1st Baron, 53
Hu Jintao, President, 173
Huddleston, General Sir Hubert, 14
Hughes, Cledwyn, Baron Cledwyn, 113
Hume, Cardinal Basil, 163–4
Hunt, Sir Rex, 142–3
Hunter, Lieutenant Colonel T.M., 34
Hurd, Douglas, Baron, 72, 78, 102
Hurst, Barbara, 73
Hussein, King, 98, 142

Inge, Field Marshal Peter, Baron, 98–9, 155
Iraq, 99
Isaacs, Sir Jeremy, 124

Israel, author's visit to, 97–8
Ivory Coast, 86

Jackson, Major General Sir William, 154
Jamaica, 109
Janvrin, Robin, Baron, 166, 171
Jawara, President, of the Gambia, 105
Jeger, Lena, Baroness, 107
Jenkins, Roy, Baron, 130, 169
Jinnah, Mohammad Ali, 49
Johnson, Sir John, 53, 54
Johnson Smith, Sir Geoffrey, 64–5
Johnston, Sir Charles, 40, 157
Jordan, state visit to, 98
Jorge, Paulo, Angola, 90, 91
Joseph, Sir Keith, Bt, 66

Kaunda, Kenneth, 87, 90, 91–2
Kealey, Dr Terence, 152
Kemp, Sir Peter, 131, 132
Kenya, author in, 52–61
Kenyatta, Jomo, 54, 59
Kent, HRH Duke of, 162–3
Kerby, Henry, 72, 73
Khama, Seretse, 91
Khan, Dr Humayun, 118
Khrushchev, Nikita, 113
King, Tom, Baron, 74, 110
Kingmaker, The, 19, 20
Kinnock, Neil, Baron, 124
Kirk, Bill, 65
Kirk-Greene, Anthony, 183
Kirkpatrick, Jeane, 139
Klaus, Vaclav, 151
Klein, Rudolph, 68, 69

Lang, Jack, 126, 130–1
Lawson, Nigel, Baron, 121, 122, 124
Leach, Admiral Sir Henry, 141
Leahy, Sir John, 85
Lee, Jennie, Baroness, 119
Lee Kwan Yew, 116, 117
Legg-Bourke, Sir Harry, 77
Lennox-Boyd, Alan, 1st Viscount Boyd,
  16–17, 18, 62–3
Letts, John, 70
Lever, Harold, Baron, 144
Lewis, Toby, 136
Liberia, 86–7, 90
Limerick, 6th Earl of, 76

Lindsay, Sir William O'Brien, 'Wob', 16
Linklater, Eric, 12
Lloyd, Selwyn, Baron Selwyn-Lloyd, 15
Lord Chamberlain, office of, 166ff
Luce, Alexander, author's son, 20, 67, 99,
  150, 176–7
Luce, Admiral Sir David, author's uncle,
  17, 64, 83
Luce, Diana, author's sister, *see* Hart Dyke
Luce, Edward, author's son, 99, 176–7;
  and wife Priya Basu, 177
Luce, Gim, author's aunt, 22
Luce, Admiral John, author's grandfather,
  11, 13, 134; and wife Gar, 23, 24, 27
Luce, Margaret, *née* Napier, author's
  mother, 11, 13, 18–21, 23–4, 26; and
  author's schooldays, 28; 63, 74, 92,
  142, 177
Luce, Major General Sir Richard, 11
Luce, Rose, *née* Nicholson, author's wife,
  12, 26, 43–4, 50 *et passim*
Luce, Ted, author's uncle, 13, 32, 34
Luce, Tom, author's cousin, 120
Luce, Sir William, Bill, author's father,
  career, 13–18; death, 18; 23; and
  author's schooldays, 28; to Eaton Hall,
  32; in Sudan, 36–8; Aden, 38–40; the
  Gulf, 40; 58, 96, 99, 155, 157
Luce family, 11
Lula, President Luiz Inácio, of Brazil,173

Macdonald, Iona, 44
Machel, President Samora, of
  Mozambique, 91
McHenry, Don, 105
Mackley, Geoffrey, 60–1
Maclaren, Martin, 74
MacLehose, Sir Murray, 100
Macleod, Iain, 17, 72
Macmillan, Harold, 1st Earl of Stockton,
  17, 53
Macmillan, Maurice, 1st Viscount, 81
McMurtrie, Peter, 65
Madden, Martin, 64, 73
Magee, Bryan, 113
Major, Sir John, 102, 117–18, 124
Makarios, Archbishop, 34, 35
Malmesbury, Wilts, 11
Manley, Norman and Michael, Jamaica,
  108

Manning, Keith, 85
Manningham-Buller. Reginald, 1st
    Viscount Dilhorne, 45; and wife Mary,
    45
Margaret, HRH Princess, 166, 168, 171
Mather, Sir Carol, 77
Matutes, Sr Abel, 161
Maudling, Reginald, 58–9, 113
Mauritius, 106
Marsh, Sir Edward, 48
Mary, HM Queen, 19
Mathews, John, 70
Mbeki, President Thabo, of South Africa,
    173
Mellor, David, 130
Melly, George, 123
Mendez, Nicanor Costa, 138, 140
Mercouri, Melina, 126–7
Merrick, Sally, 79
Middleton, Sir George, 40
Mitterand, François, 128, 131
Mobbs, Sir Nigel, 148, 150
Moberly, Sir John, 99
Moberly, Sir Patrick, 97
Mobutu, Joseph (Mobutu Sese Seko),
    85–6
Mogwe, Archie, Botswana, 90
Molloy, Colonel Peter, 134–5
Montgomery, 2nd Viscount, 110
Morris, Denis, 72, 79
Morrison, Sir Charles, 74
Morrison, John, 1st Baron Margadale, 62
Moyes, Adrian, 68
Mozambique, 90, 91
Mudge, Dirk, Namibia, 105
Mugabe, Robert, 80, 84, 88, 89, 90, 94–5
Mugabe, Sally, 89, 90, 95
Museveni, Yoweri Kaguta, Uganda, 106
Muzorewa, Bishop Abel, Zimbabwe, 84,
    86, 87, 94

Nabarro, Sir Gerald, 73
Nairne, Sir Patrick, 144
Napier, Anne, later Hamilton, 23
Napier, Sir Charles, 11–12
Napier, Joan, author's aunt, 19, 21, 23
Napier, John, 11
Napier, Lavinia, later Robinson, 23, 94,
    113
Napier, Lennox, 177

Napier, Miles, 23, 25
Napier, Priscilla, *née* Hayter, author's
    aunt, 23, 24, 113
Napier, Commander Trevylyan, 'Trevie',
    author's uncle, 12, 21, 23, 24, 177
Napier of Magdala, 1st Baron, 12, 156
Nasser, Gamal Abdel, 16
National Service, author's period of, 31–5
Neguib, General Mohammed, 15
Nehru, Pandit Jawaharlal, 49
Neill, Sir Brian, 165
Newens, Stan, 107
Nguza Karl I Bond, 85–6
Nicholson, Brigadier Claude, 44, 48
Nicholson, Emma, later Baroness, 45, 47
Nicholson, Sir Godfrey, Bt, 44–51 *passim*;
    59, 62, 63, 64, 66, 81, 143
Nicholson, Harriet, later Flower, 45
Nicholson, Lady Katharine, 44, 45, 49,
    50–1, 66, 177
Nicholson, Laura, later Lady
    Montgomery-Cuninghame, 45, 57–8
Nicholson, Richard, 45
Nicholson, Rose, *see* Luce
Nicholson, Willie, 44
Nigeria, 90
Nimeiry, Gaafar, Sudan, 87
Nkomo, Joshua, 89, 90, 94
Norfolk, Bernard, 16th Duke of, and wife
    Lavinia, 76
Norfolk, Edward, 18th Duke of, 170
Norway, King Harald and Queen Sonja
    of, 173
Nott, Sir John, 140, 141, 145
Nujoma, Sam, Namibia, 104
Nyerere, Julius, Tanzania, 90, 139

Obote, Milton, 105, 106; and wife Miria,
    105
O'Brien, Conor Cruise. 43
Ogilvy, Sir Angus, 163, 172
Old Malt House, The, 24–6
Onslow, Cranley, Baron, 144
Oppenheim, Sally, Baroness Oppenheim-
    Barnes, 75
Oxford, author at, 42, 52

Pack, Major General Simon, 156
Palliser, Sir Michael, 88, 89
Parkinson, Cecil, Baron, 72, 77, 110

Parsons, Sir Anthony, 20, 138
Parsons, Sir Richard, 159
Patch, Air Chief Marshal Sir Hubert, 39
Patten, Chris, Baron, 100, 102, 103, 148;
   and wife Lavender, 103
Paul, Robin, 52
Pearsall, Phyllis, 79, 179
Peat, Sir Michael, 167, 171
Peel, 3rd Earl, 173
Peres, Shimon, 97
Perez de Cuellar, Javier, 139
Perle, Richard, 112
Phillips, Melanie, 120
Pierrepoint, Albert, 81
Plumb, Sir Jack, 20, 42, 149
Podgorny, Nikolai, 113, 114
Pompidou, Georges, 128
Poncet, François, 84–5
Pott, Henry Percivall, 62
Powell, Colin, 112
Powell, Enoch, 60, 78–9, 143
Power, Michael, 53
Powys, Gilfrid, 57–8
Price, George, 108
Putin, Vladimir, 115
Pym, Francis, Baron, 73, 78, 94, 107,
   144

Quinton, Anthony, Baron, 130

Ramsden, James, 64
Ramus, Tony, 39
Reagan, President Ronald, 97, 109, 114,
   115, 139, 141
Rees, Merlyn, Baron Merlyn-Rees, 144
Reid, Sir Alan, 167
Renison, Sir Patrick, 17, 52
Renwick, Robin, Baron, 88
Rhoda, Ricky, 165
Rhodesia/Zimbabwe, 80ff; and Deputy
   Governorship, 92
Rhys Williams, Sir Brandon, Bt, 96
Rice, Condoleezza, 112
Ridley, Matthew, 4th Viscount, 170
Ridley, Nicholas, Baron, 75, 137
Rifkind, Sir Malcolm, 82, 107–8, 154,
   155, 157, 161
Risso, Major Colin. 162
Robbins, Major 'Dim', 34
Roberts, Sir Hugh, 167

Robertson, Sir James, 15
Robinson, Michael, 156
Rockingham Castle, 19, 24, 25, 125
Rogers, Harold, 79
Ros, Enrique, 138, 139
Rosas, Carlos Ortiz de, 138
Ross, Lieutenant Colonel Sir Malcolm,
   167
Rothschild, Sir Evelyn de, 151; and wife
   Victoria (*née* Schott), 151
Ruark, Robert, 58

Saddam Hussein, 99
Sainsbury, John, Baron, 124
Sandys, Duncan, Baron Duncan-Sandys,
   39
Sankey, Colonel, 163
Saunders Watson, Michael, 130
Sayed Osman, 37
Schofield, Derek, 156
Schultz, George P., 98, 112
Scott, Sir Nicholas, 74
Searle, Dominic, 161
Sedgehill, Wilts, 23–4
Semprun, Jorge, 126
Senegal, 86
Senghor, Léopold, Senegal, 86
Seth, Vikram, 118
Shackleton Report, 137, 138, 146
Shagari, Shehu, Nigeria, 90, 91
Shaker, General Sharif Zaid Ben, 98
Shamir, Yitzchak, 97
Singapore, 116–7
Skinner, Dennis, 78
Slim, Field Marshal 1st Viscount, 38–9
Smith, Arnold, 185
Smith, Ian, 80, 81, 88
Smuts, Field Marshal Jan, 14, 82
Snook, Glenys, 22–3
Soames, Christopher, Baron, 89, 90, 92–3;
   and wife Mary, 95
Soames, Nicholas, 75
Solana, Javier, 126
Soviet Union, 112–15
Stanley, Sir John, 72
Sterling, Jeffrey Maurice, Baron, 171
Stevas, Norman St John, Baron St John of
   Fawsley, 119, 129
Stirling, Sir Alexander, 37
Stockwood, Rt Revd Mervyn, 43, 113

Stokes, Sir John, 63
Stonehouse, John, 82
Strong, Sir Roy, 123
Sudan, 14ff, 36–8, 52, 53
Swaziland, King Sobhuza II of, 106

Tanzania, 90
Tariq Aziz, 99
Taylor, Professor Robert, 152
Taylor, Sir Teddy, 75
Tedder, Marshal of the Royal Air Force
    Arthur, 1st Baron, 39
Templer, Field Marshal Sir Gerald, 17
Thatcher, Sir Denis, 98, 151, 163
Thatcher, Margaret, Baroness, 66–7, 80,
    81, 82, 83, 84, 87, 90, 92, 94, 97, 98,
    100, 101–2, 107, 109, 114, 117, 119,
    120, 122, 124, 128, 129, 130, 131,
    132, 137, 139, 141, 144, 147, 151,
    152, 163
Thesiger, Sir Wilfred, 40, 58, 107
Tolbert, William, Liberia, 87, 91
Tongogara, Josiah, 88
Trefgarne, David, 2nd Baron, 139
Trinidad, 108
Tugendhat, Christopher, Baron, 32, 43
Tyrie, Andrew, 121

Uganda, 105–6
Ure, Sir John, 137
Urquhart, Sir Brian, 104
Urwick, Sir Alan, 98

Valois, Dame Ninette de, 123
van der Byl, Pieter, 82, 89
Vance, Cyrus, 112
Vaughan, Denis, 124
Viola, General Roberto, 138

Wainwright, Robin, 52
Waite, Sir John, 165
Walden, George, 91
Wales, HRH Prince of, 116, 130, 168,
    171, 172, 173, 180; and Princess of,
    159; and Camilla Parker Bowles, 172

Walker, Air Vice Marshal David Allan,
    167
Walker, Peter, Baron, 76, 110
Wall, Sir Patrick, 81
Walls, Lieutenant General Peter, 93
Walters, Sir Dennis, 96
Warren-Gash, Haydon, 133
Watkinson, Harold, 1st Viscount, 144
Watson, Professor Peter, 148, 149–50
Wauchope, John, 65
Wavell, Field Marshal Archibald, 1st Earl,
    49
Weatherill, Jack, Baron, 77, 78, 169
Weinberger, Caspar, 98, 112, 151
Wellington College, 26–8
Wessex, HRH Prince Edward, Earl of, and
    Countess of, 170–1
Westbrook, Roger, 155
Westmacott, Sir Peter, 133
Whistler, General Sir Lashmar ('Bolo'), 32
White, Admiral Sir Hugo, 154
Whitelaw, William, 1st Viscount, 73–4, 91
Wilding, Richard, 120, 128
Williams, Alma, 69
Williams, Sir Anthony, 138, 146
Williams, Dr Eric, Trinidad, 108
Williams, Shirley, Baroness, 64, 65, 66, 67
Williamson, Robin, 52
Wilson, Sir Colin St John, 130
Wilson Sir David, 127
Wilson, David, Baron, and wife Natasha,
    102–3
Wilson, Harold, Baron, 11, 64, 66, 73,
    106, 119
Winning, Cardinal Thomas, 164
Woolf, Leonard, 183

York, HRH Duke of, 170
Youde, Sir Edward, 101, 102; and wife
    Pamela, 101
Young, Michael, Baron, 68–9, 71, 72

Zaid, Sheikh, 99
Zaire, 85–6, 90
Zambia, 90